MAKER

BAKE LIKE A PRO!

COMICS

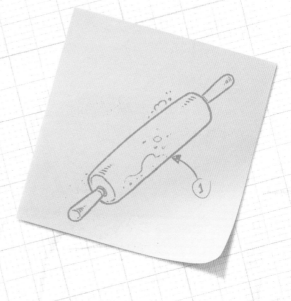

BAKE LIKE A PRO!

Falynn Koch

:01

First Second
New York

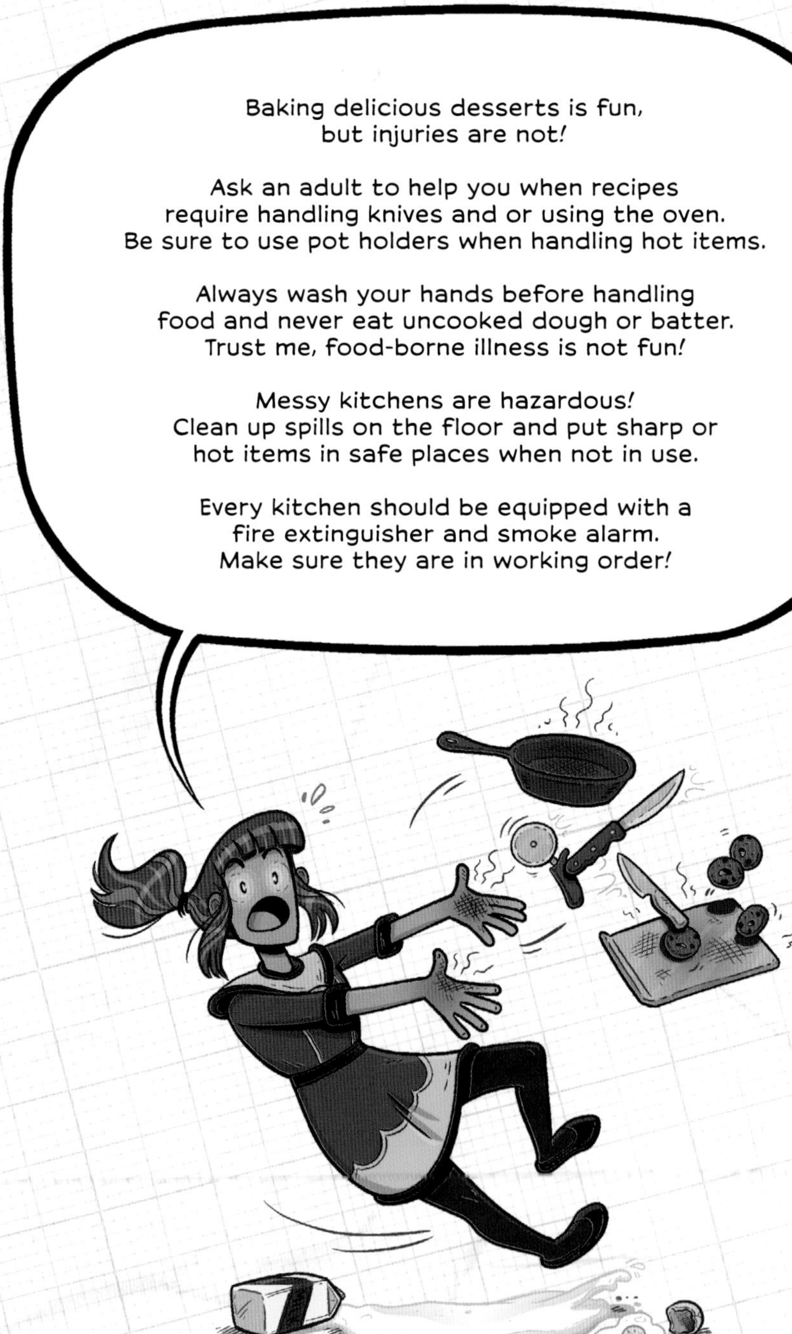
Baking delicious desserts is fun, but injuries are not! Ask an adult to help you when recipes require handling knives and or using the oven. Be sure to use pot holders when handling hot items. Always wash your hands before handling food and never eat uncooked dough or batter. Trust me, food-borne illness is not fun! Messy kitchens are hazardous! Clean up spills on the floor and put sharp or hot items in safe places when not in use. Every kitchen should be equipped with a fire extinguisher and smoke alarm. Make sure they are in working order!

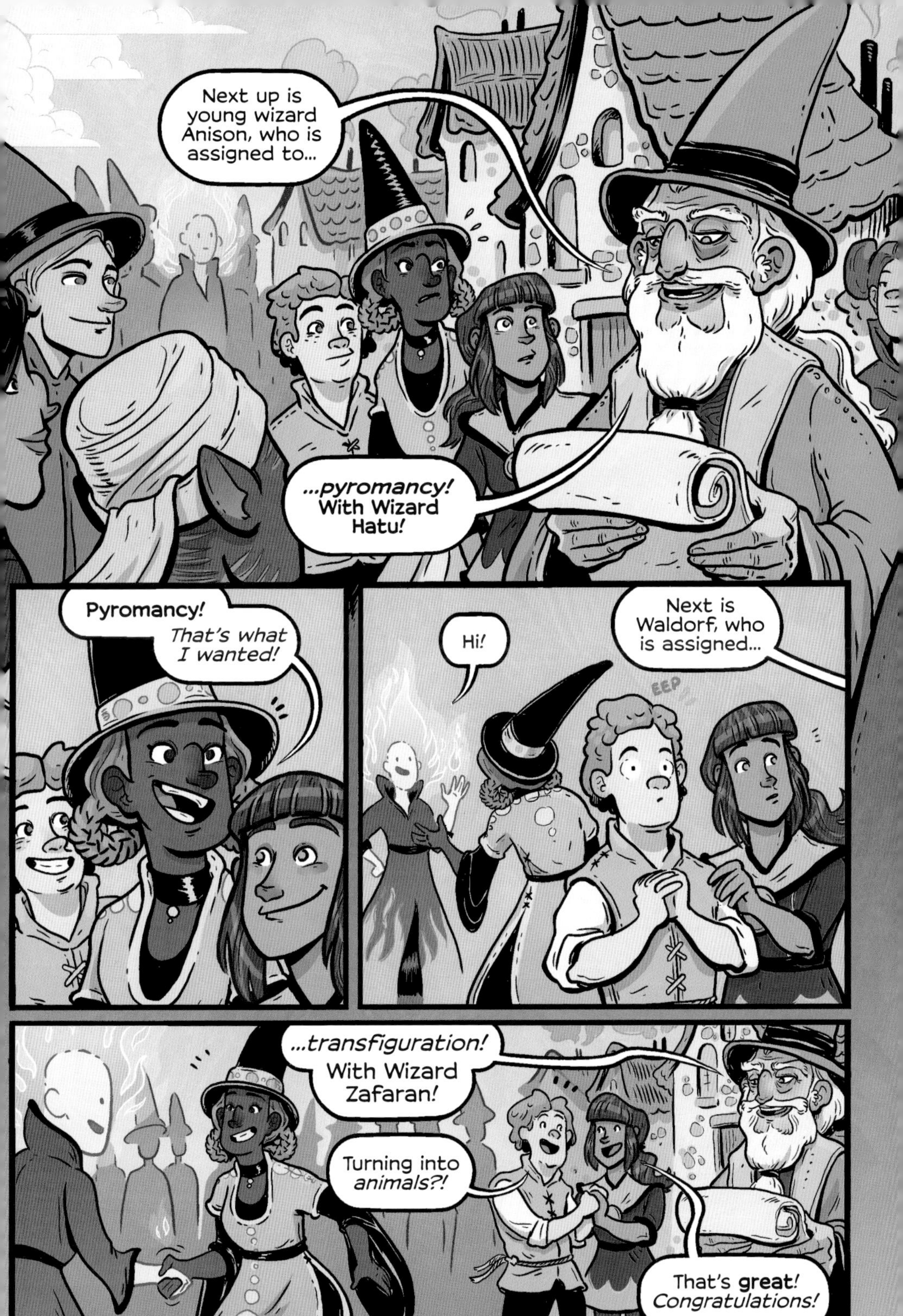
Next up is young wizard Anison, who is assigned to...
...pyromancy! With Wizard Hatu!
Pyromancy! That's what I wanted!
Hi!
Next is Waldorf, who is assigned...
EEP
...transfiguration! With Wizard Zafaran!
Turning into animals?!
That's great! Congratulations!

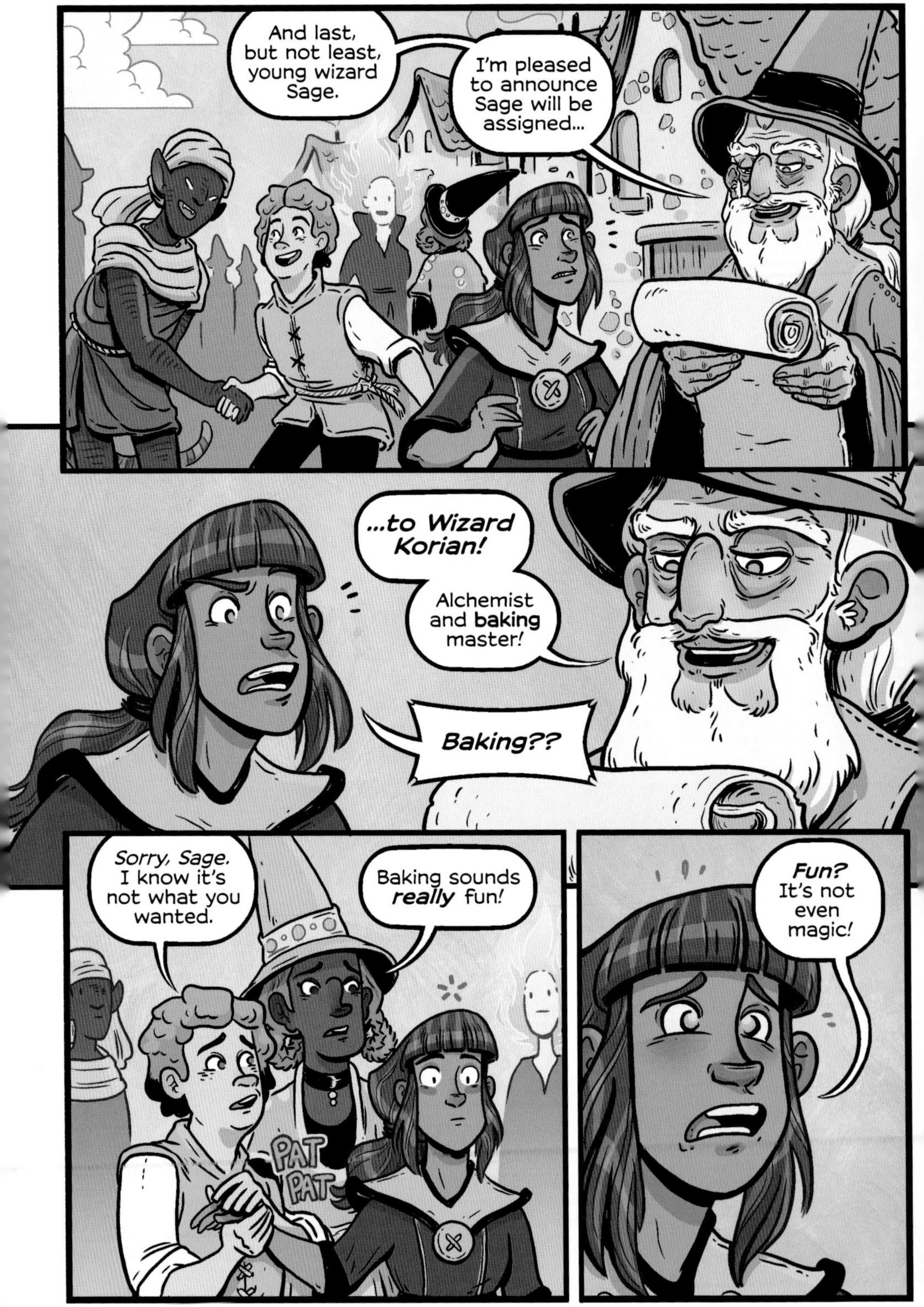
And last, but not least, young wizard Sage.
I'm pleased to announce Sage will be assigned...
...to Wizard Korian!
Alchemist and baking master!
Baking??
Sorry, Sage. I know it's not what you wanted.
Baking sounds really fun!
PAT PAT
Fun? It's not even magic!

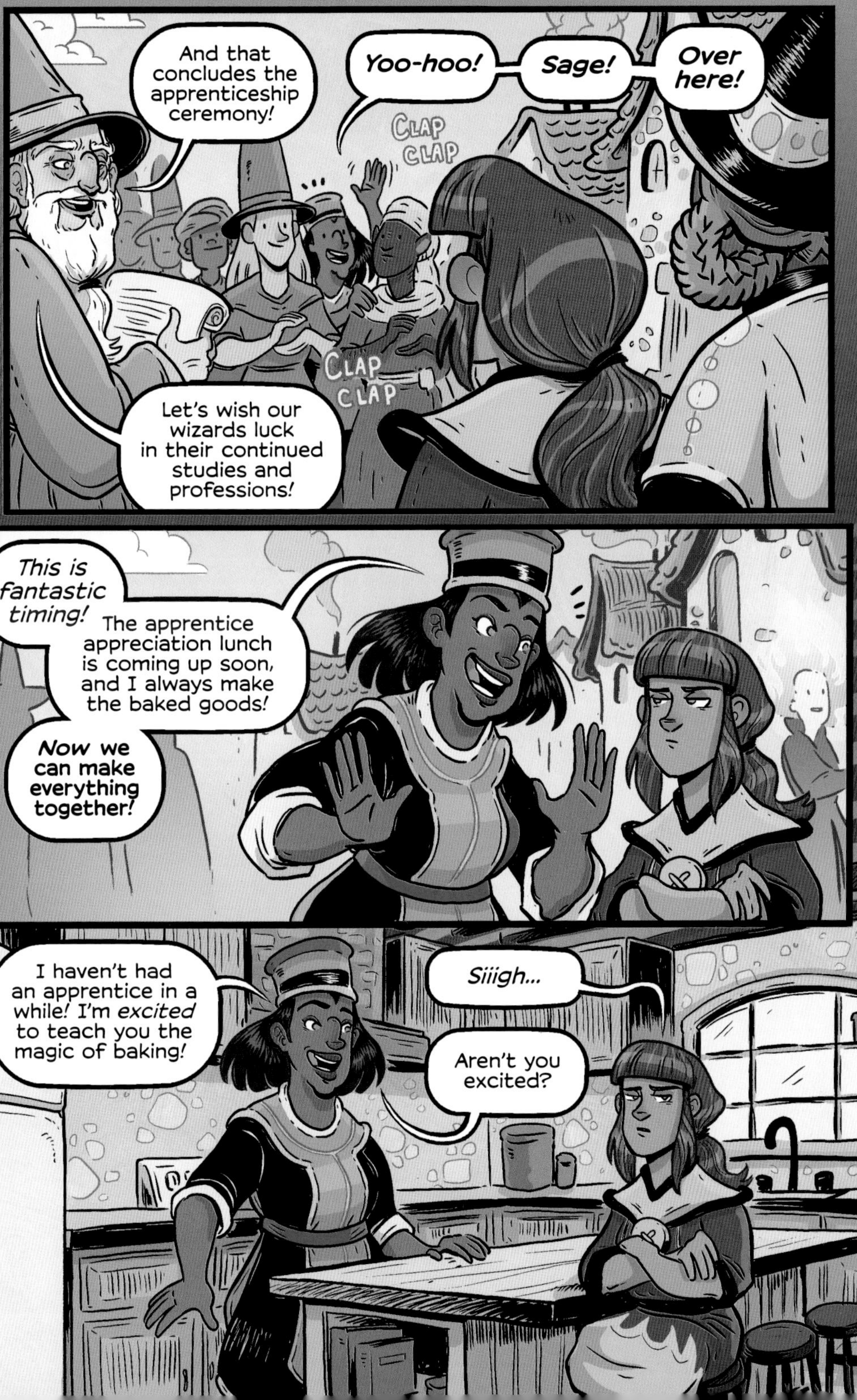
And that concludes the apprenticeship ceremony!
Yoo-hoo!
Sage!
Over here!
CLAP CLAP
CLAP CLAP
Let's wish our wizards luck in their continued studies and professions!
This is fantastic timing!
The apprentice appreciation lunch is coming up soon, and I always make the baked goods!
Now we can make everything together!
I haven't had an apprentice in a while! I'm excited to teach you the magic of baking!
Siiigh...
Aren't you excited?

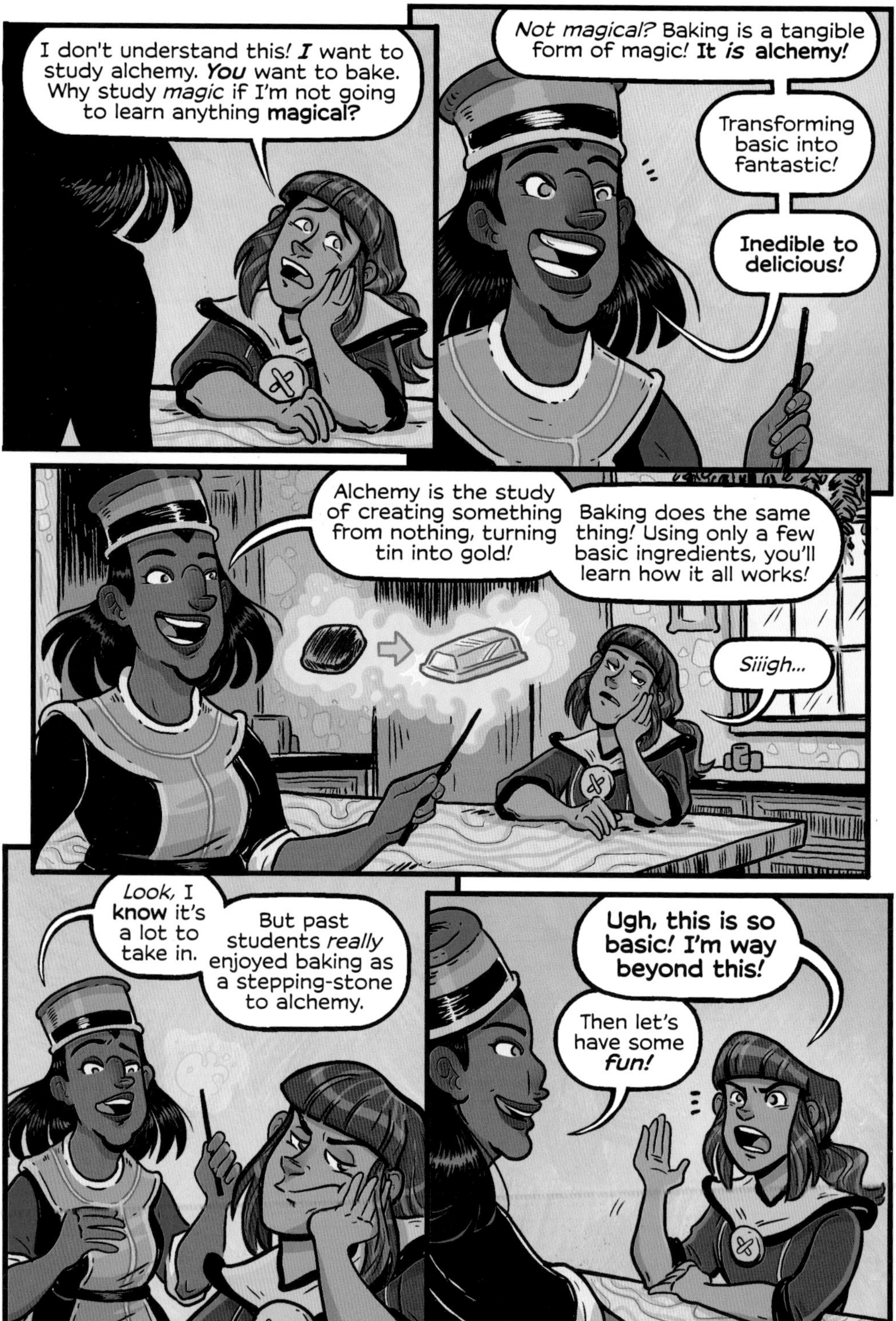
I don't understand this! *I* want to study alchemy. *You* want to bake. Why study *magic* if I'm not going to learn anything **magical?**
Not magical? Baking is a tangible form of magic! **It *is* alchemy!**
Transforming basic into fantastic!
Inedible to delicious!
Alchemy is the study of creating something from nothing, turning tin into gold!
Baking does the same thing! Using only a few basic ingredients, you'll learn how it all works!
Siiigh...
Look, I **know** it's a lot to take in.
But past students *really* enjoyed baking as a stepping-stone to alchemy.
Ugh, this is so basic! I'm way beyond this!
Then let's have some ***fun!***

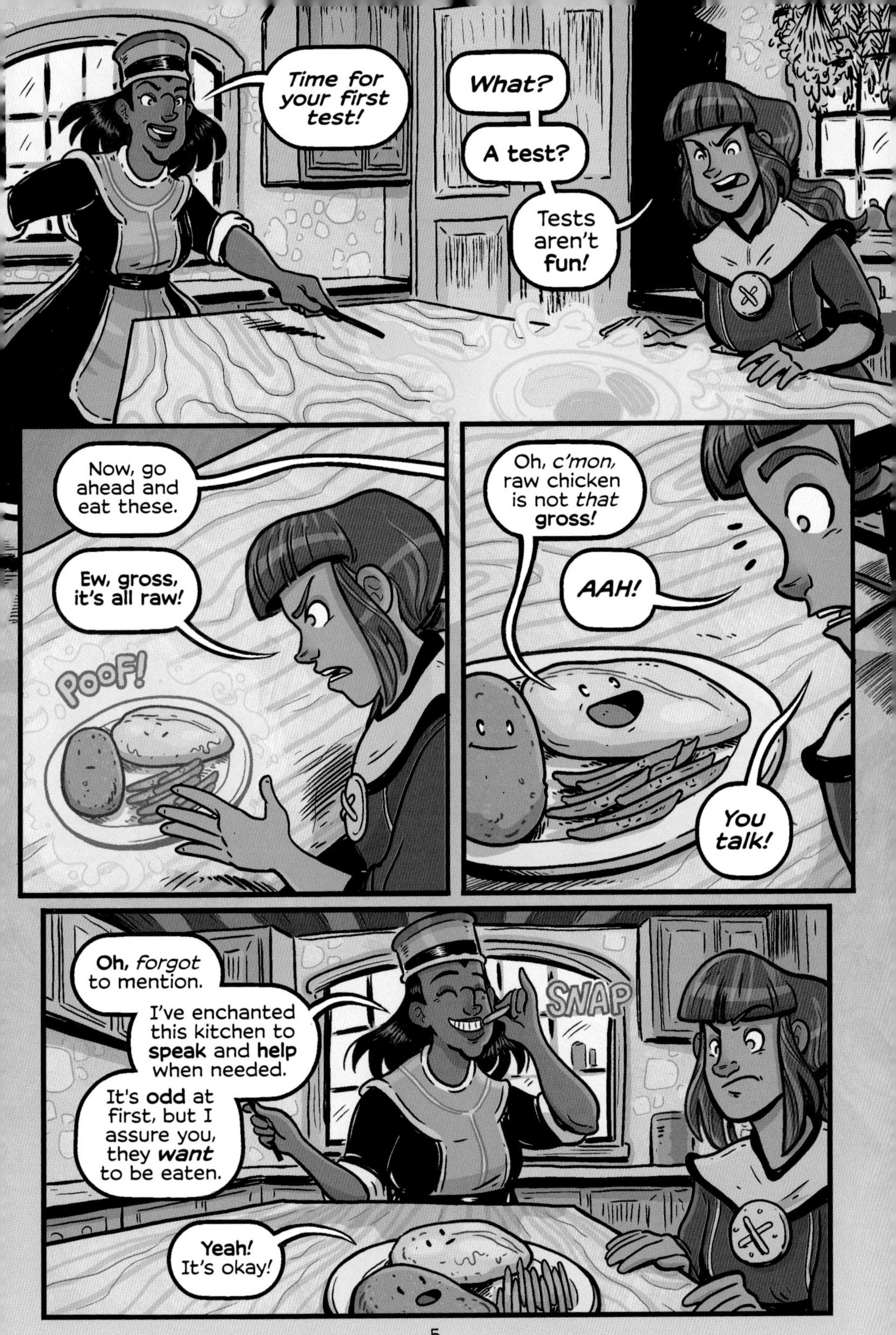
Time for your first test!
What?
A test?
Tests aren't fun!
Now, go ahead and eat these.
Ew, gross, it's all raw!
POOF!
Oh, c'mon, raw chicken is not that gross!
AAH!
You talk!
Oh, forgot to mention.
I've enchanted this kitchen to speak and help when needed.
SNAP
It's odd at first, but I assure you, they want to be eaten.
Yeah! It's okay!

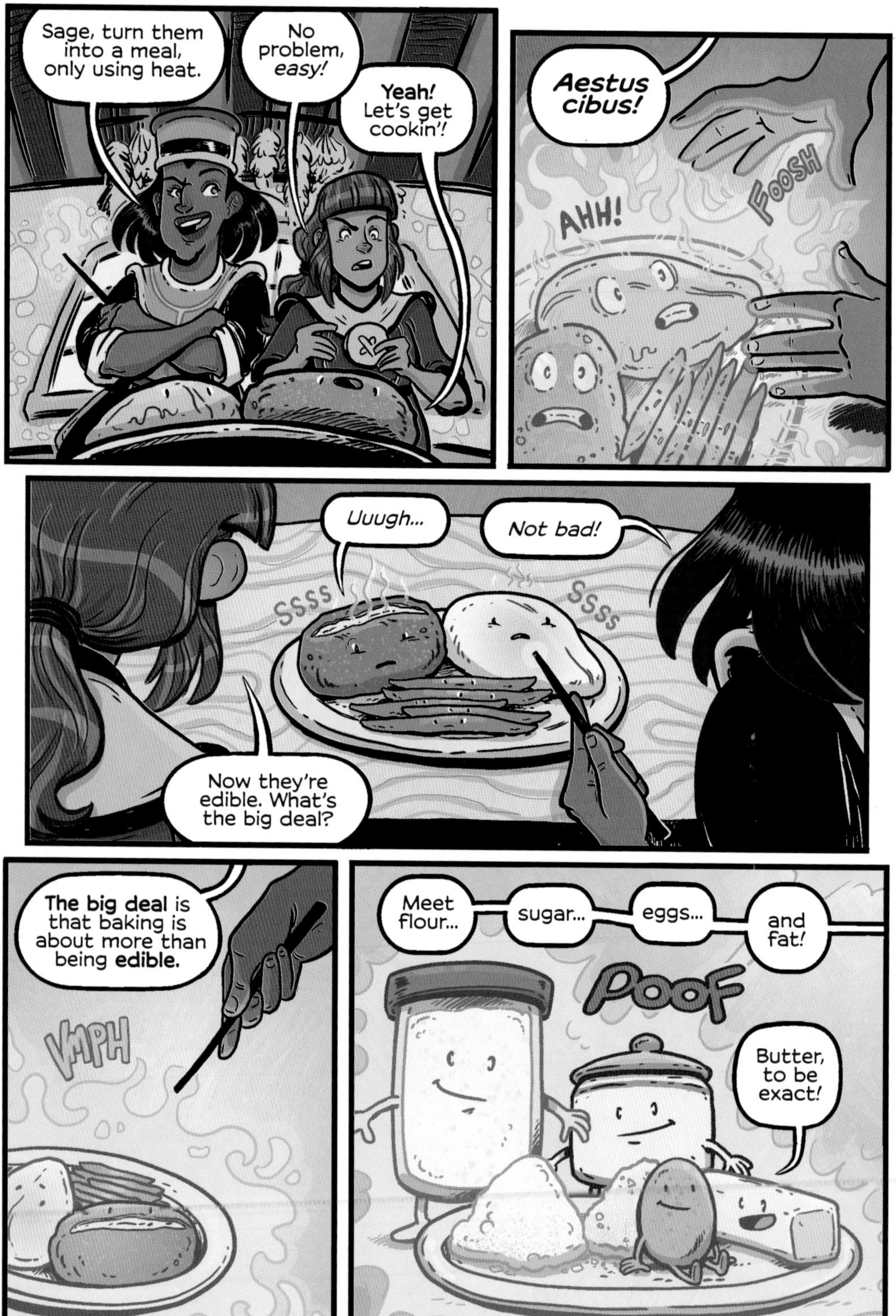
Sage, turn them into a meal, only using heat.
No problem, *easy!*
Yeah! Let's get cookin'!
Aestus cibus!
AHH!
FOOSH
Uuugh...
Not bad!
SSSS
SSSS
Now they're edible. What's the big deal?
The big deal is that baking is about more than being **edible.**
VMPH
Meet flour...
sugar...
eggs...
and fat!
POOF
Butter, to be exact!

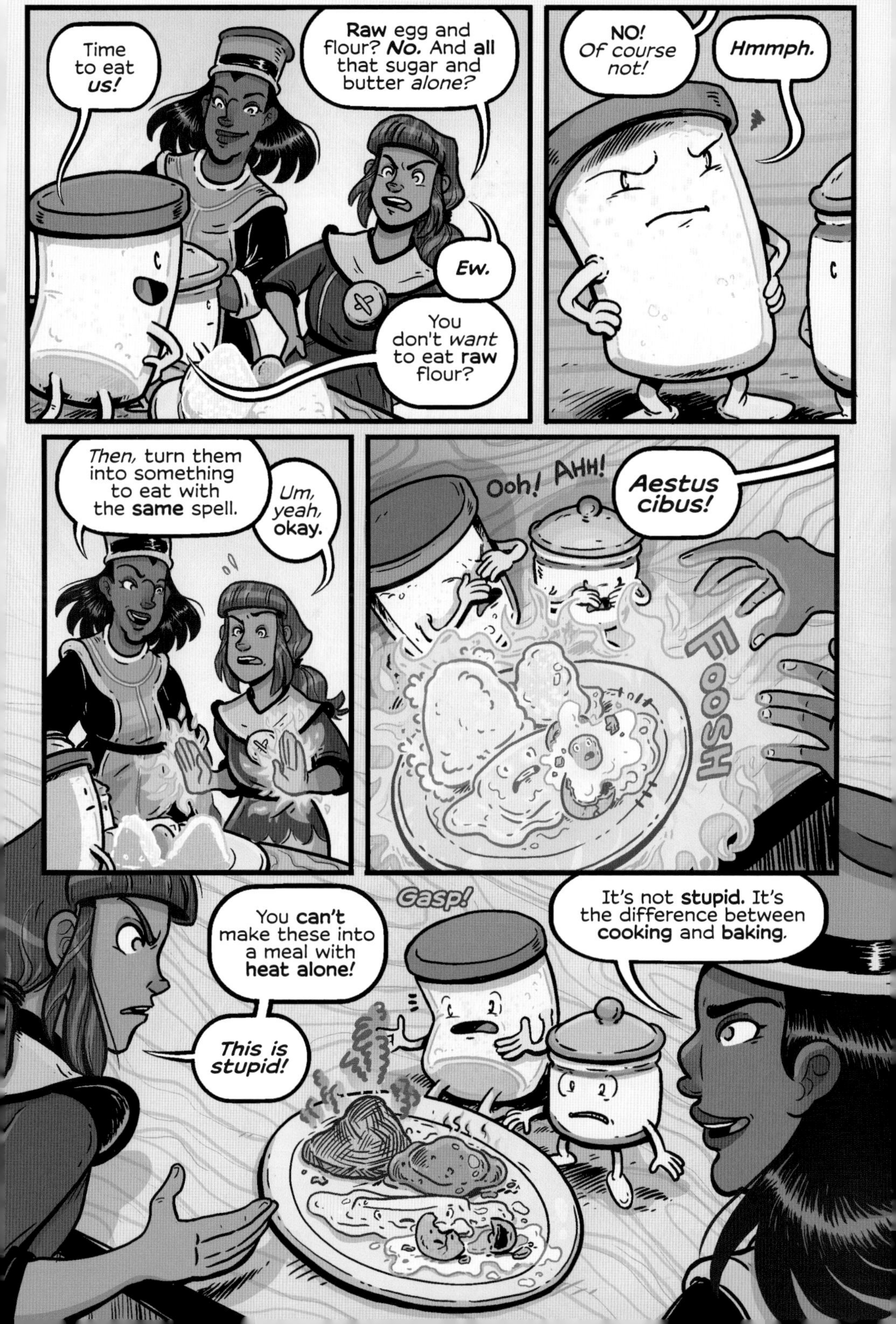

Time to eat **us!**
Raw egg and flour? ***No.*** And **all** that sugar and butter *alone?*
Ew.
You don't *want* to eat **raw** flour?
NO! *Of course not!*
Hmmph.
Then, turn them into something to eat with the **same** spell.
Um, yeah, **okay.**
Ooh! AHH!
Aestus cibus!
FOOSH
Gasp!
You **can't** make these into a meal with **heat alone!**
This is stupid!
It's not **stupid.** It's the difference between **cooking** and **baking.**

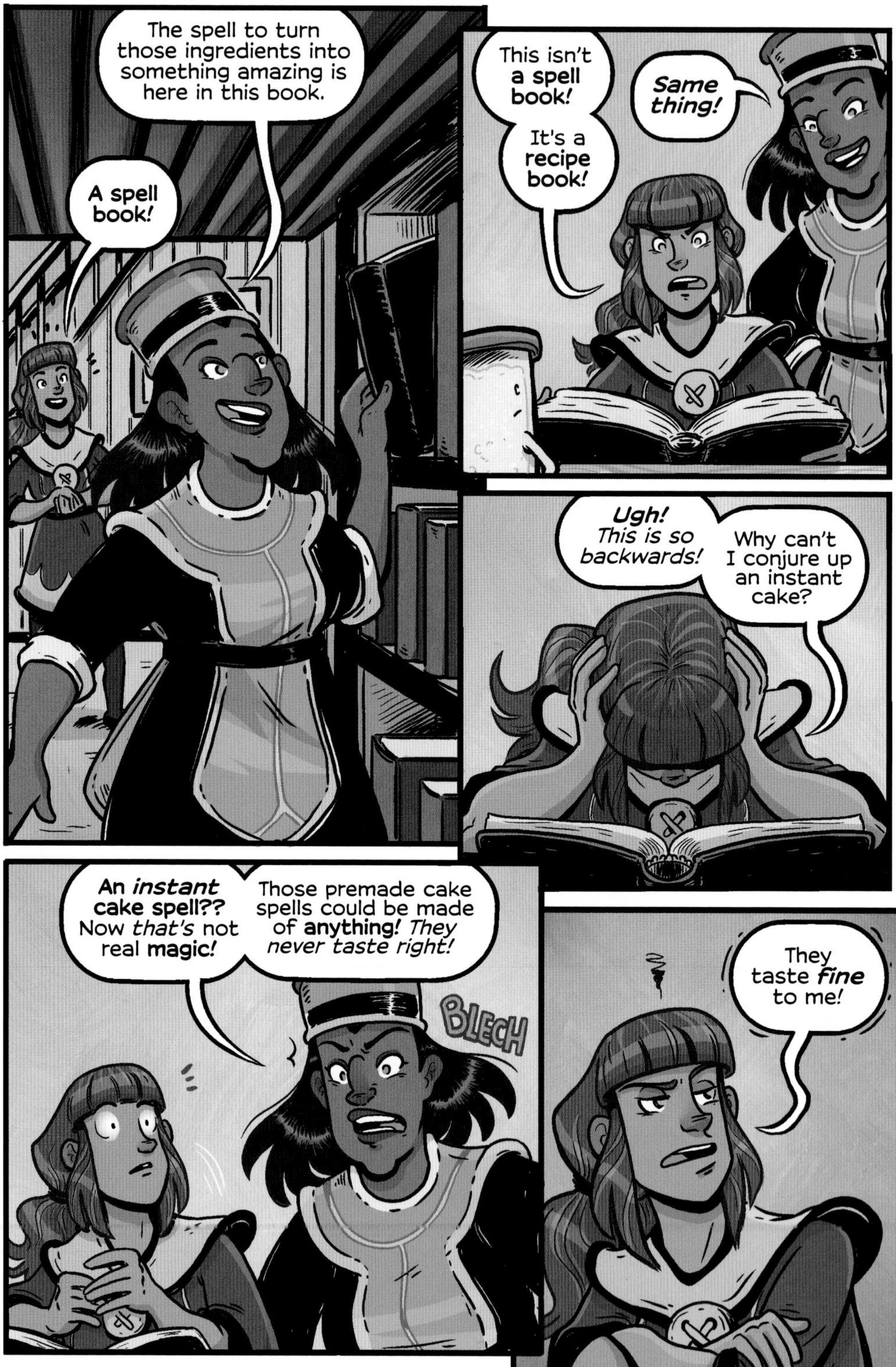
The spell to turn those ingredients into something amazing is here in this book.
A spell book!
This isn't **a spell** book!
It's a **recipe** book!
Same thing!
Ugh! *This is so backwards!*
Why can't I conjure up an instant cake?
An *instant* cake spell?? Now *that's* not real **magic!**
Those premade cake spells could be made of **anything!** *They never taste right!*
BLECH
They taste ***fine*** to me!

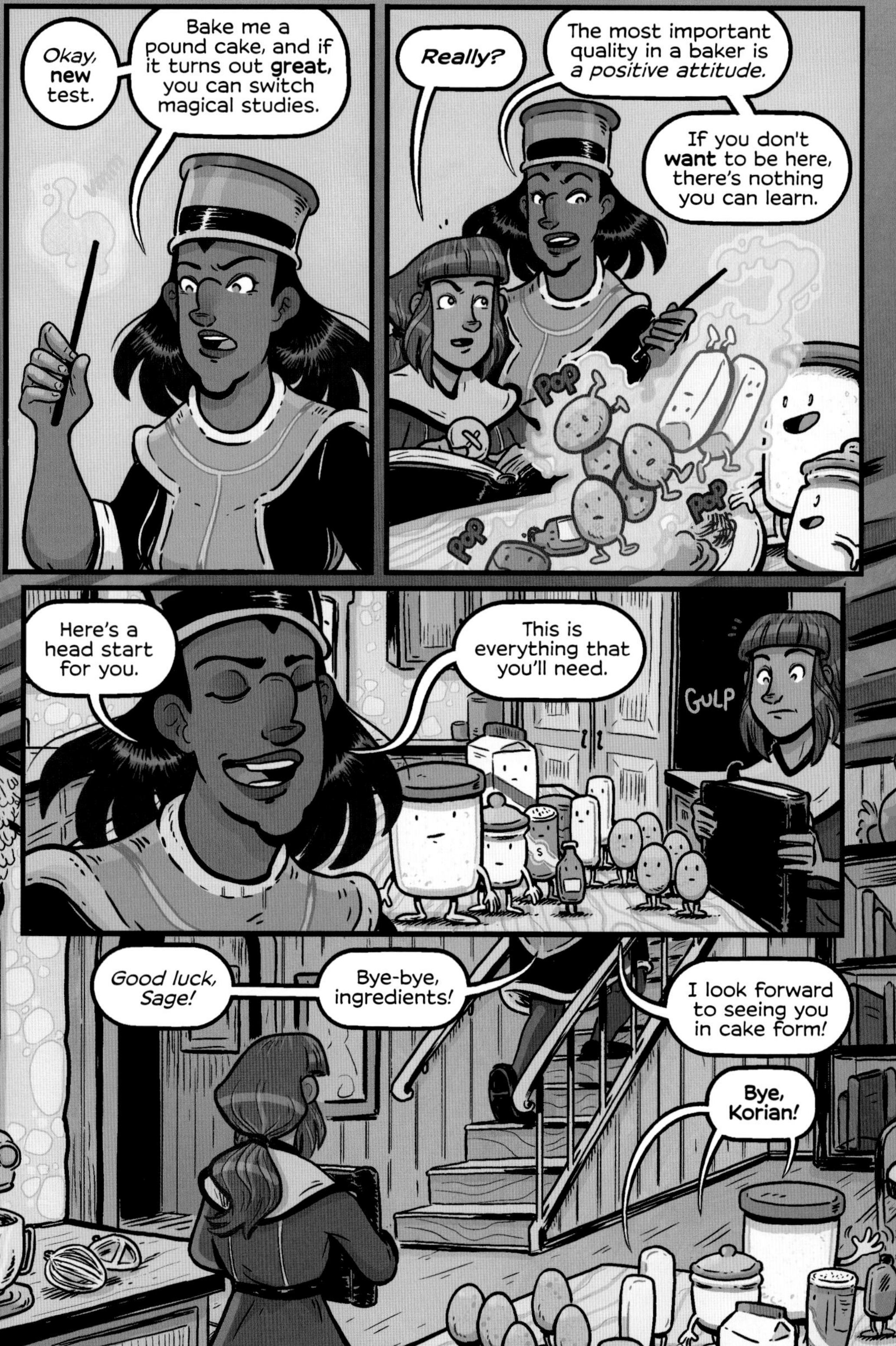
Okay, **new** test.
Bake me a pound cake, and if it turns out **great**, you can switch magical studies.
Really?
The most important quality in a baker is *a positive attitude.*
If you don't **want** to be here, there's nothing you can learn.
POP
POP
POP
Here's a head start for you.
This is everything that you'll need.
GULP
Good luck, Sage!
Bye-bye, ingredients!
I look forward to seeing you in cake form!
Bye, Korian!

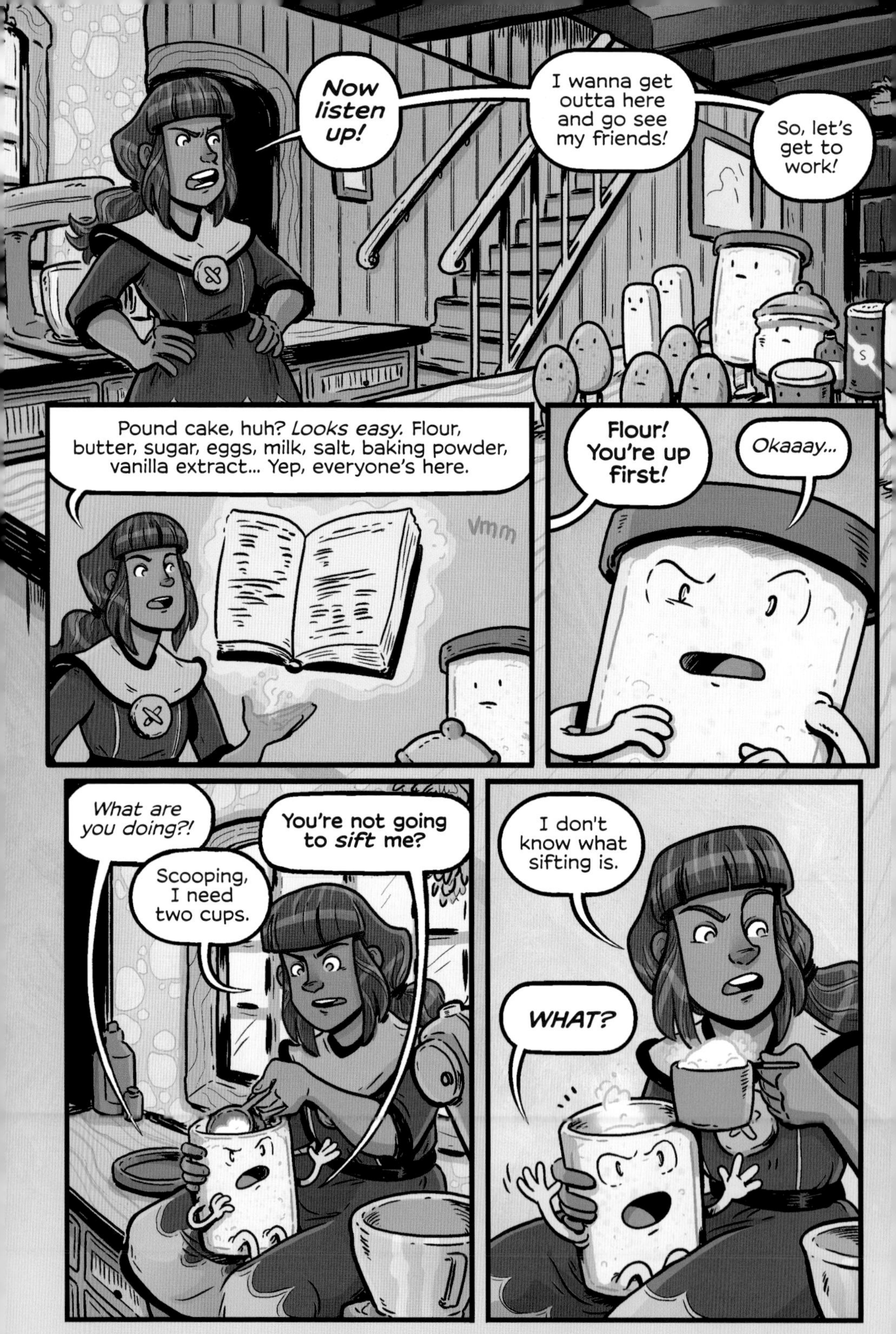

Now listen up!
I wanna get outta here and go see my friends!
So, let's get to work!
Pound cake, huh? *Looks easy.* Flour, butter, sugar, eggs, milk, salt, baking powder, vanilla extract... Yep, everyone's here.
vmm
Flour! You're up first!
Okaaay...
What are you doing?!
You're not going to *sift* me?
Scooping, I need two cups.
I don't know what sifting is.
WHAT?

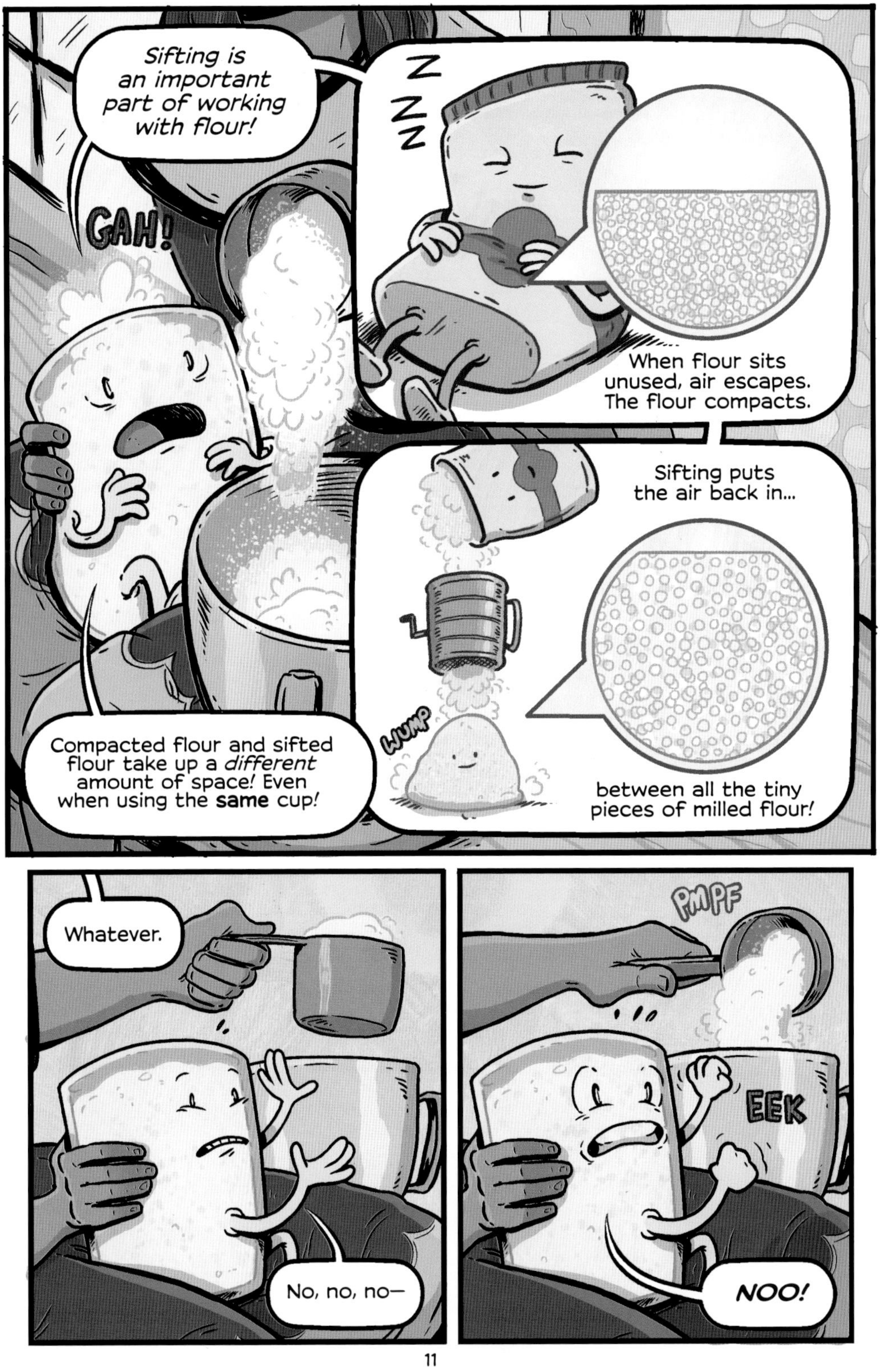
Sifting is an important part of working with flour!
GAH!
Z Z Z
When flour sits unused, air escapes. The flour compacts.
Sifting puts the air back in...
WUMP
between all the tiny pieces of milled flour!
Compacted flour and sifted flour take up a *different* amount of space! Even when using the **same** cup!
Whatever.
No, no, no—
PMPF
EEK
NOO!

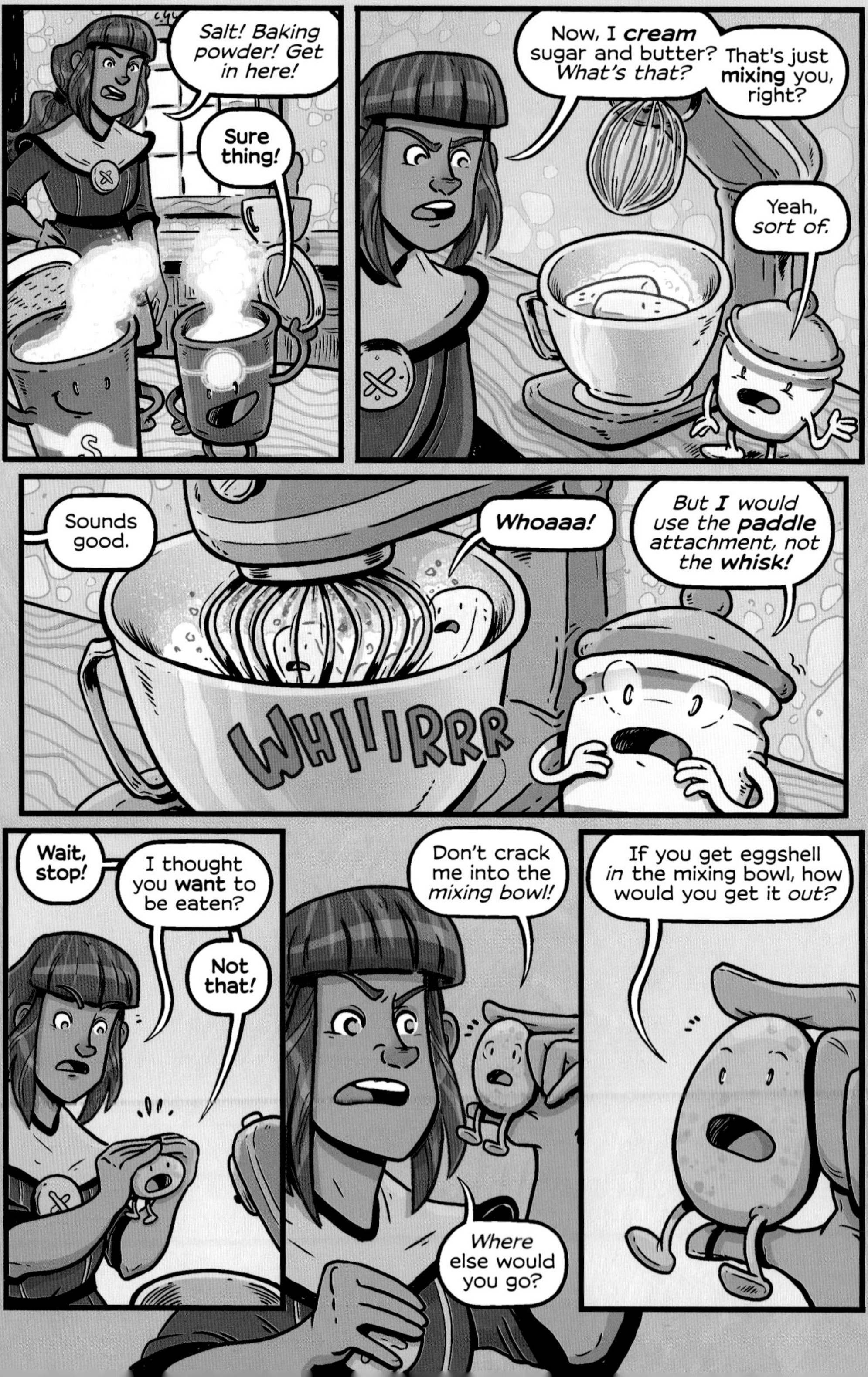
Salt! Baking powder! Get in here!
Sure thing!
Now, I cream sugar and butter? What's that?
That's just mixing you, right?
Yeah, sort of.
Sounds good.
Whoaaa!
But I would use the paddle attachment, not the whisk!
WHIIIRRR
Wait, stop!
I thought you want to be eaten?
Not that!
Don't crack me into the mixing bowl!
Where else would you go?
If you get eggshell in the mixing bowl, how would you get it out?

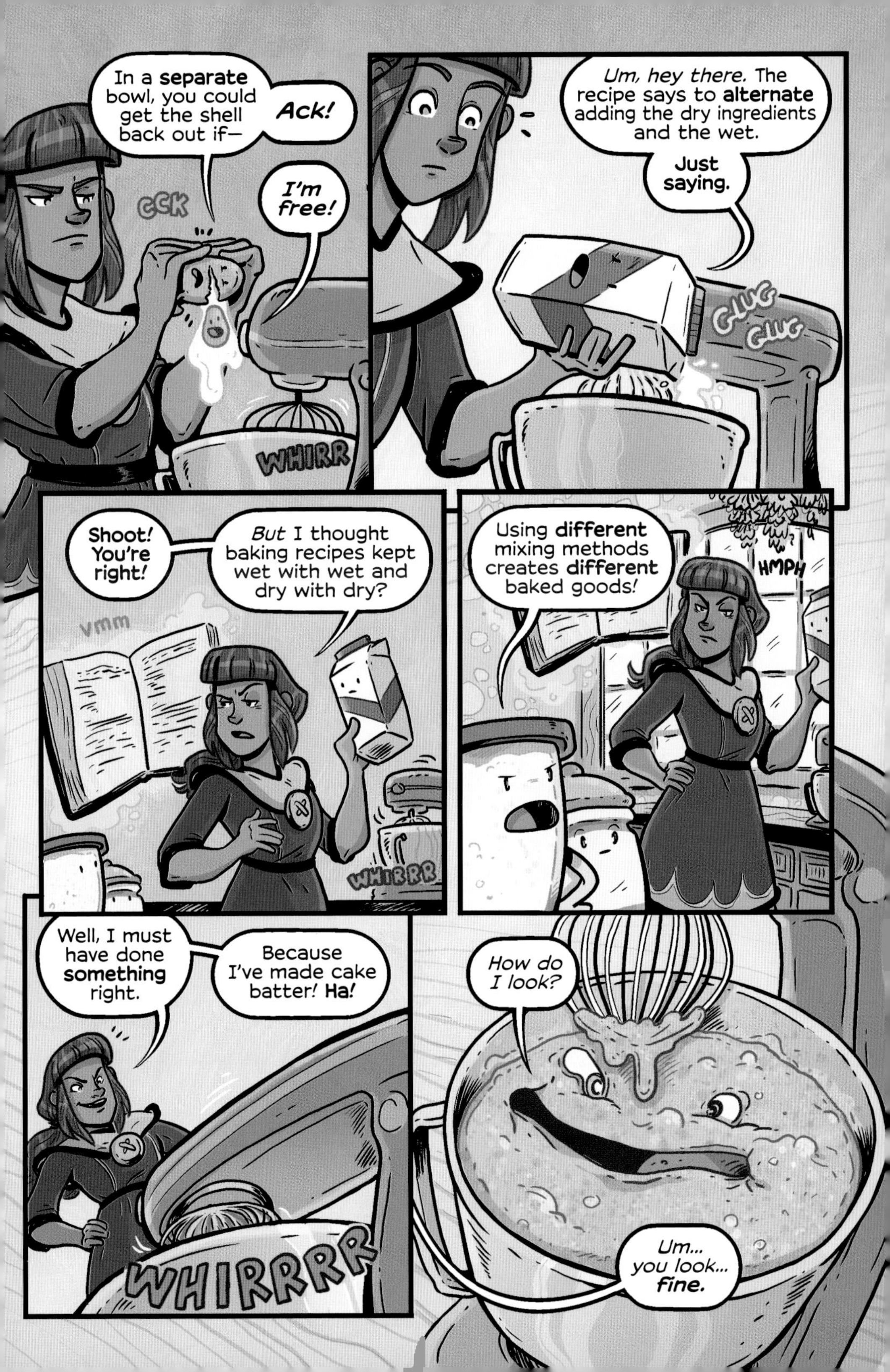
In a **separate** bowl, you could get the shell back out if—
CCK
Ack!
I'm free!
WHIRR
Um, hey there. The recipe says to **alternate** adding the dry ingredients and the wet.
Just saying.
GLUG
GLUG
Shoot! You're right!
But I thought baking recipes kept wet with wet and dry with dry?
vmm
WHIRRR
Using **different** mixing methods creates **different** baked goods!
HMPH
Well, I must have done **something** right.
Because I've made cake batter! **Ha!**
WHIRRRR
How do I look?
Um... you look... ***fine.***

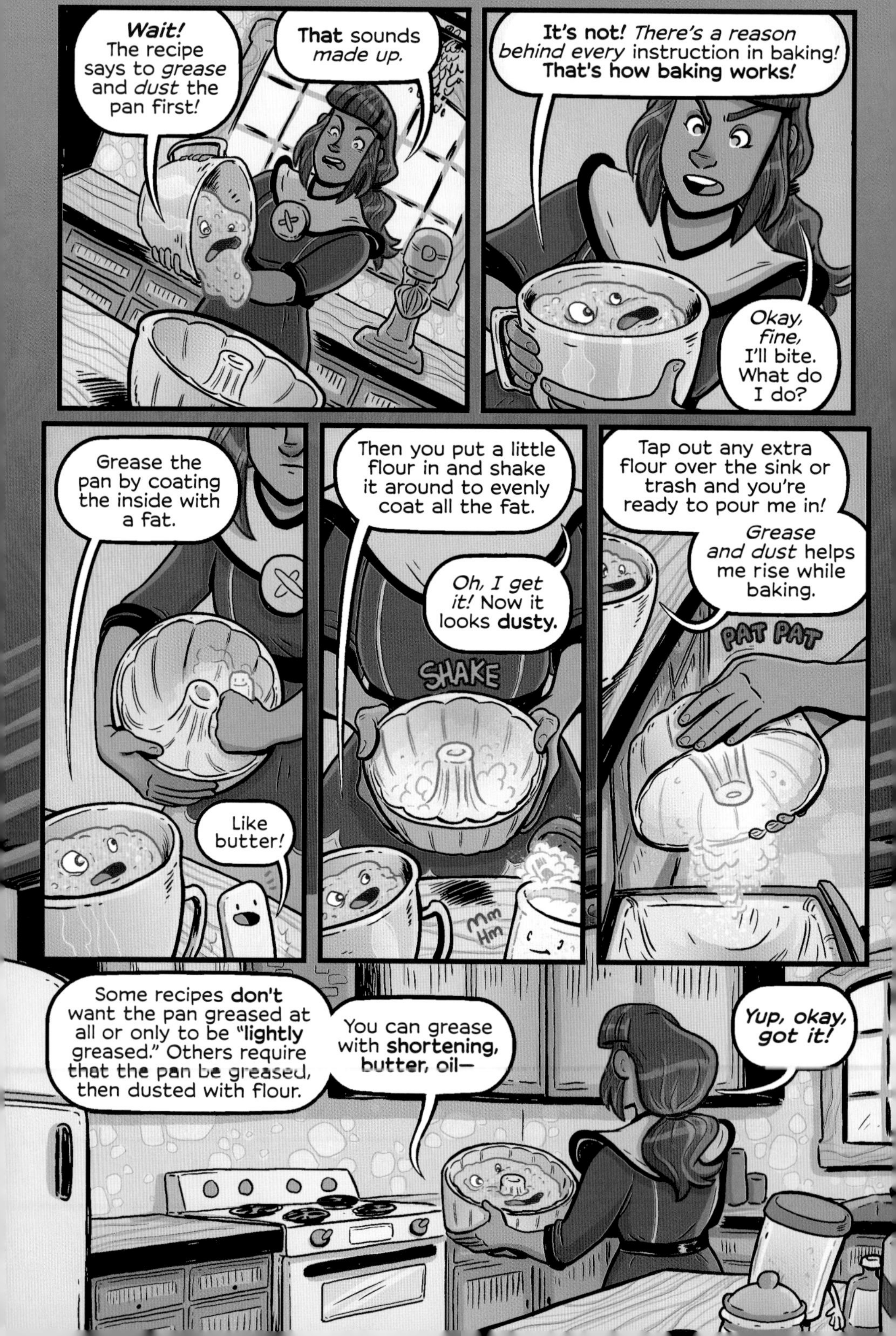
Wait! The recipe says to grease and dust the pan first!
That sounds made up.
It's not! There's a reason behind every instruction in baking! That's how baking works!
Okay, fine, I'll bite. What do I do?
Grease the pan by coating the inside with a fat.
Like butter!
Then you put a little flour in and shake it around to evenly coat all the fat.
Oh, I get it! Now it looks dusty.
SHAKE
Mm Hm
Tap out any extra flour over the sink or trash and you're ready to pour me in!
Grease and dust helps me rise while baking.
PAT PAT
Some recipes don't want the pan greased at all or only to be "lightly greased." Others require that the pan be greased, then dusted with flour.
You can grease with shortening, butter, oil—
Yup, okay, got it!

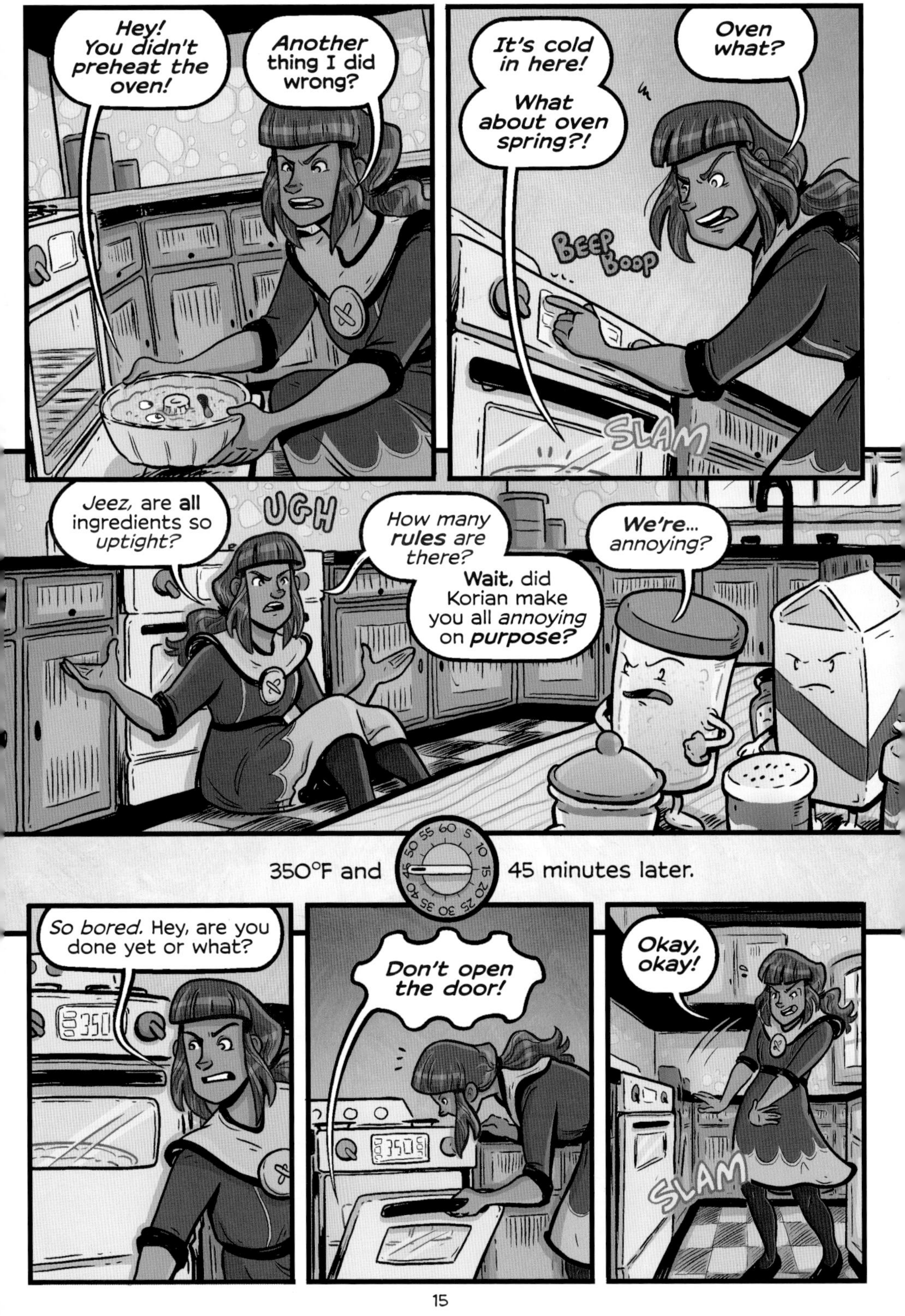
Hey! You didn't preheat the oven!
Another thing I did wrong?
It's cold in here!
What about oven spring?!
Oven what?
BEEP BOOP
SLAM
Jeez, are all ingredients so uptight?
UGH
How many rules are there?
Wait, did Korian make you all annoying on purpose?
We're... annoying?
350°F and 45 minutes later.
So bored. Hey, are you done yet or what?
Don't open the door!
Okay, okay!
SLAM

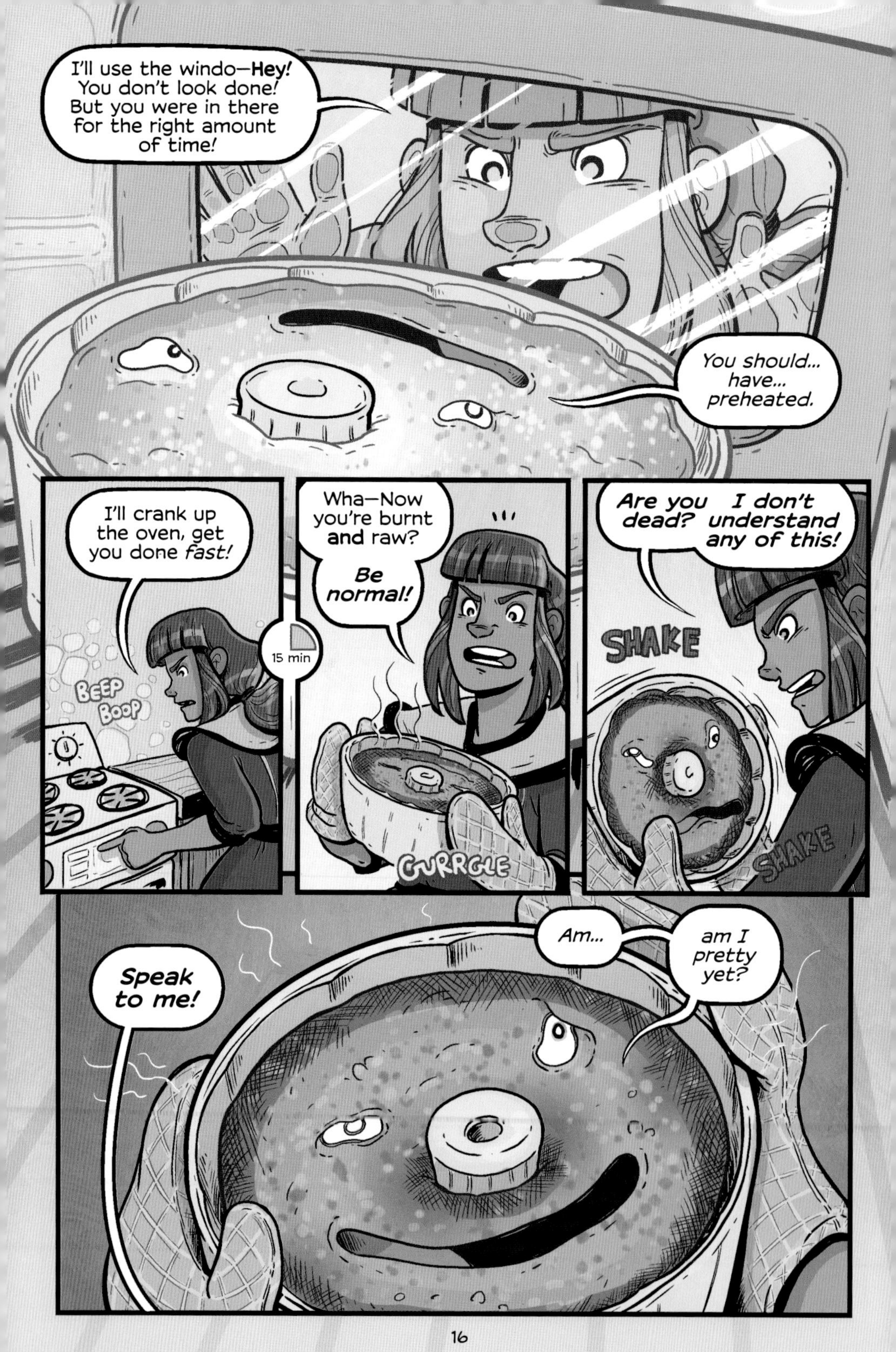

I'll use the windo—**Hey!** You don't look done! But you were in there for the right amount of time!
You should... have... preheated.
I'll crank up the oven, get you done *fast!*
BEEP BOOP
15 min
Wha—Now you're burnt **and** raw?
Be normal!
GURRGLE
Are you dead?
I don't understand any of this!
SHAKE
SHAKE
Speak to me!
Am...
am I pretty yet?

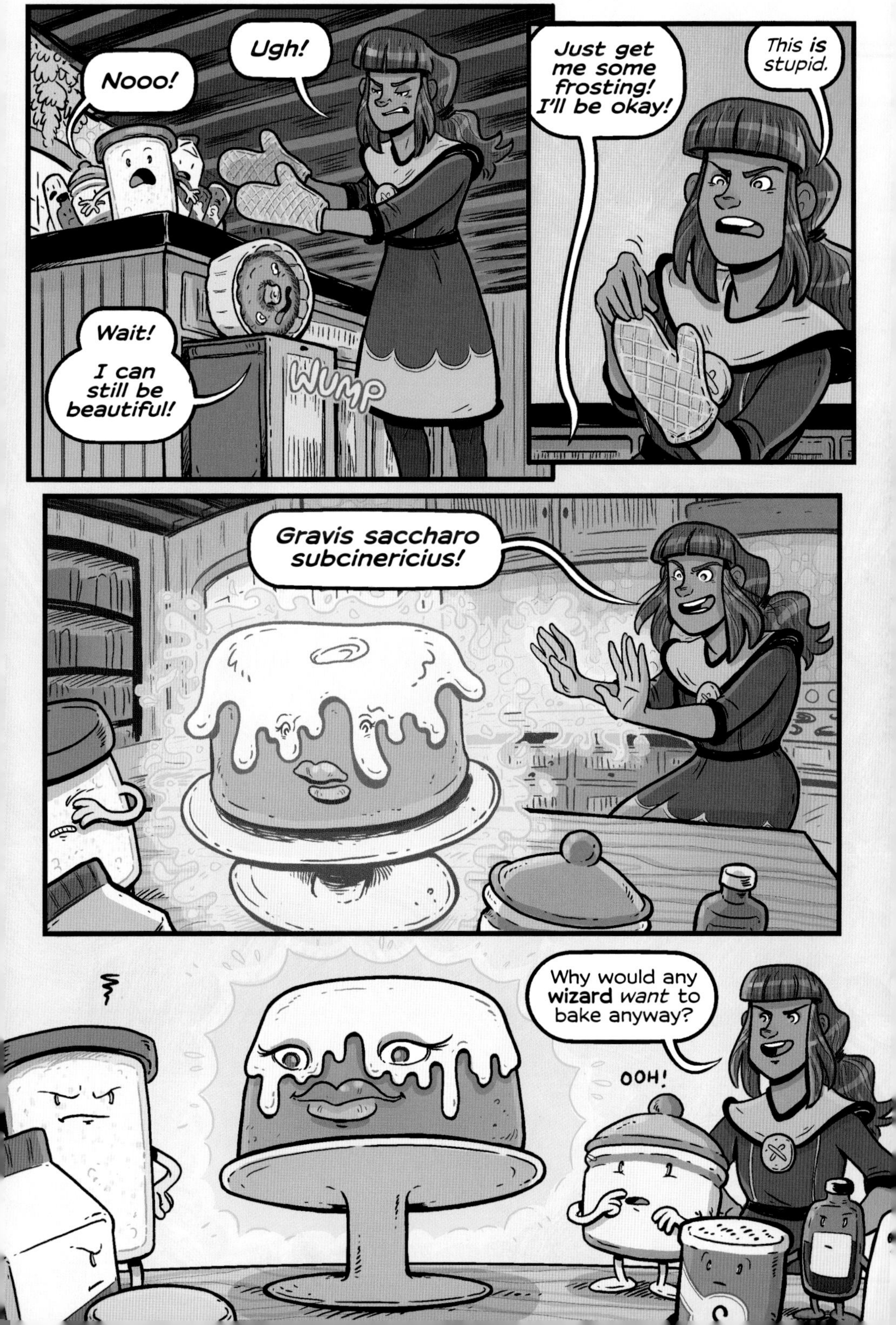
Ugh!
Nooo!
Wait!
I can still be beautiful!
WUMP
Just get me some frosting! I'll be okay!
This is stupid.
Gravis saccharo subcinericius!
Why would any **wizard** *want* to bake anyway?
OOH!

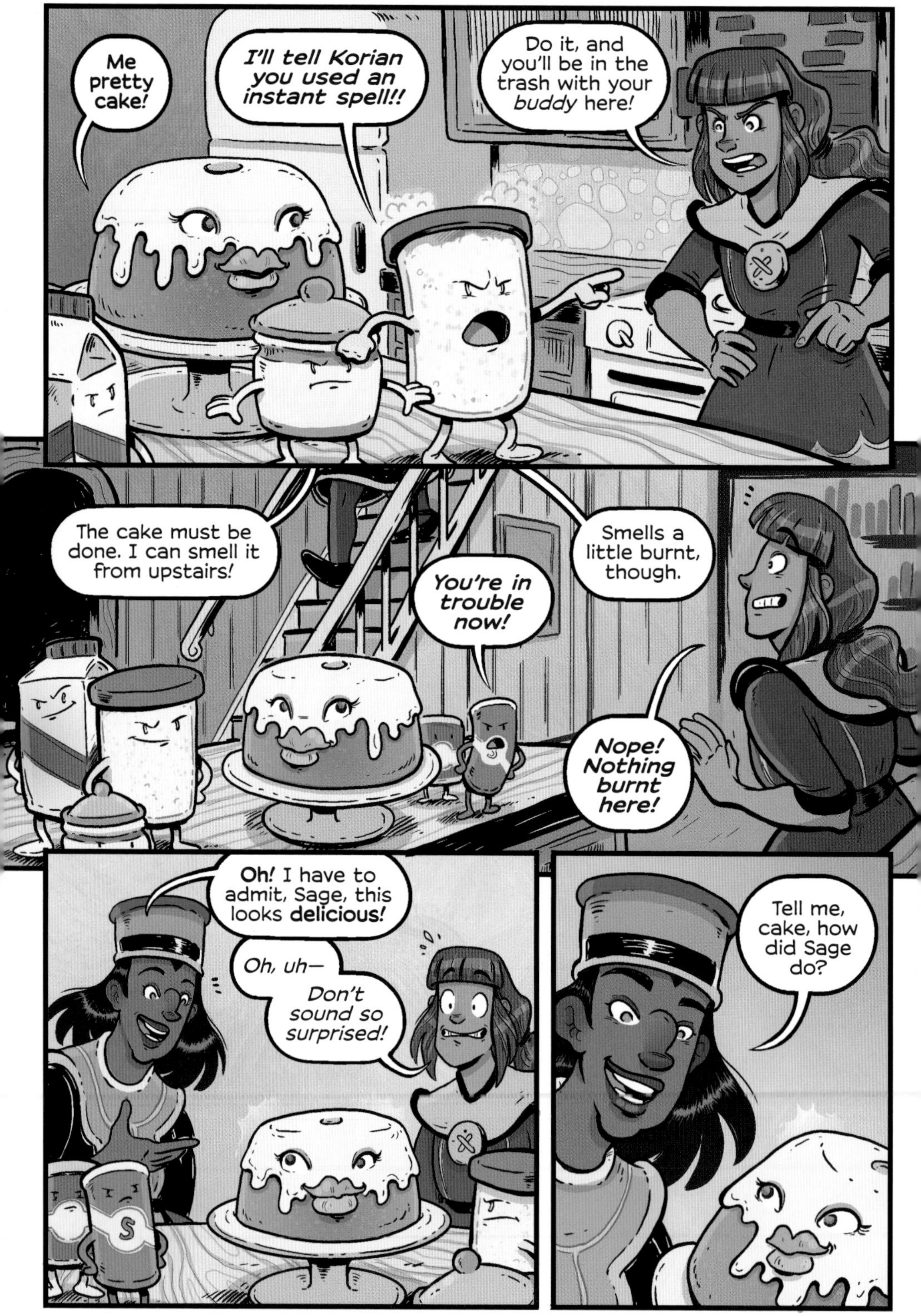
Me pretty cake!
I'll tell Korian you used an instant spell!!
Do it, and you'll be in the trash with your buddy here!
The cake must be done. I can smell it from upstairs!
Smells a little burnt, though.
You're in trouble now!
Nope! Nothing burnt here!
Oh! I have to admit, Sage, this looks delicious!
Oh, uh—
Don't sound so surprised!
Tell me, cake, how did Sage do?
S

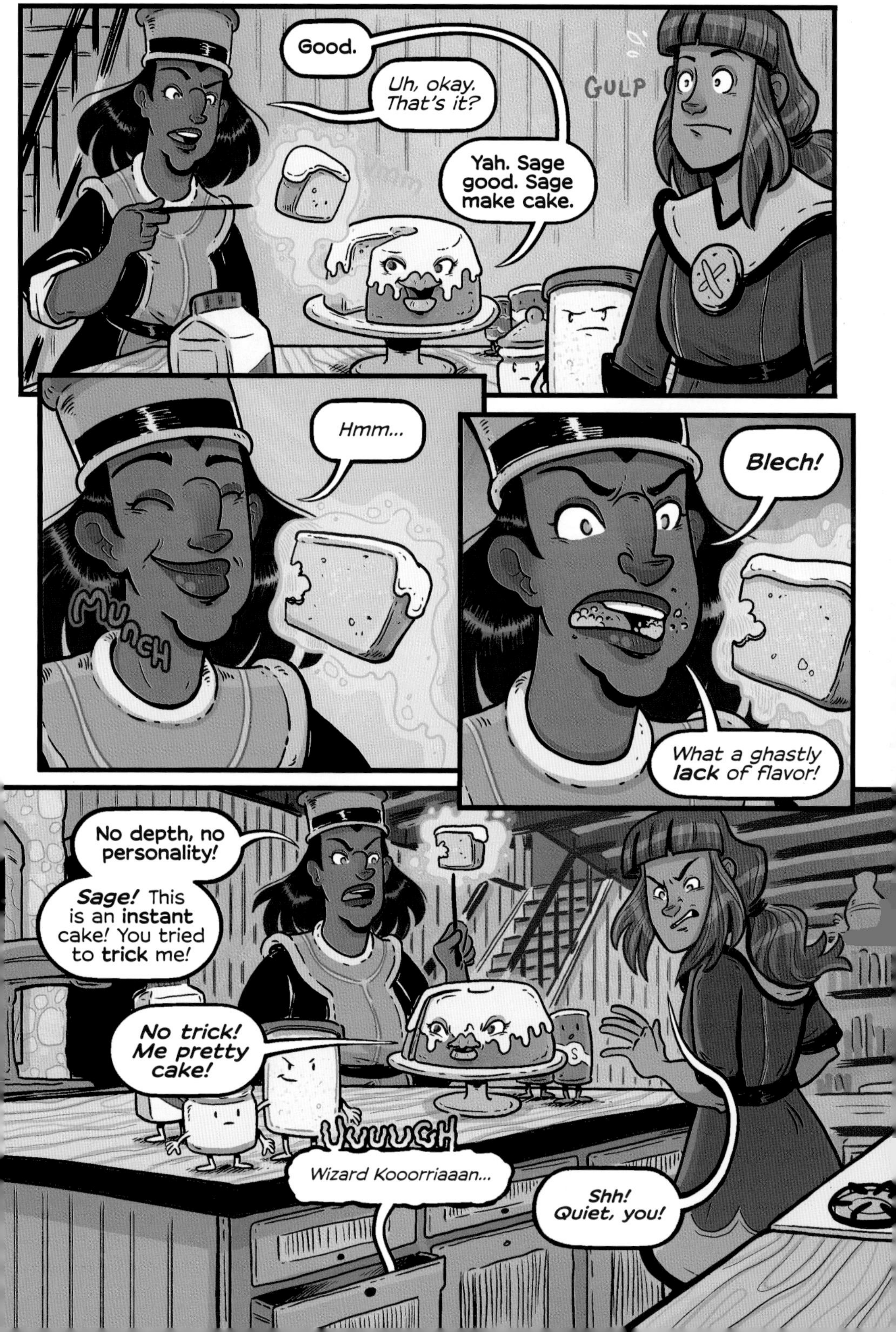

Good.
Uh, okay. That's it?
GULP
Yah. Sage good. Sage make cake.
Hmm...
MUNCH
Blech!
What a ghastly lack of flavor!
No depth, no personality!
Sage! This is an instant cake! You tried to trick me!
No trick! Me pretty cake!
UUUUGH
Wizard Kooorriaaan...
Shh! Quiet, you!

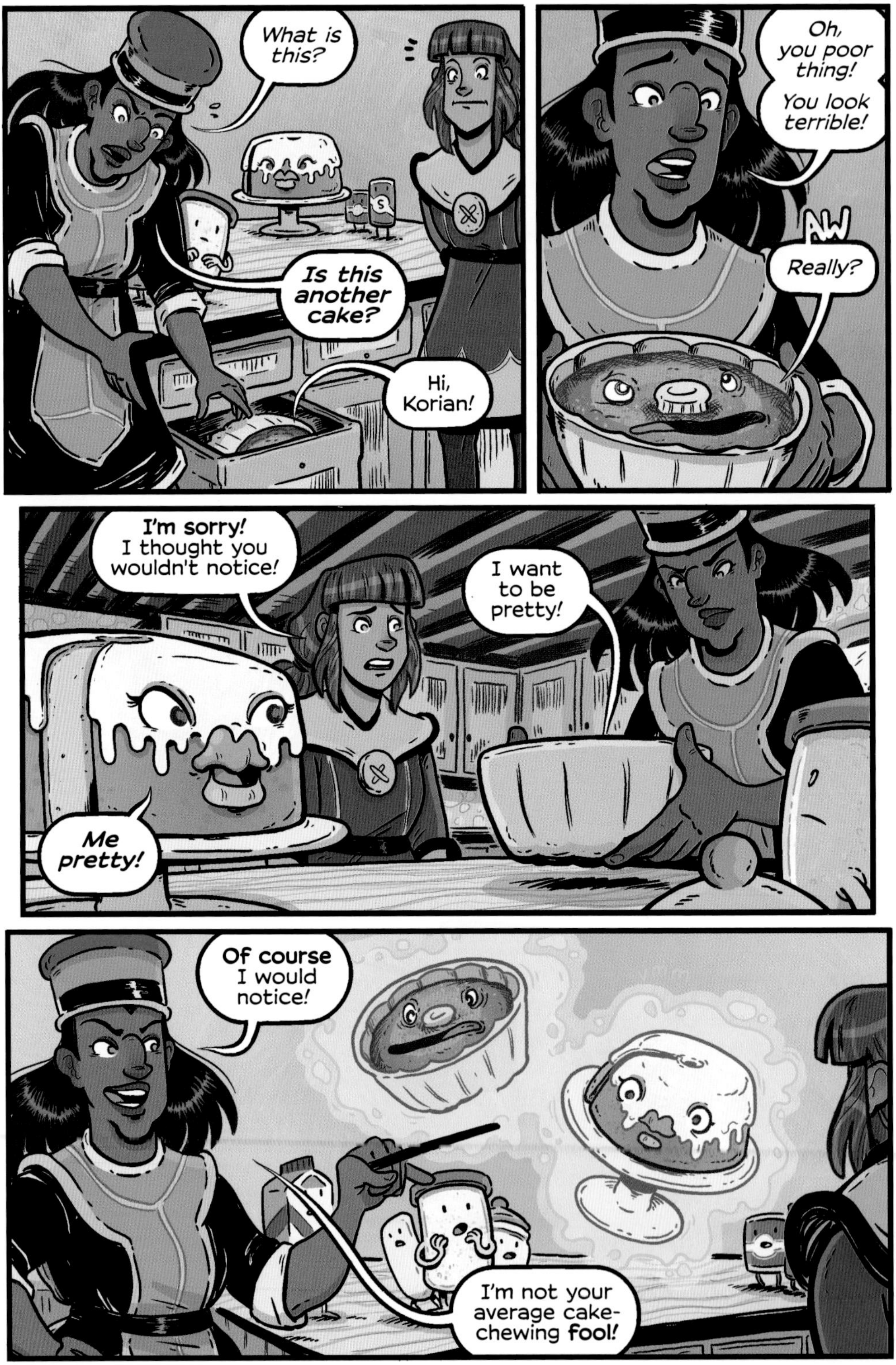
What is this?
Is this another cake?
Hi, Korian!
Oh, you poor thing!
You look terrible!
AW
Really?
I'm sorry! I thought you wouldn't notice!
I want to be pretty!
Me pretty!
Of course I would notice!
I'm not your average cake-chewing fool!

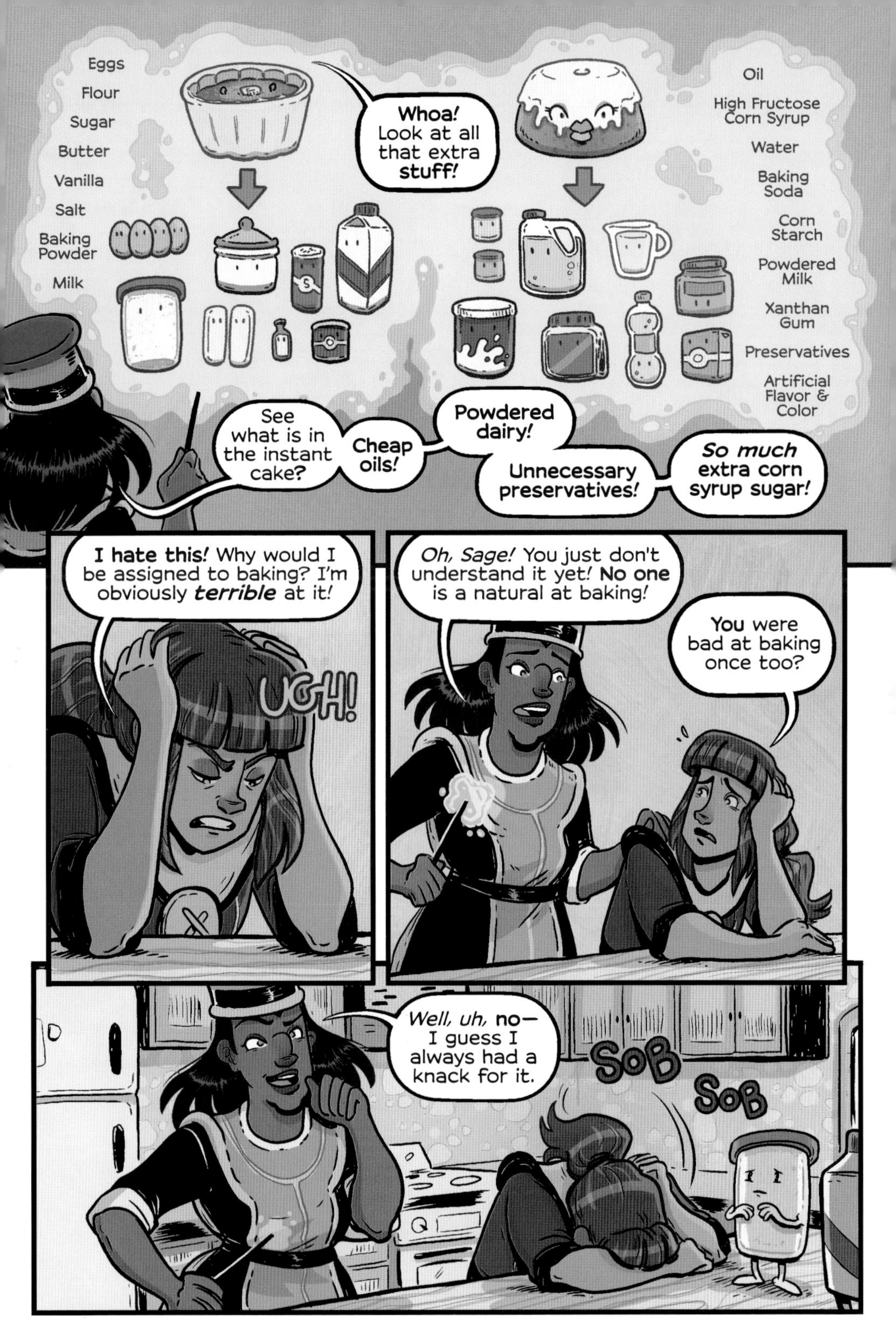
Eggs
Flour
Sugar
Butter
Vanilla
Salt
Baking Powder
Milk
Whoa! Look at all that extra stuff!
Oil
High Fructose Corn Syrup
Water
Baking Soda
Corn Starch
Powdered Milk
Xanthan Gum
Preservatives
Artificial Flavor & Color
See what is in the instant cake?
Cheap oils!
Powdered dairy!
Unnecessary preservatives!
So much extra corn syrup sugar!
I hate this! Why would I be assigned to baking? I'm obviously terrible at it!
UGH!
Oh, Sage! You just don't understand it yet! No one is a natural at baking!
You were bad at baking once too?
Well, uh, no— I guess I always had a knack for it.
SOB
SOB

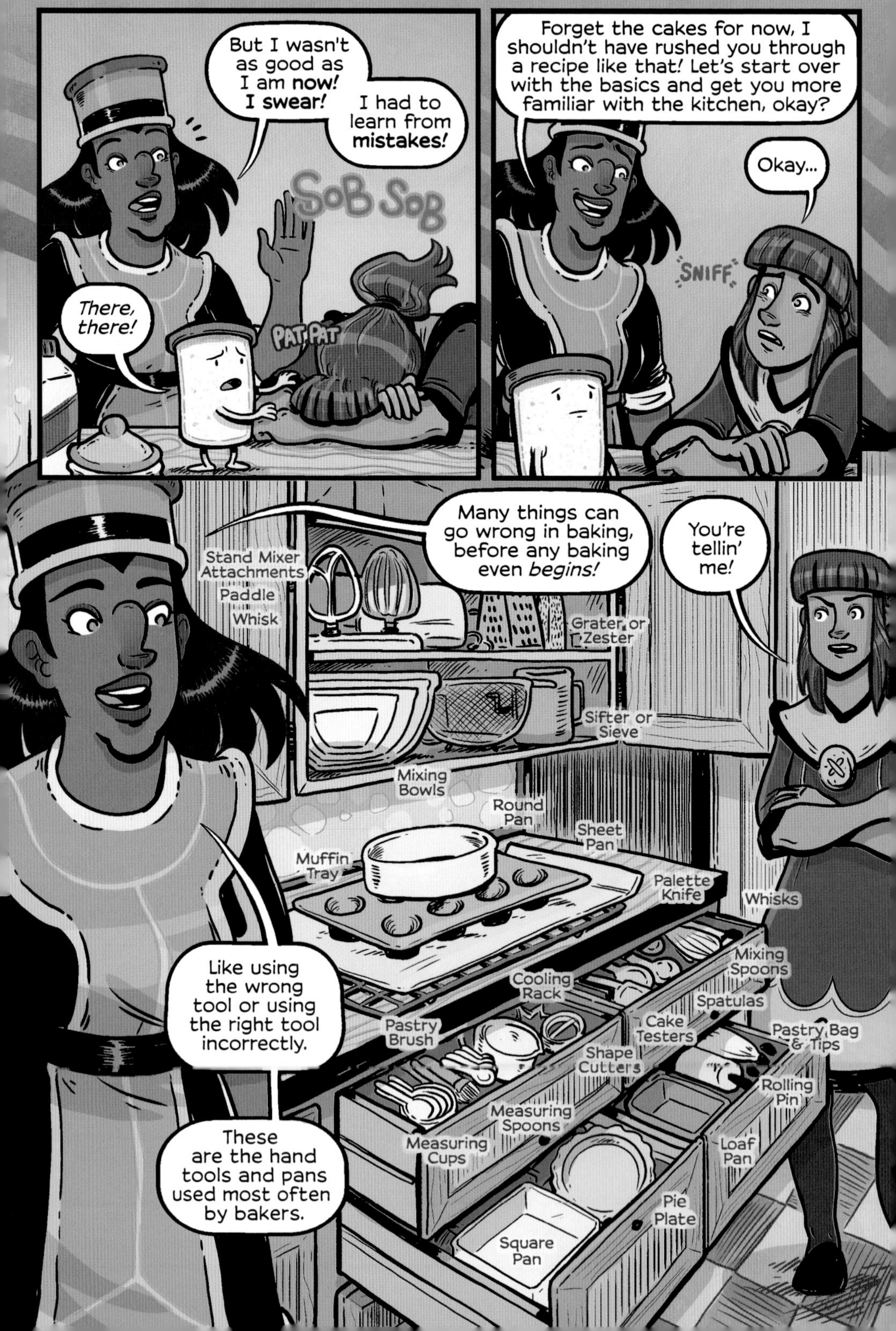
But I wasn't as good as I am **now!** **I swear!**
I had to learn from **mistakes!**
SOB SOB
There, there!
PAT PAT
Forget the cakes for now, I shouldn't have rushed you through a recipe like that! Let's start over with the basics and get you more familiar with the kitchen, okay?
Okay...
SNIFF
Many things can go wrong in baking, before any baking even *begins!*
You're tellin' me!
Stand Mixer Attachments
Paddle
Whisk
Grater or Zester
Sifter or Sieve
Mixing Bowls
Round Pan
Sheet Pan
Muffin Tray
Palette Knife
Whisks
Mixing Spoons
Cooling Rack
Spatulas
Pastry Brush
Cake Testers
Pastry Bag & Tips
Shape Cutters
Rolling Pin
Measuring Spoons
Measuring Cups
Loaf Pan
Pie Plate
Square Pan
Like using the wrong tool or using the right tool incorrectly.
These are the hand tools and pans used most often by bakers.

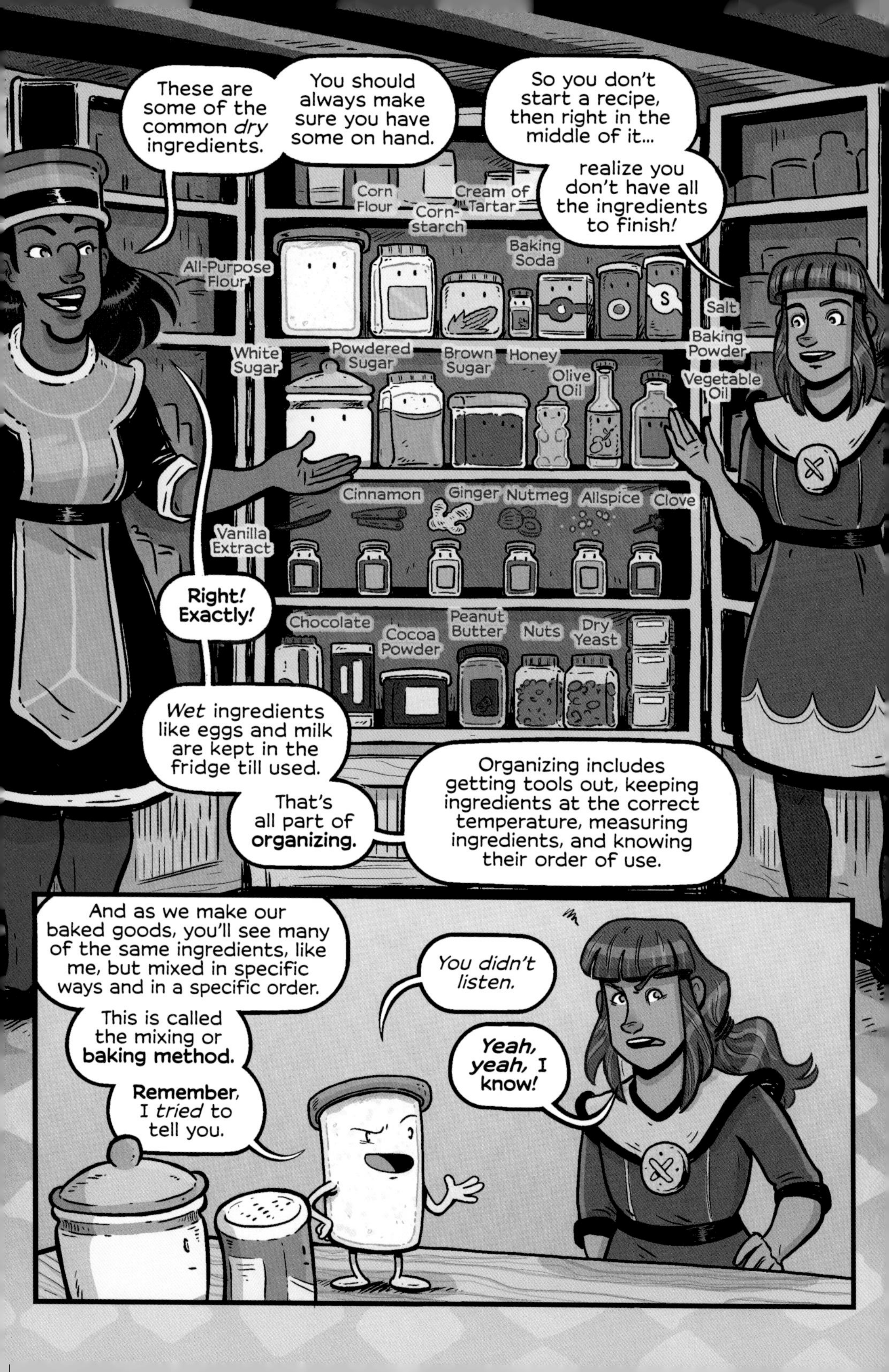
These are some of the common *dry* ingredients.
You should always make sure you have some on hand.
So you don't start a recipe, then right in the middle of it...
realize you don't have all the ingredients to finish!
Corn Flour
Corn-starch
Cream of Tartar
All-Purpose Flour
Baking Soda
Salt
Baking Powder
White Sugar
Powdered Sugar
Brown Sugar
Honey
Olive Oil
Vegetable Oil
Cinnamon
Ginger
Nutmeg
Allspice
Clove
Vanilla Extract
Right! Exactly!
Chocolate
Cocoa Powder
Peanut Butter
Nuts
Dry Yeast
Wet ingredients like eggs and milk are kept in the fridge till used.
That's all part of **organizing.**
Organizing includes getting tools out, keeping ingredients at the correct temperature, measuring ingredients, and knowing their order of use.
And as we make our baked goods, you'll see many of the same ingredients, like me, but mixed in specific ways and in a specific order.
This is called the mixing or **baking method.**
Remember, I *tried* to tell you.
You didn't listen.
***Yeah, yeah,* I know!**

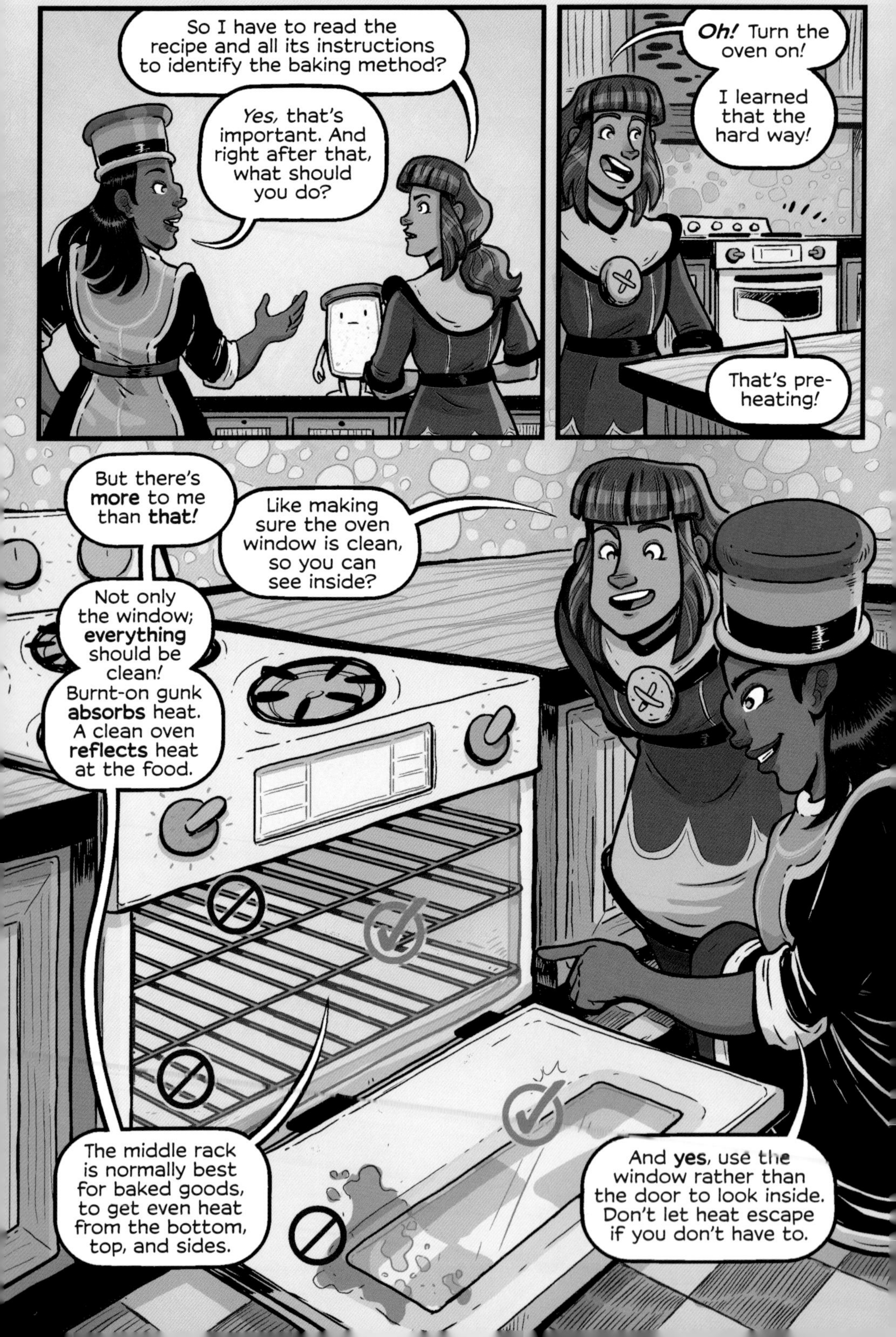
So I have to read the recipe and all its instructions to identify the baking method?
Yes, that's important. And right after that, what should you do?
Oh! Turn the oven on*!*
I learned that the hard way*!*
That's pre-heating*!*
But there's **more** to me than **that***!*
Like making sure the oven window is clean, so you can see inside?
Not only the window; **everything** should be clean*!* Burnt-on gunk **absorbs** heat. A clean oven **reflects** heat at the food.
The middle rack is normally best for baked goods, to get even heat from the bottom, top, and sides.
And **yes**, use the window rather than the door to look inside. Don't let heat escape if you don't have to.

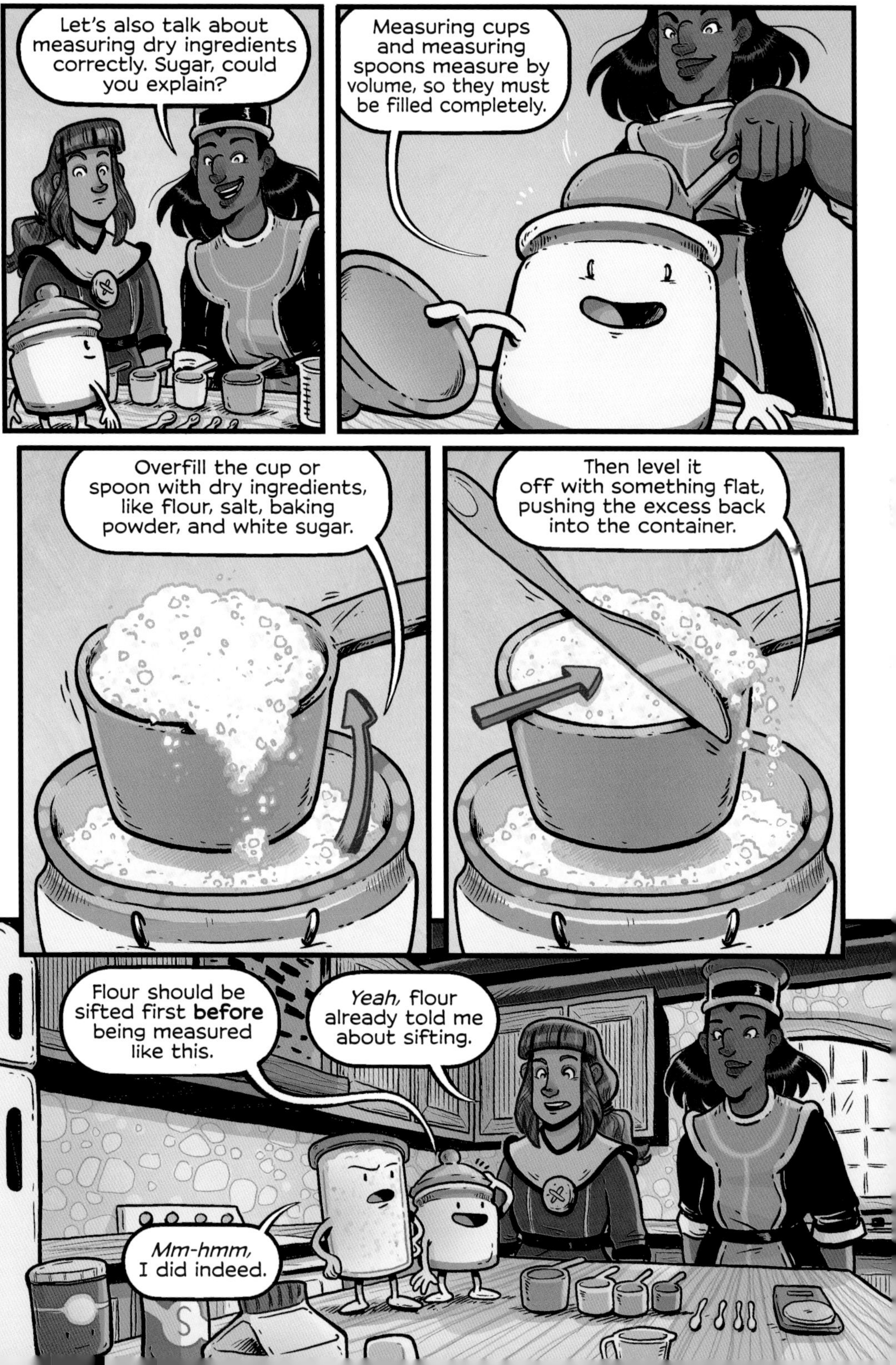
Let's also talk about measuring dry ingredients correctly. Sugar, could you explain?
Measuring cups and measuring spoons measure by volume, so they must be filled completely.
Overfill the cup or spoon with dry ingredients, like flour, salt, baking powder, and white sugar.
Then level it off with something flat, pushing the excess back into the container.
Flour should be sifted first **before** being measured like this.
Yeah, flour already told me about sifting.
Mm-hmm, I did indeed.
S

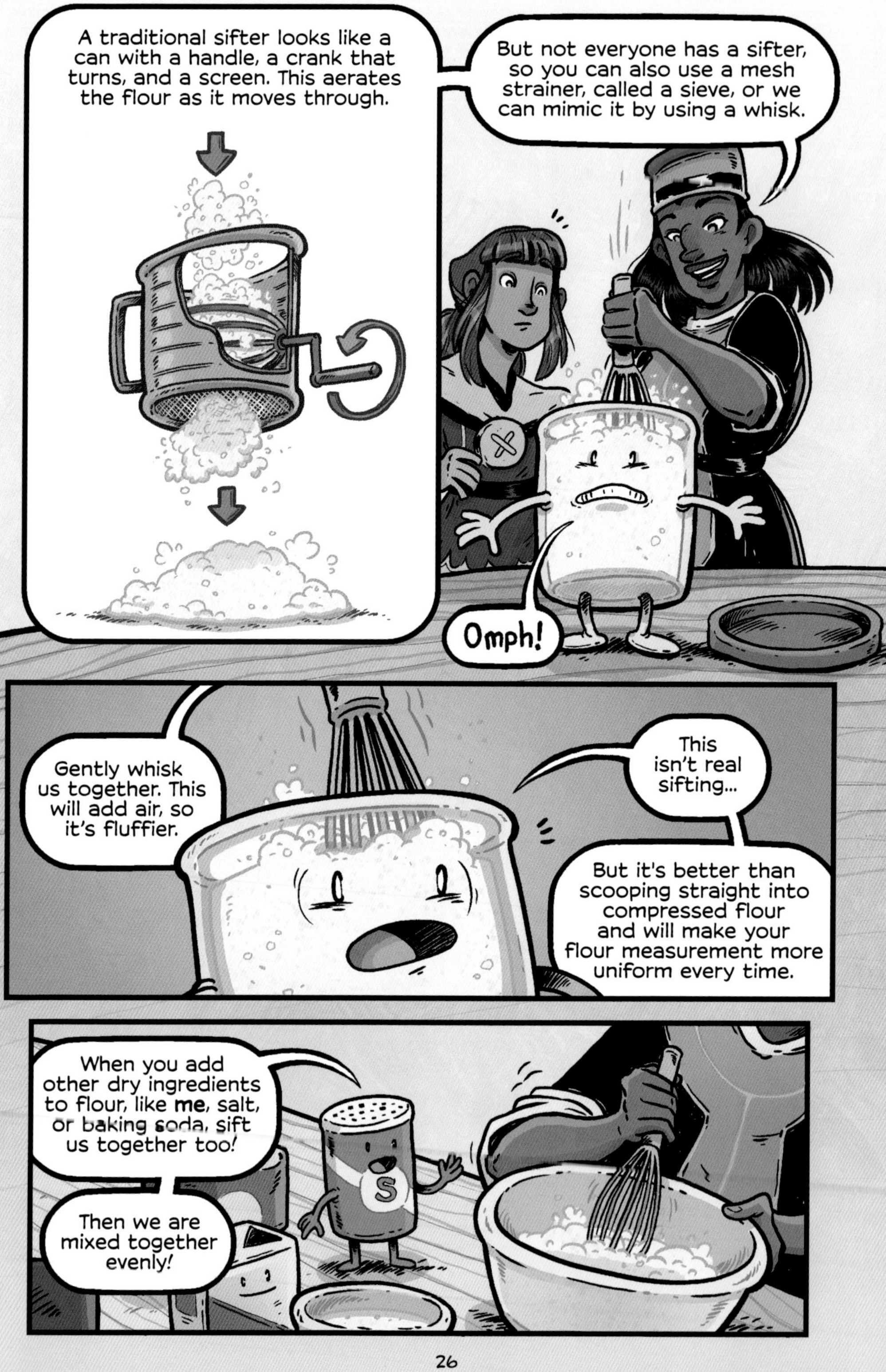
A traditional sifter looks like a can with a handle, a crank that turns, and a screen. This aerates the flour as it moves through.
But not everyone has a sifter, so you can also use a mesh strainer, called a sieve, or we can mimic it by using a whisk.
Omph!
Gently whisk us together. This will add air, so it's fluffier.
This isn't real sifting...
But it's better than scooping straight into compressed flour and will make your flour measurement more uniform every time.
When you add other dry ingredients to flour, like **me**, salt, or baking soda, sift us together too!
Then we are mixed together evenly!

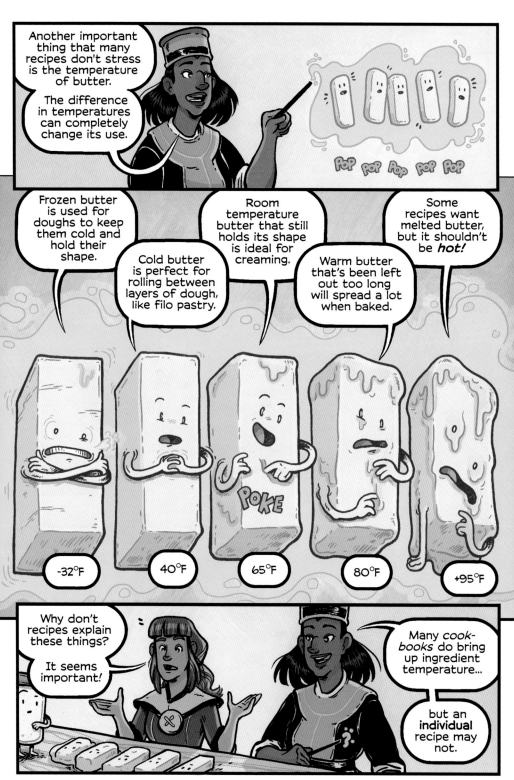

Another important thing that many recipes don't stress is the temperature of butter.

The difference in temperatures can completely change its use.

POP POP POP POP POP

Frozen butter is used for doughs to keep them cold and hold their shape.

Cold butter is perfect for rolling between layers of dough, like filo pastry.

Room temperature butter that still holds its shape is ideal for creaming.

Warm butter that's been left out too long will spread a lot when baked.

Some recipes want melted butter, but it shouldn't be *hot!*

POKE

-32°F

40°F

65°F

80°F

+95°F

Why don't recipes explain these things?

It seems important!

Many *cook-books* do bring up ingredient temperature...

but an **individual** recipe may not.

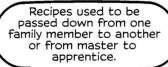

Recipes used to be passed down from one family member to another or from master to apprentice.

People learned by *example.*

Bakers learned *how* different baking methods worked...

without knowing exactly *why* they did.

Understanding the science of baking improves the skills of both the expert and the amateur baker especially since recipes don't always explain every word or technique.

I'll never remember all this.

It's best to learn by doing it.

Whaddya say we make some cookies?

Chocolate chip?

CHOCOLATE CHIP COOKIES

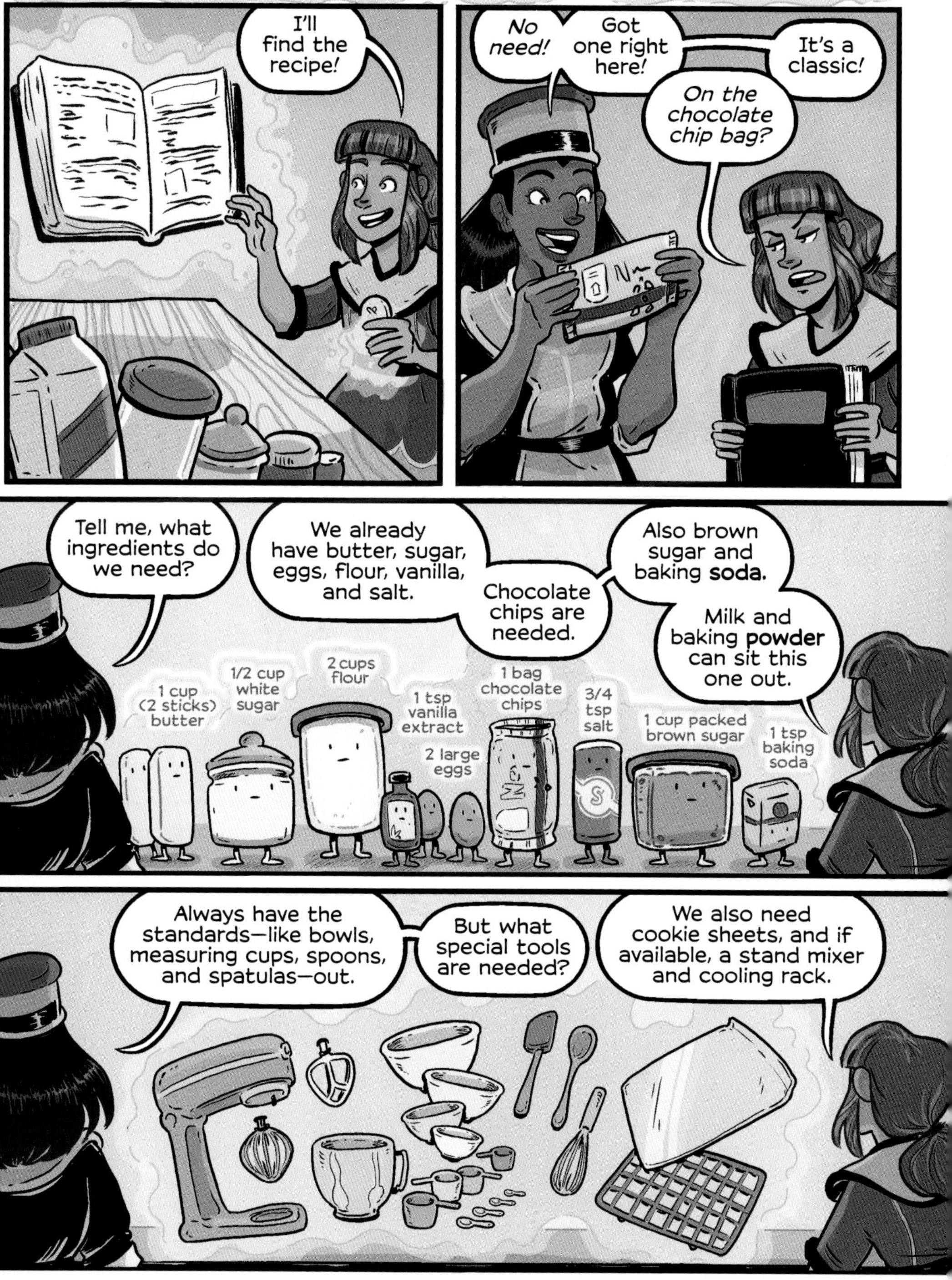

I'll find the recipe!
No need!
Got one right here!
It's a classic!
On the chocolate chip bag?
Tell me, what ingredients do we need?
We already have butter, sugar, eggs, flour, vanilla, and salt.
Chocolate chips are needed.
Also brown sugar and baking **soda.**
Milk and baking **powder** can sit this one out.
1 cup (2 sticks) butter
1/2 cup white sugar
2 cups flour
1 tsp vanilla extract
2 large eggs
1 bag chocolate chips
3/4 tsp salt
1 cup packed brown sugar
1 tsp baking soda
Always have the standards—like bowls, measuring cups, spoons, and spatulas—out.
But what special tools are needed?
We also need cookie sheets, and if available, a stand mixer and cooling rack.

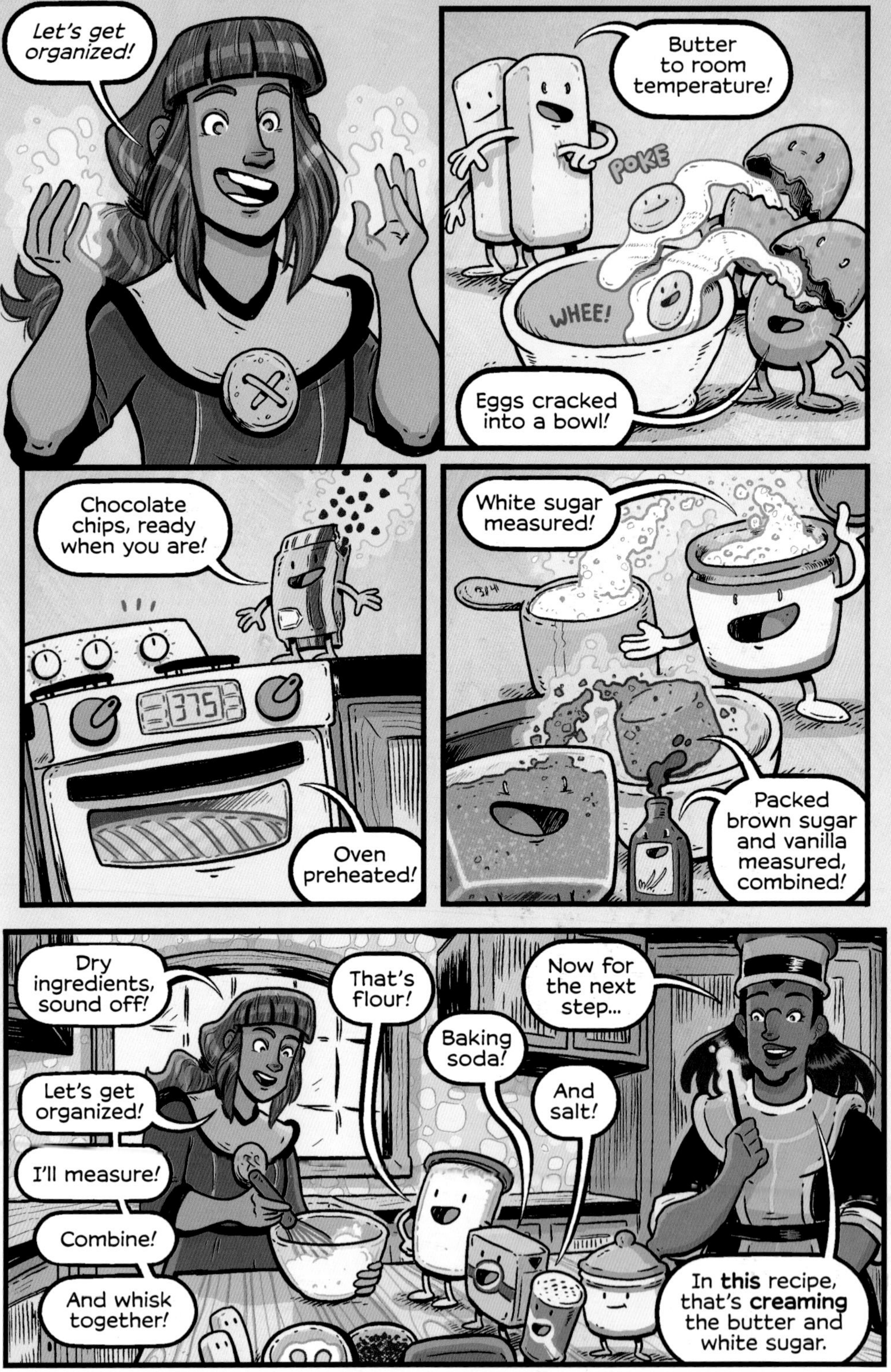
Let's get organized!
Butter to room temperature!
POKE
WHEE!
Eggs cracked into a bowl!
Chocolate chips, ready when you are!
375
Oven preheated!
White sugar measured!
3/4
Packed brown sugar and vanilla measured, combined!
Dry ingredients, sound off!
That's flour!
Baking soda!
And salt!
Now for the next step...
Let's get organized!
I'll measure!
Combine!
And whisk together!
In **this** recipe, that's **creaming** the butter and white sugar.

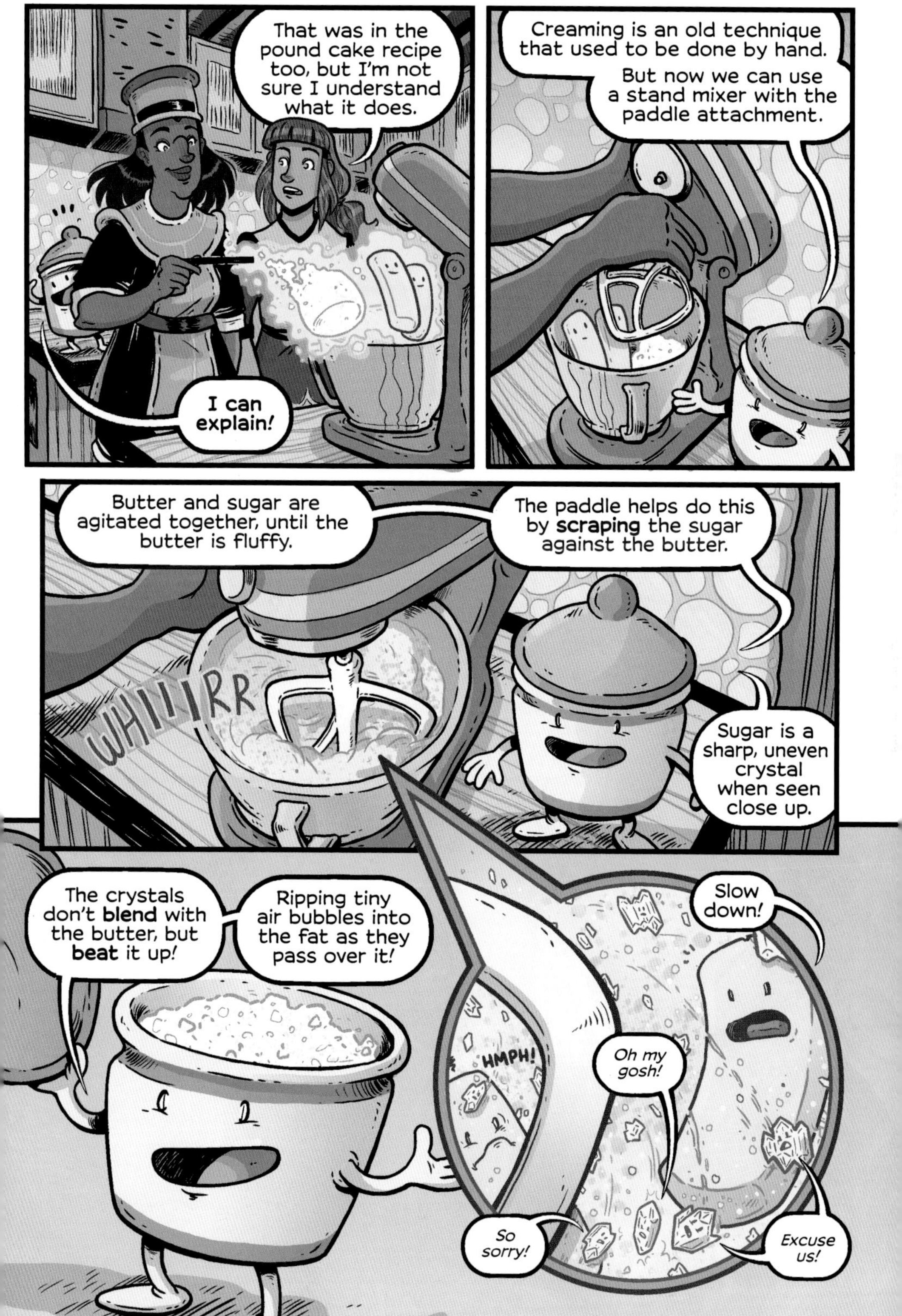
That was in the pound cake recipe too, but I'm not sure I understand what it does.
I can explain!
Creaming is an old technique that used to be done by hand.
But now we can use a stand mixer with the paddle attachment.
Butter and sugar are agitated together, until the butter is fluffy.
The paddle helps do this by scraping the sugar against the butter.
WHIIIRR
Sugar is a sharp, uneven crystal when seen close up.
The crystals don't blend with the butter, but beat it up!
Ripping tiny air bubbles into the fat as they pass over it!
Slow down!
HMPH!
Oh my gosh!
So sorry!
Excuse us!

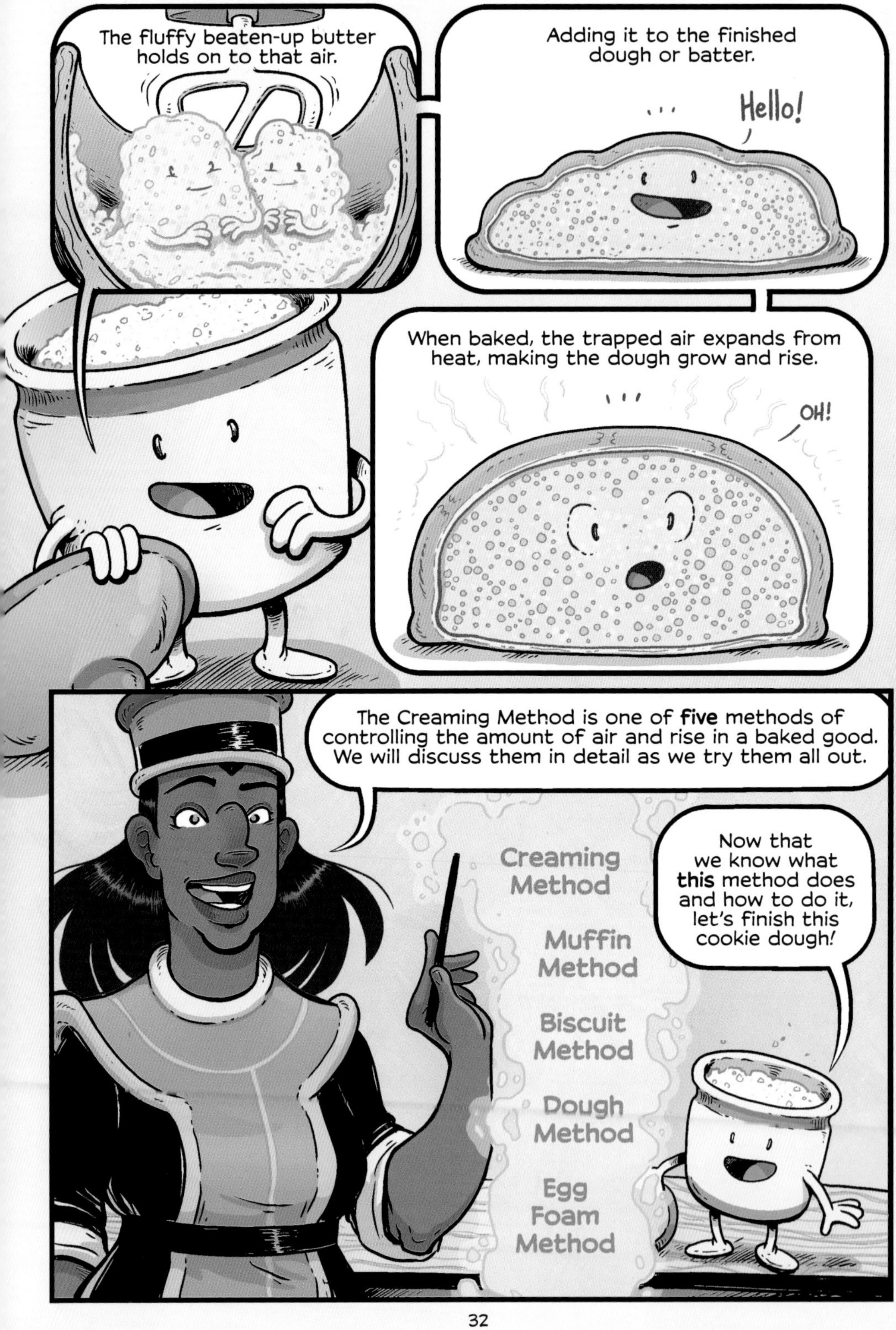

The fluffy beaten-up butter holds on to that air.
Adding it to the finished dough or batter.
...
Hello!
When baked, the trapped air expands from heat, making the dough grow and rise.
...
OH!
The Creaming Method is one of **five** methods of controlling the amount of air and rise in a baked good. We will discuss them in detail as we try them all out.
Creaming Method
Muffin Method
Biscuit Method
Dough Method
Egg Foam Method
Now that we know what **this** method does and how to do it, let's finish this cookie dough!

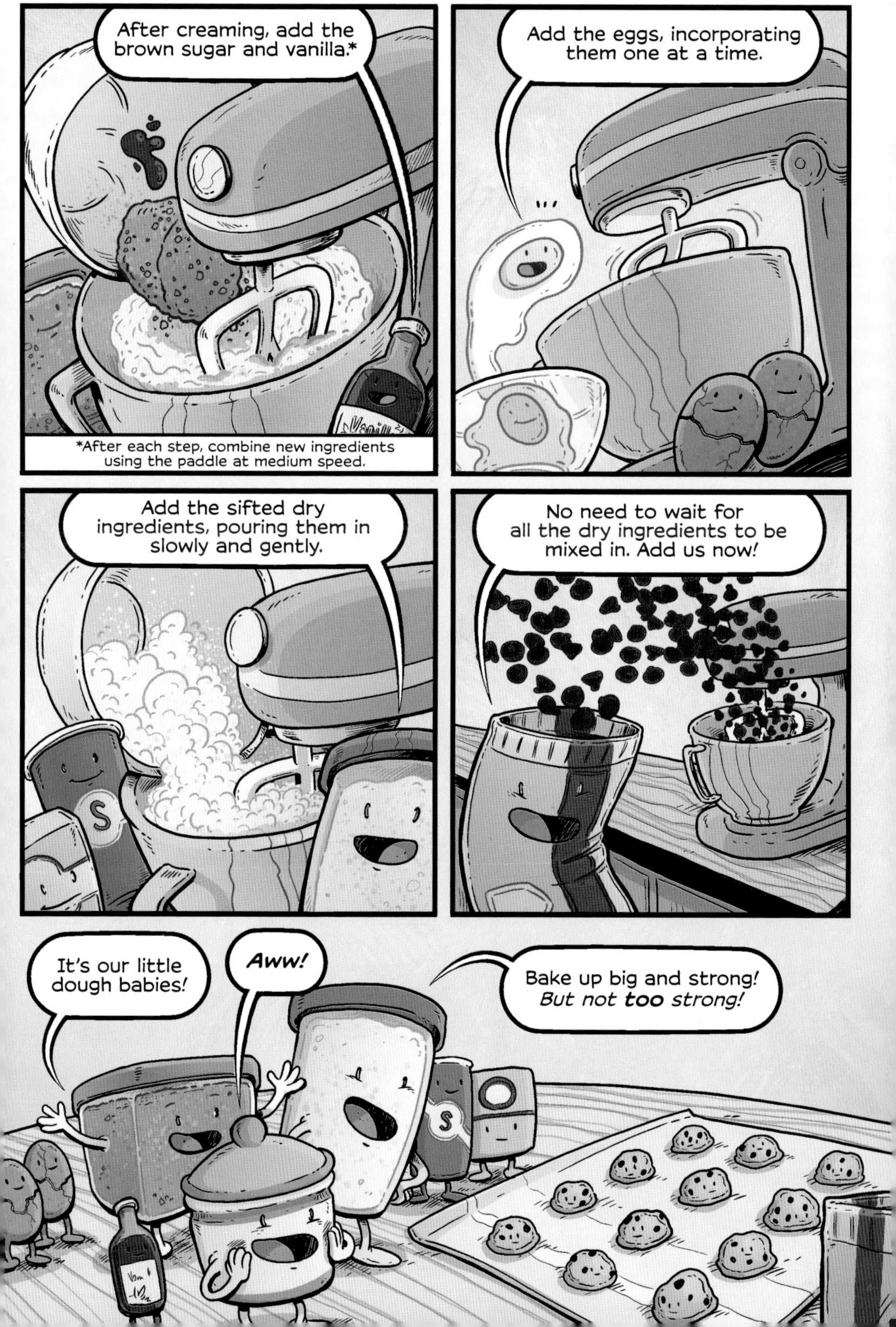
After creaming, add the brown sugar and vanilla.*
*After each step, combine new ingredients using the paddle at medium speed.
Add the eggs, incorporating them one at a time.
Add the sifted dry ingredients, pouring them in slowly and gently.
No need to wait for all the dry ingredients to be mixed in. Add us now!
It's our little dough babies!
Aww!
Bake up big and strong! *But not **too** strong!*

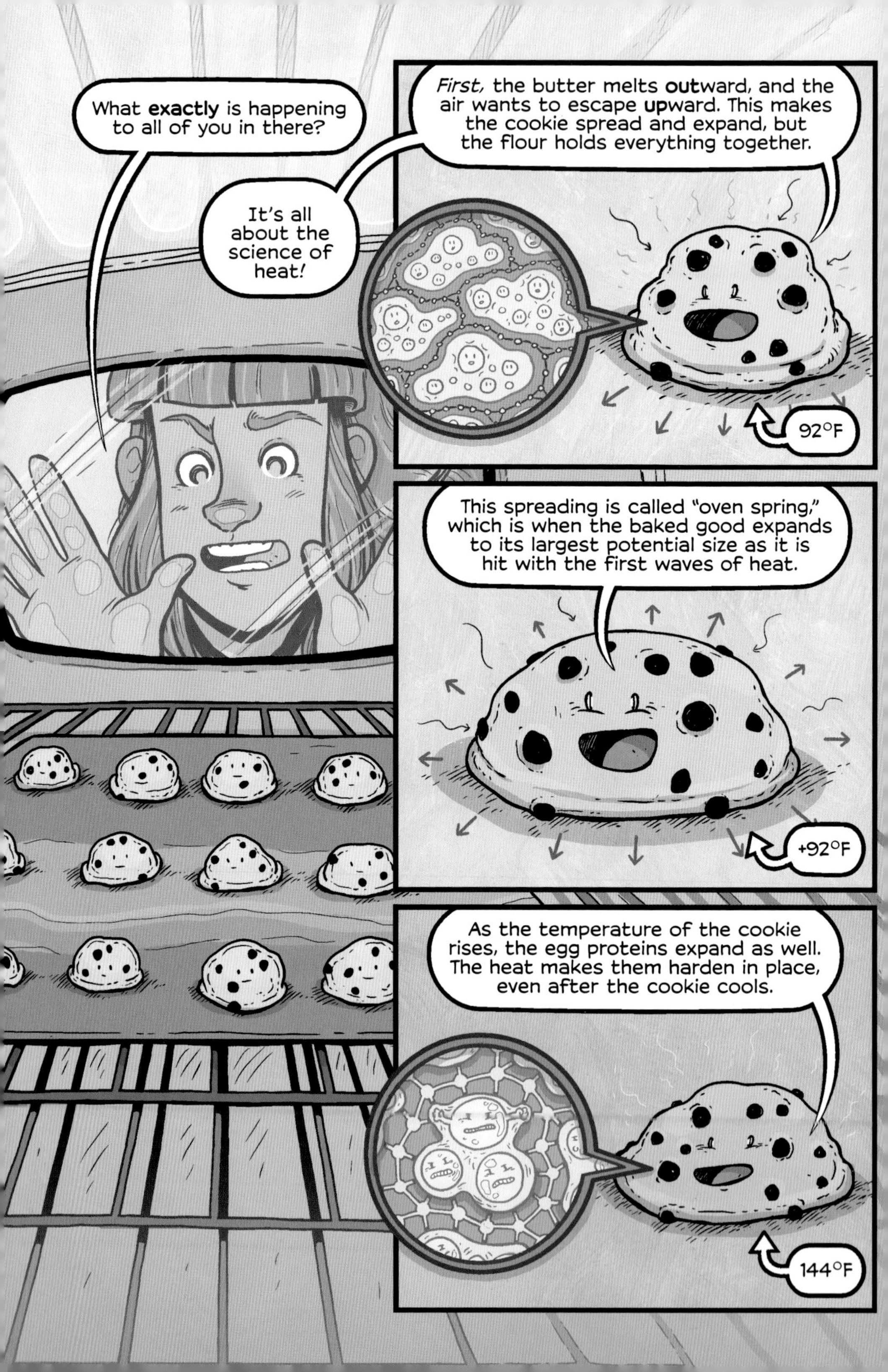
What exactly is happening to all of you in there?
It's all about the science of heat!
First, the butter melts outward, and the air wants to escape upward. This makes the cookie spread and expand, but the flour holds everything together.
92°F
This spreading is called "oven spring," which is when the baked good expands to its largest potential size as it is hit with the first waves of heat.
+92°F
As the temperature of the cookie rises, the egg proteins expand as well. The heat makes them harden in place, even after the cookie cools.
144°F

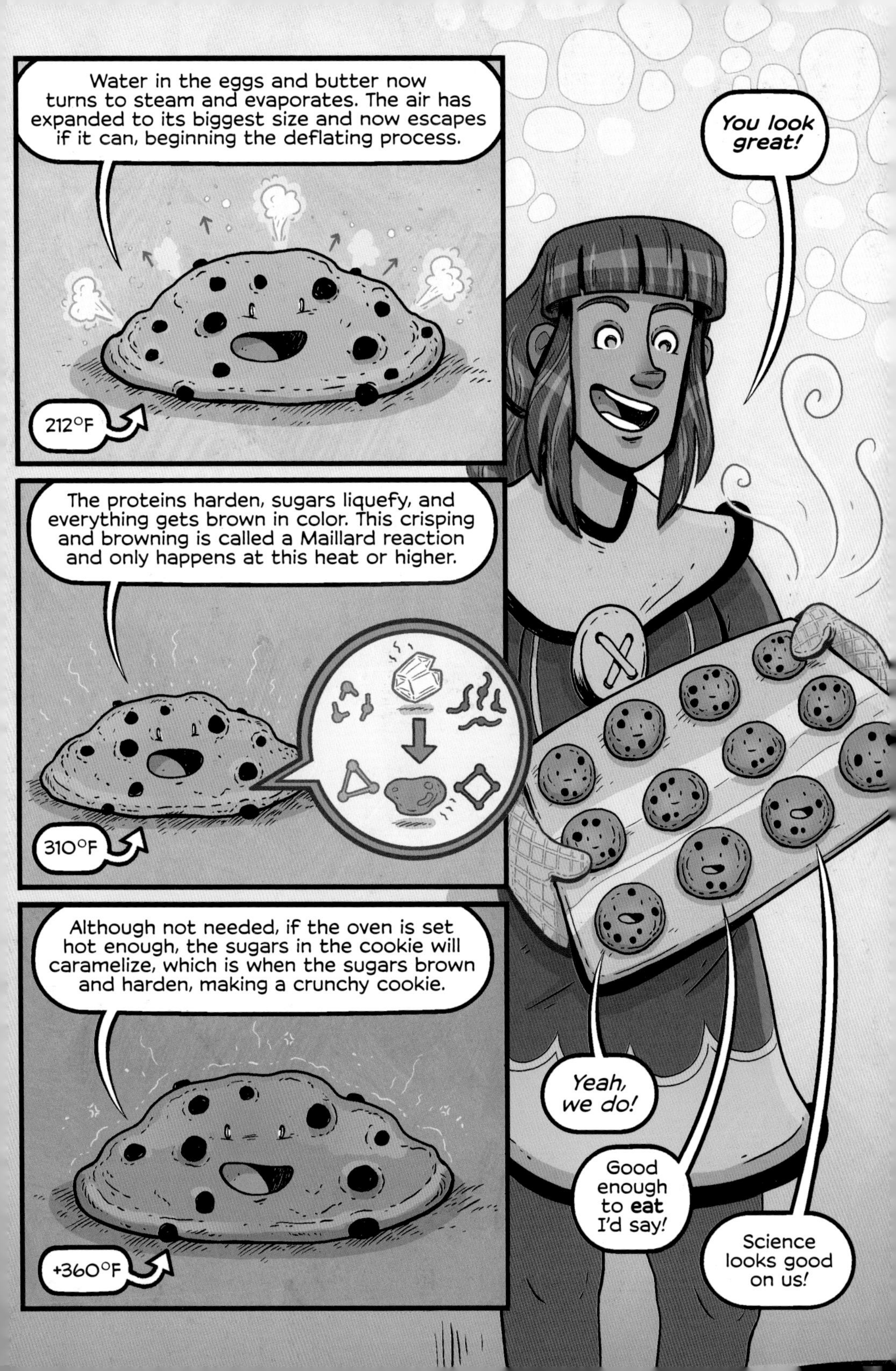
Water in the eggs and butter now turns to steam and evaporates. The air has expanded to its biggest size and now escapes if it can, beginning the deflating process.
212°F
You look great!
The proteins harden, sugars liquefy, and everything gets brown in color. This crisping and browning is called a Maillard reaction and only happens at this heat or higher.
310°F
Although not needed, if the oven is set hot enough, the sugars in the cookie will caramelize, which is when the sugars brown and harden, making a crunchy cookie.
+360°F
Yeah, we do!
Good enough to **eat** I'd say!
Science looks good on us!

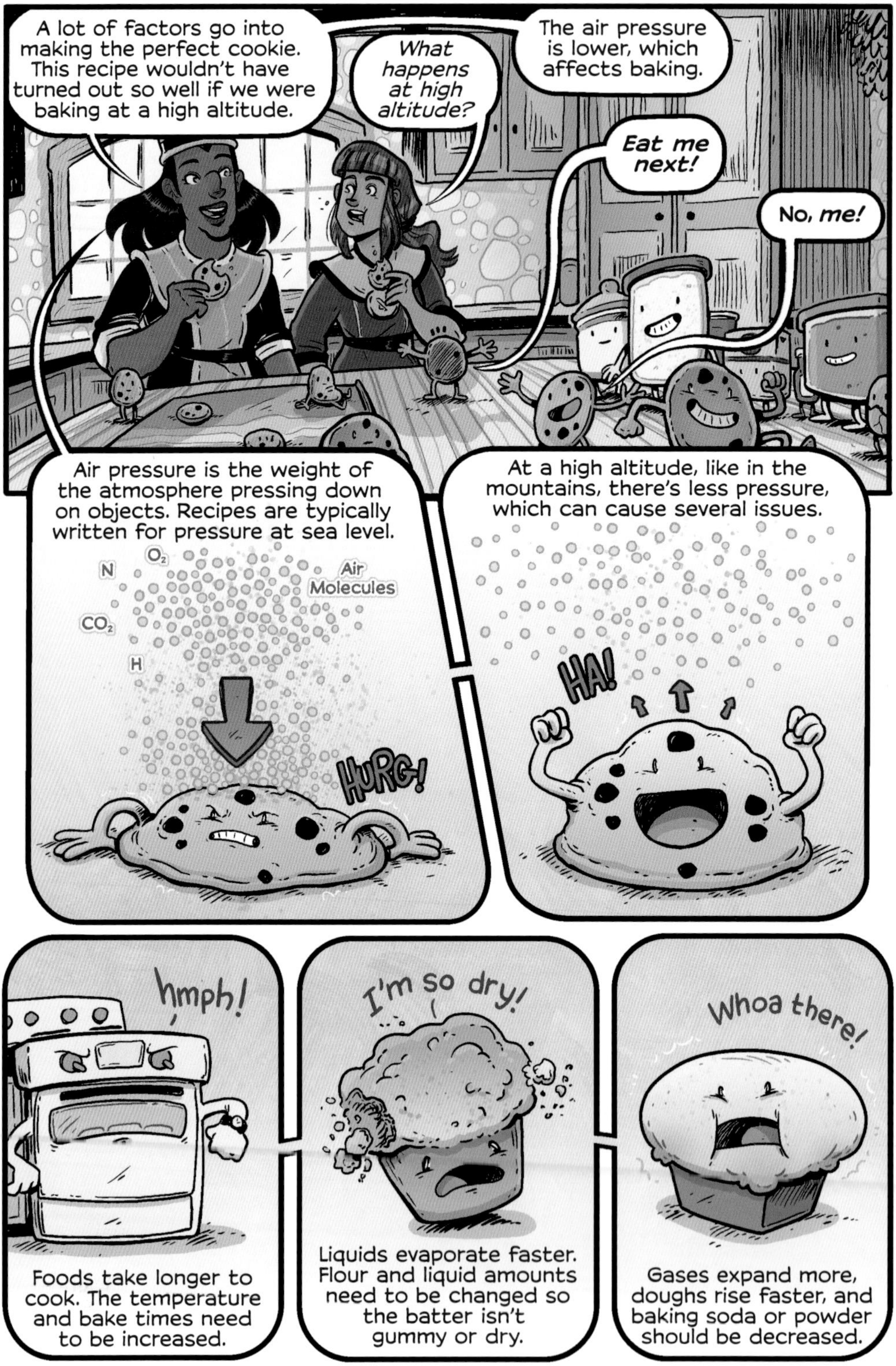
A lot of factors go into making the perfect cookie. This recipe wouldn't have turned out so well if we were baking at a high altitude.
What happens at high altitude?
The air pressure is lower, which affects baking.
Eat me next!
No, me!
Air pressure is the weight of the atmosphere pressing down on objects. Recipes are typically written for pressure at sea level.
N
O2
CO2
H
Air Molecules
HURG!
At a high altitude, like in the mountains, there's less pressure, which can cause several issues.
HA!
hmph!
Foods take longer to cook. The temperature and bake times need to be increased.
I'm so dry!
Liquids evaporate faster. Flour and liquid amounts need to be changed so the batter isn't gummy or dry.
Whoa there!
Gases expand more, doughs rise faster, and baking soda or powder should be decreased.

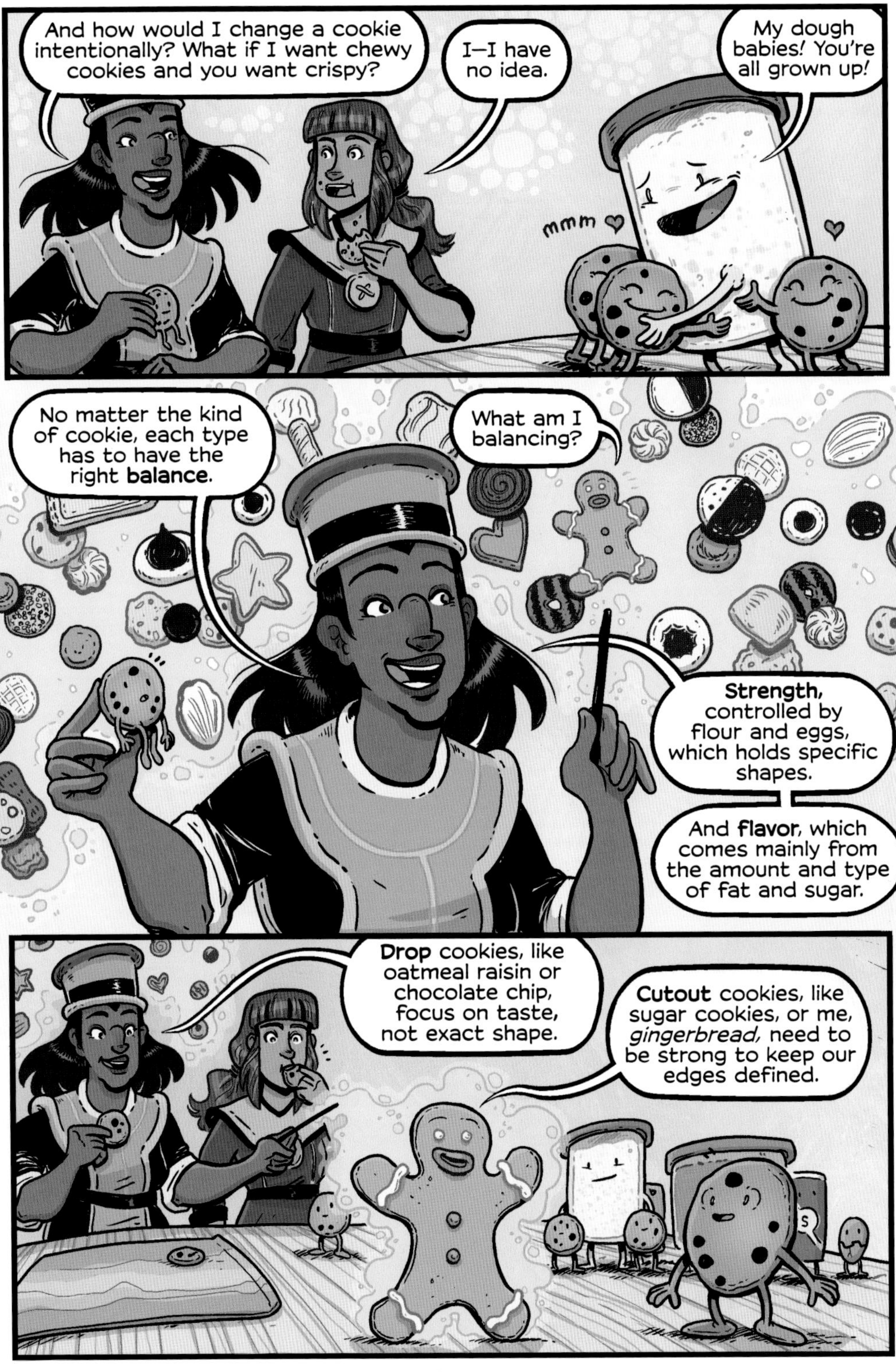

And how would I change a cookie intentionally? What if I want chewy cookies and you want crispy?
I—I have no idea.
My dough babies! You're all grown up!
mmm
No matter the kind of cookie, each type has to have the right **balance**.
What am I balancing?
Strength, controlled by flour and eggs, which holds specific shapes.
And **flavor**, which comes mainly from the amount and type of fat and sugar.
Drop cookies, like oatmeal raisin or chocolate chip, focus on taste, not exact shape.
Cutout cookies, like sugar cookies, or me, *gingerbread,* need to be strong to keep our edges defined.

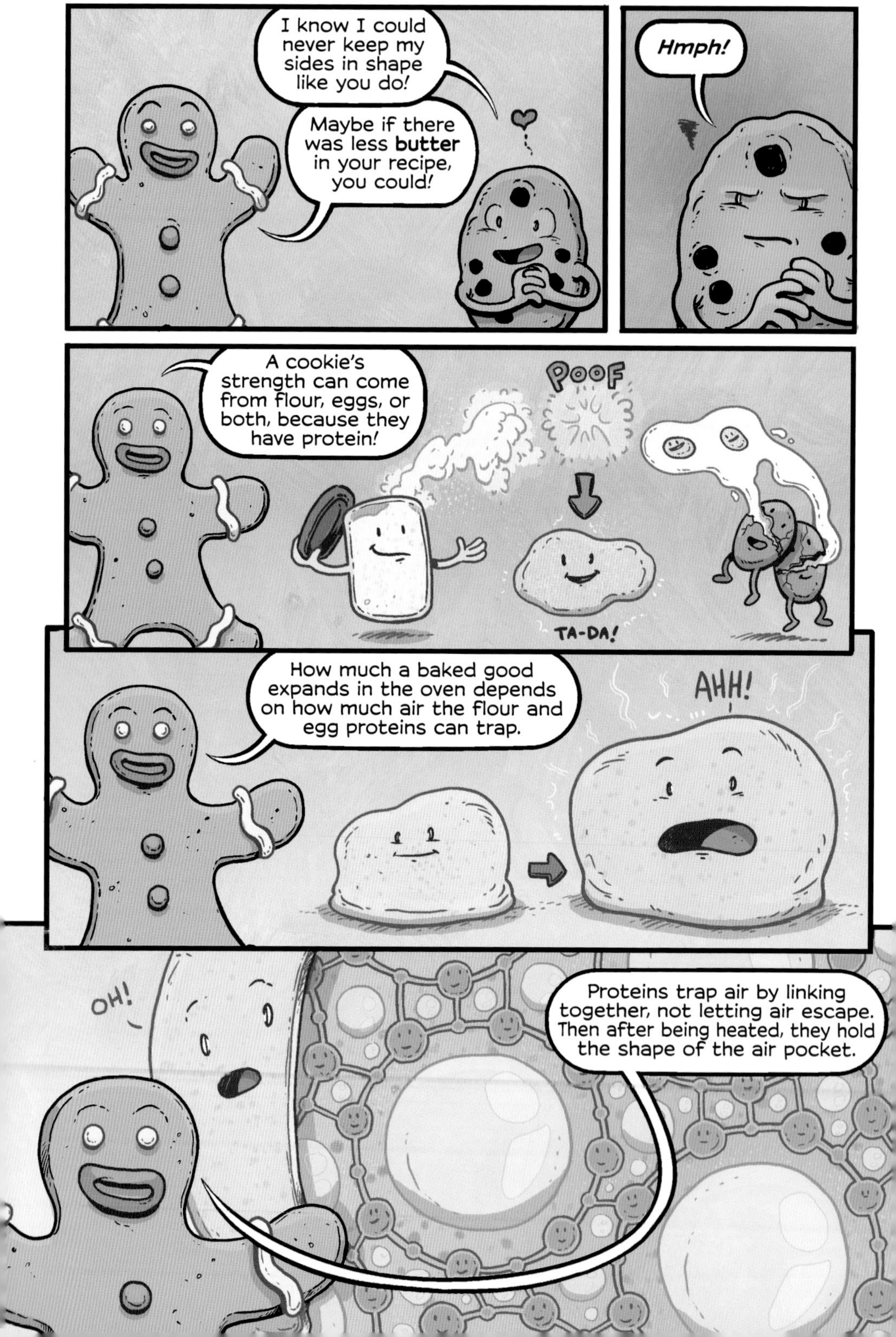
I know I could never keep my sides in shape like you do!
Maybe if there was less **butter** in your recipe, you could!
Hmph!
A cookie's strength can come from flour, eggs, or both, because they have protein!
POOF
TA-DA!
How much a baked good expands in the oven depends on how much air the flour and egg proteins can trap.
AHH!
OH!
Proteins trap air by linking together, not letting air escape. Then after being heated, they hold the shape of the air pocket.

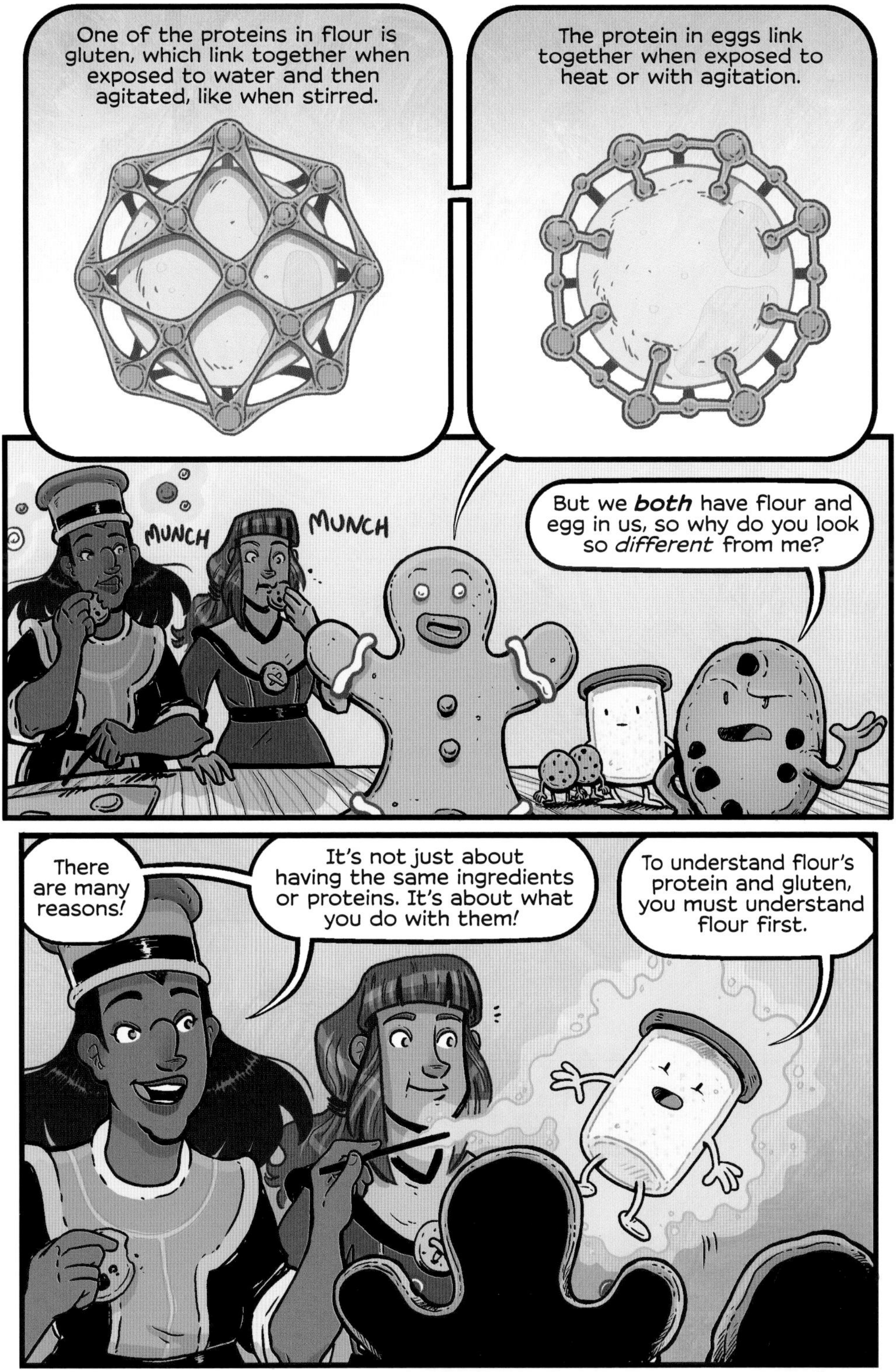
One of the proteins in flour is gluten, which link together when exposed to water and then agitated, like when stirred.
The protein in eggs link together when exposed to heat or with agitation.
MUNCH
MUNCH
But we **both** have flour and egg in us, so why do you look so *different* from me?
There are many reasons!
It's not just about having the same ingredients or proteins. It's about what you do with them!
To understand flour's protein and gluten, you must understand flour first.

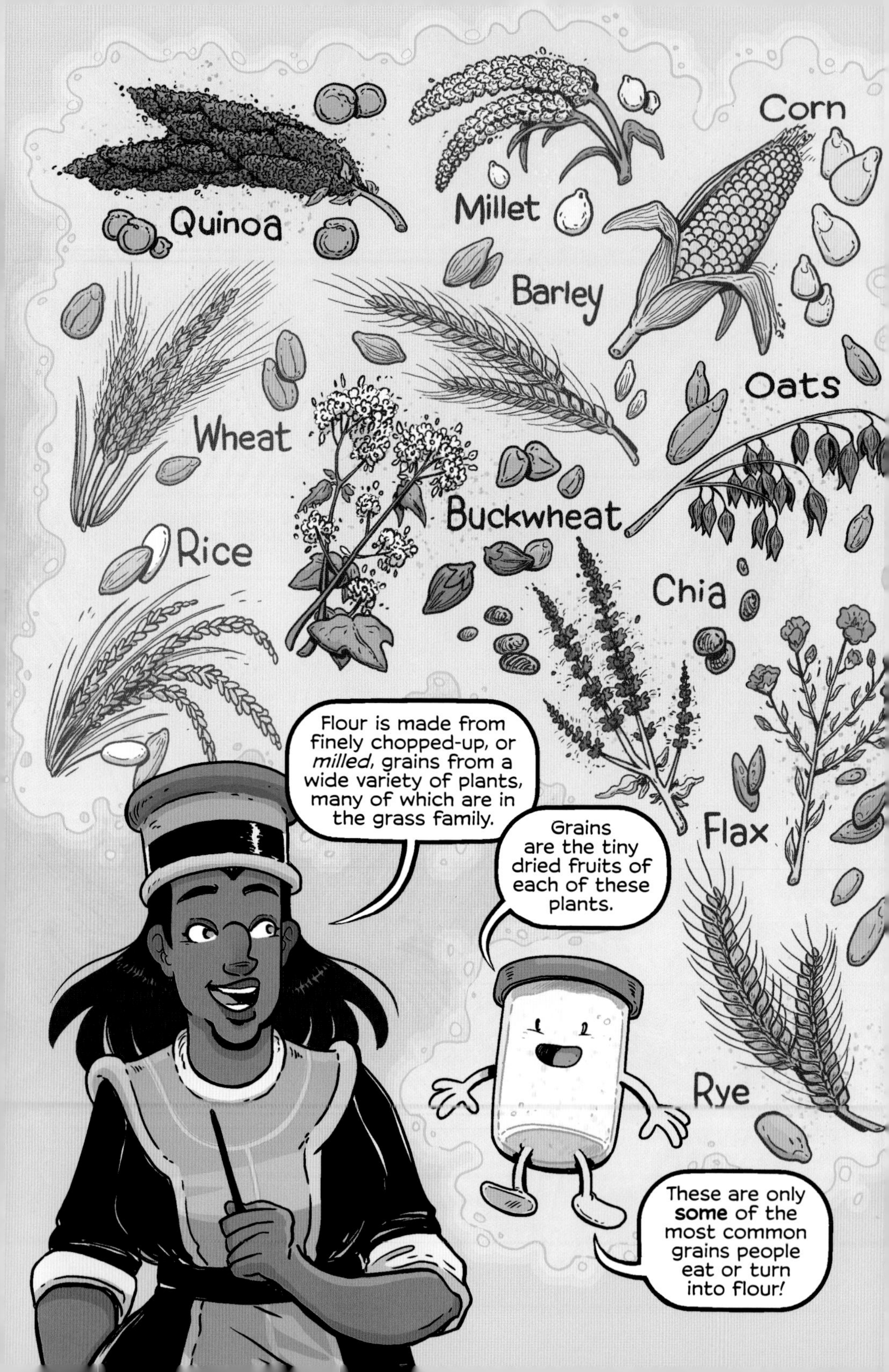

Quinoa
Millet
Corn
Barley
Oats
Wheat
Buckwheat
Rice
Chia
Flax
Rye
Flour is made from finely chopped-up, or *milled*, grains from a wide variety of plants, many of which are in the grass family.
Grains are the tiny dried fruits of each of these plants.
These are only **some** of the most common grains people eat or turn into flour!

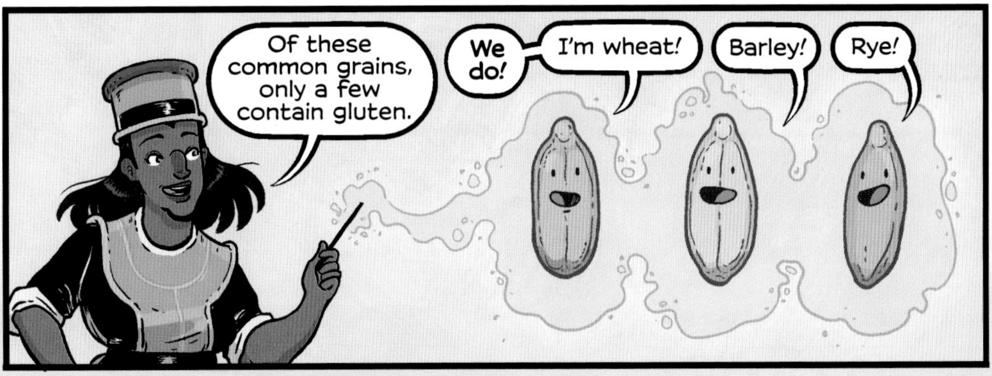
Of these common grains, only a few contain gluten.
We do!
I'm wheat!
Barley!
Rye!

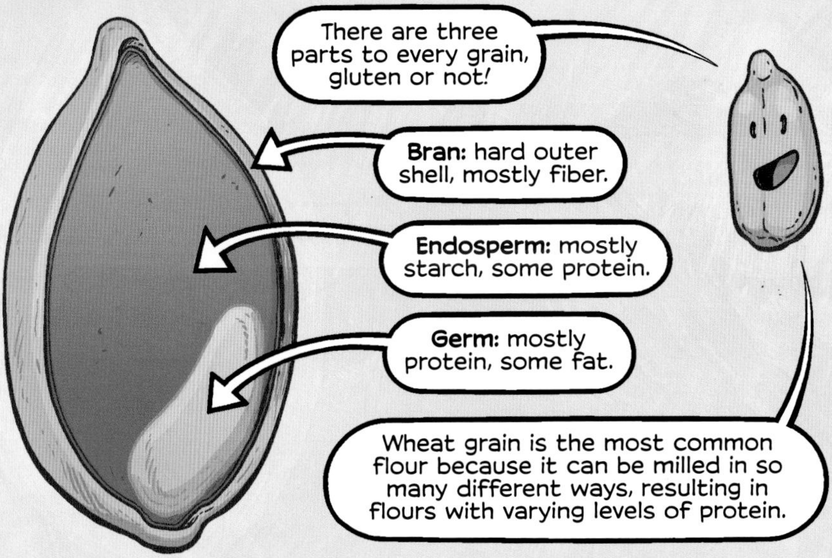
There are three parts to every grain, gluten or not!
Bran: hard outer shell, mostly fiber.
Endosperm: mostly starch, some protein.
Germ: mostly protein, some fat.
Wheat grain is the most common flour because it can be milled in so many different ways, resulting in flours with varying levels of protein.

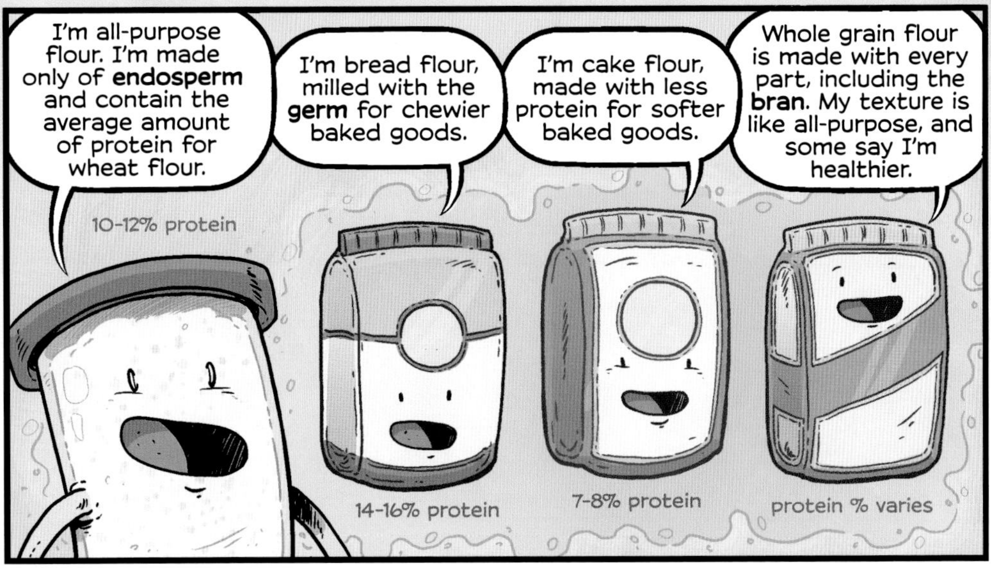
I'm all-purpose flour. I'm made only of **endosperm** and contain the average amount of protein for wheat flour.
I'm bread flour, milled with the **germ** for chewier baked goods.
I'm cake flour, made with less protein for softer baked goods.
Whole grain flour is made with every part, including the **bran**. My texture is like all-purpose, and some say I'm healthier.
10-12% protein
14-16% protein
7-8% protein
protein % varies

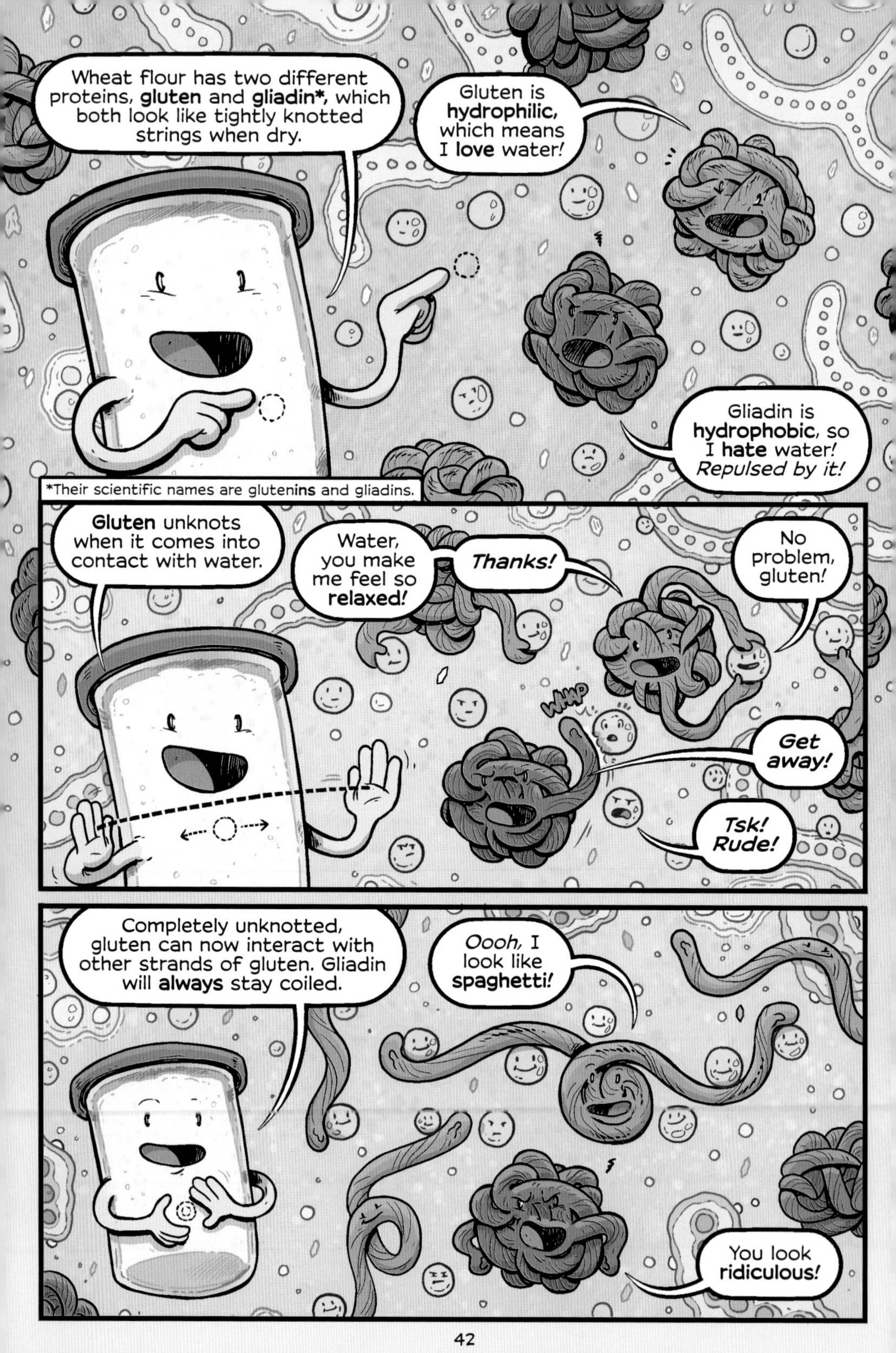

Wheat flour has two different proteins, gluten and gliadin*, which both look like tightly knotted strings when dry.
Gluten is hydrophilic, which means I love water!
Gliadin is hydrophobic, so I hate water! Repulsed by it!
*Their scientific names are glutenins and gliadins.
Gluten unknots when it comes into contact with water.
Water, you make me feel so relaxed!
Thanks!
No problem, gluten!
WHAP
Get away!
Tsk! Rude!
Completely unknotted, gluten can now interact with other strands of gluten. Gliadin will always stay coiled.
Oooh, I look like spaghetti!
You look ridiculous!

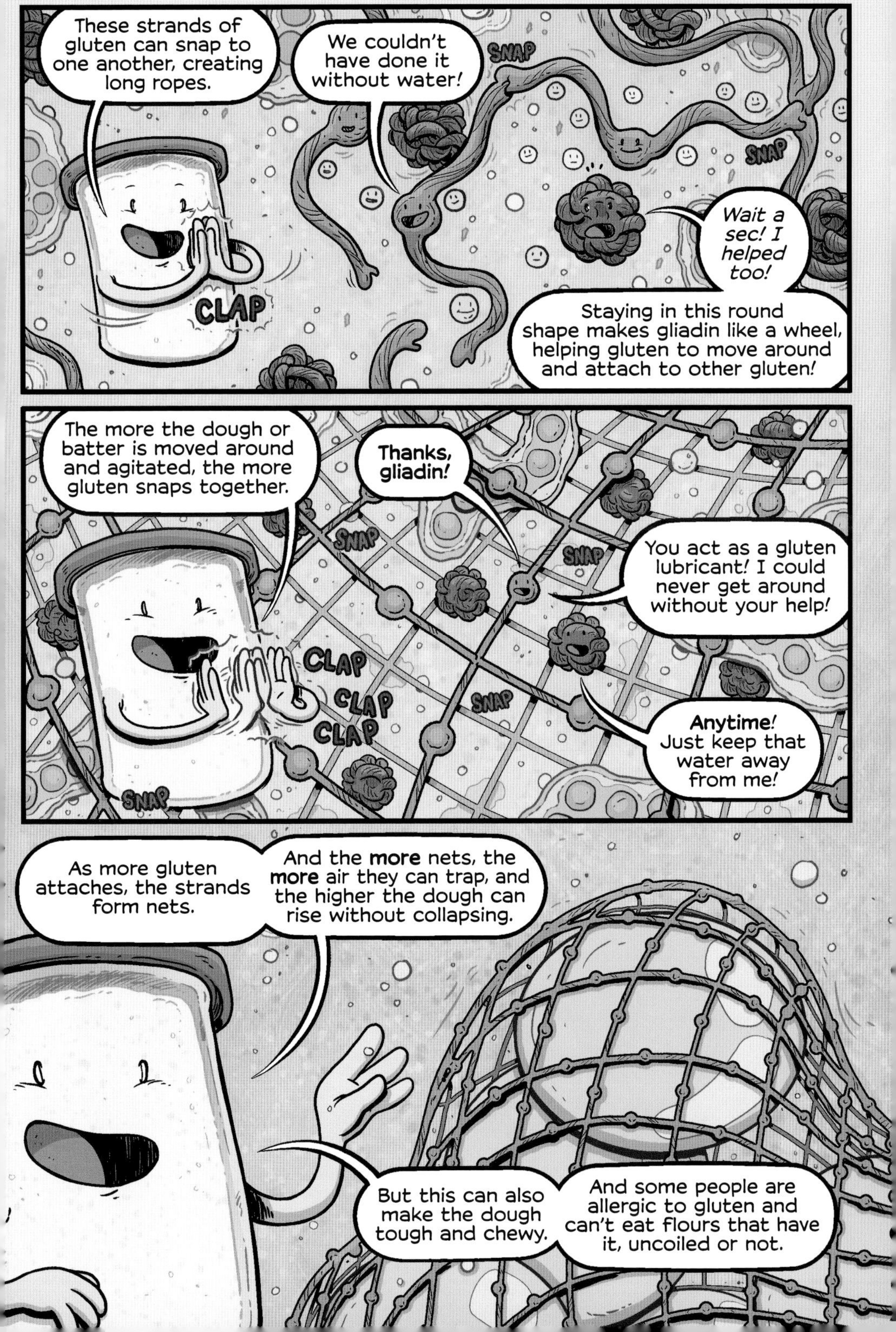
These strands of gluten can snap to one another, creating long ropes.
We couldn't have done it without water!
SNAP
SNAP
CLAP
Wait a sec! I helped too!
Staying in this round shape makes gliadin like a wheel, helping gluten to move around and attach to other gluten!
The more the dough or batter is moved around and agitated, the more gluten snaps together.
Thanks, gliadin!
SNAP
SNAP
You act as a gluten lubricant! I could never get around without your help!
CLAP
CLAP
CLAP
SNAP
Anytime! Just keep that water away from me!
SNAP
As more gluten attaches, the strands form nets.
And the more nets, the more air they can trap, and the higher the dough can rise without collapsing.
But this can also make the dough tough and chewy.
And some people are allergic to gluten and can't eat flours that have it, uncoiled or not.

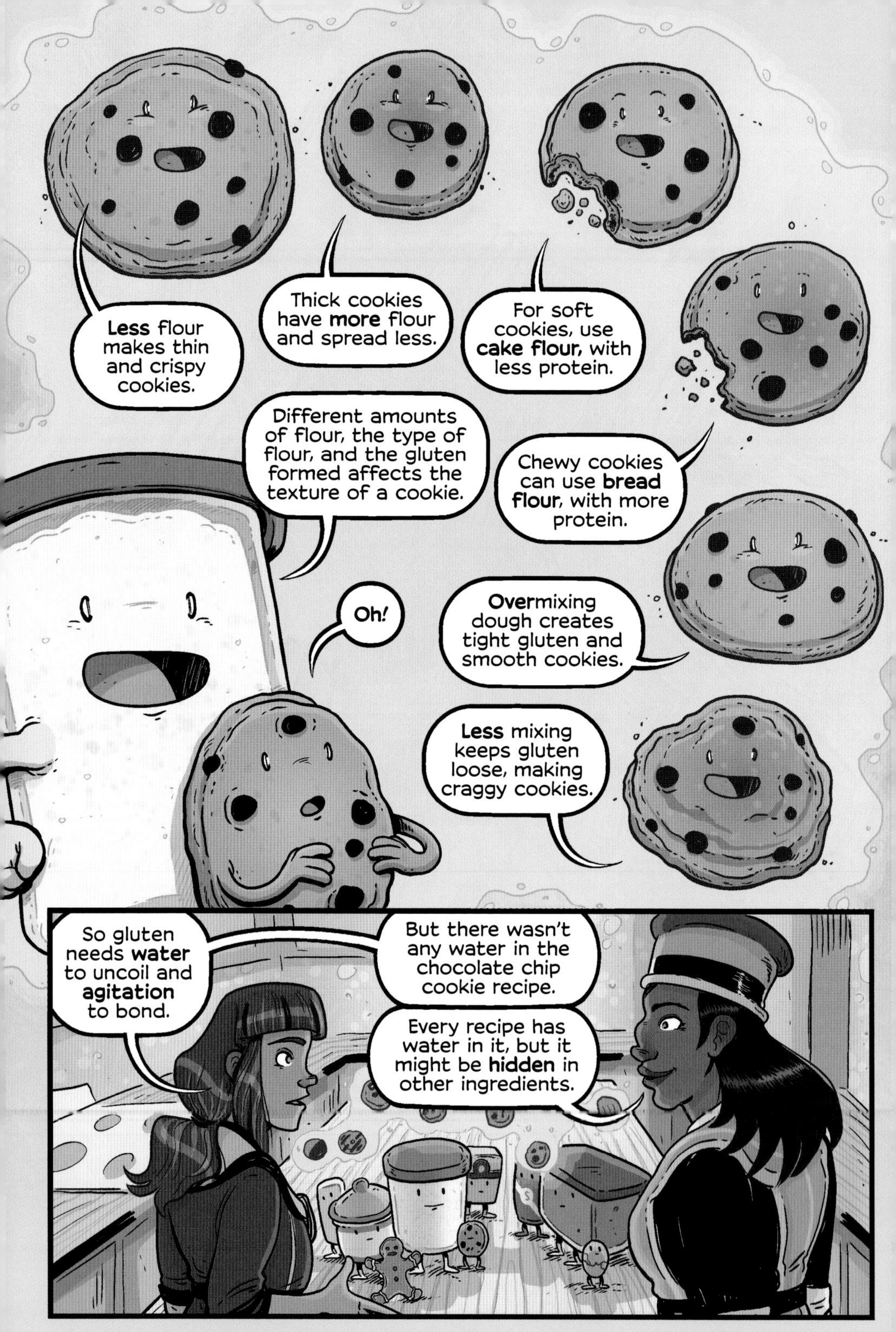

Less flour makes thin and crispy cookies.
Thick cookies have **more** flour and spread less.
For soft cookies, use **cake flour,** with less protein.
Different amounts of flour, the type of flour, and the gluten formed affects the texture of a cookie.
Chewy cookies can use **bread flour**, with more protein.
Oh!
Overmixing dough creates tight gluten and smooth cookies.
Less mixing keeps gluten loose, making craggy cookies.
So gluten needs **water** to uncoil and **agitation** to bond.
But there wasn't any water in the chocolate chip cookie recipe.
Every recipe has water in it, but it might be **hidden** in other ingredients.

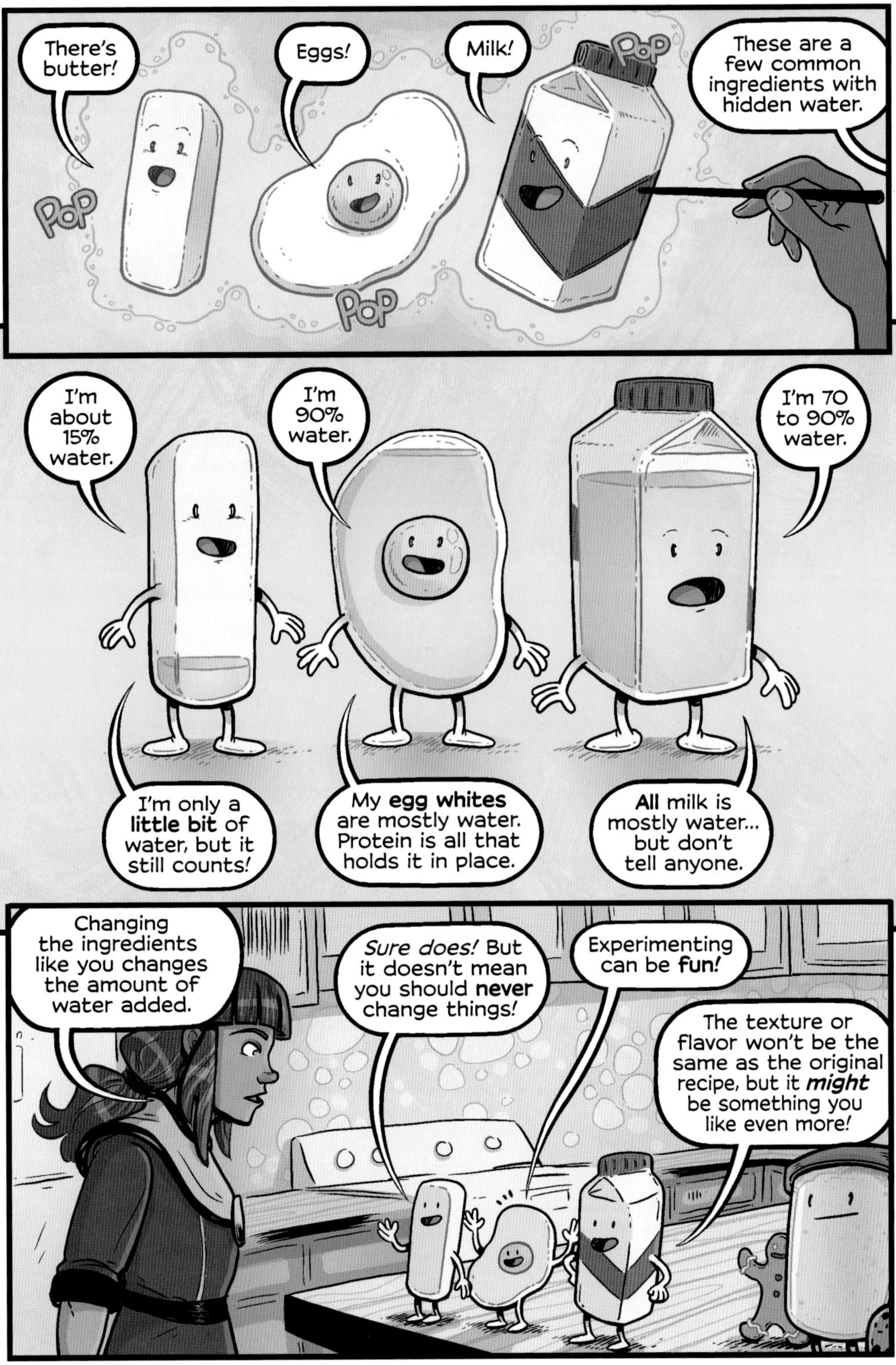
There's butter!
POP
Eggs!
POP
Milk!
POP
These are a few common ingredients with hidden water.
I'm about 15% water.
I'm 90% water.
I'm 70 to 90% water.
I'm only a **little bit** of water, but it still counts!
My **egg whites** are mostly water. Protein is all that holds it in place.
All milk is mostly water... but don't tell anyone.
Changing the ingredients like you changes the amount of water added.
Sure does! But it doesn't mean you should **never** change things!
Experimenting can be **fun!**
The texture or flavor won't be the same as the original recipe, but it ***might*** be something you like even more!

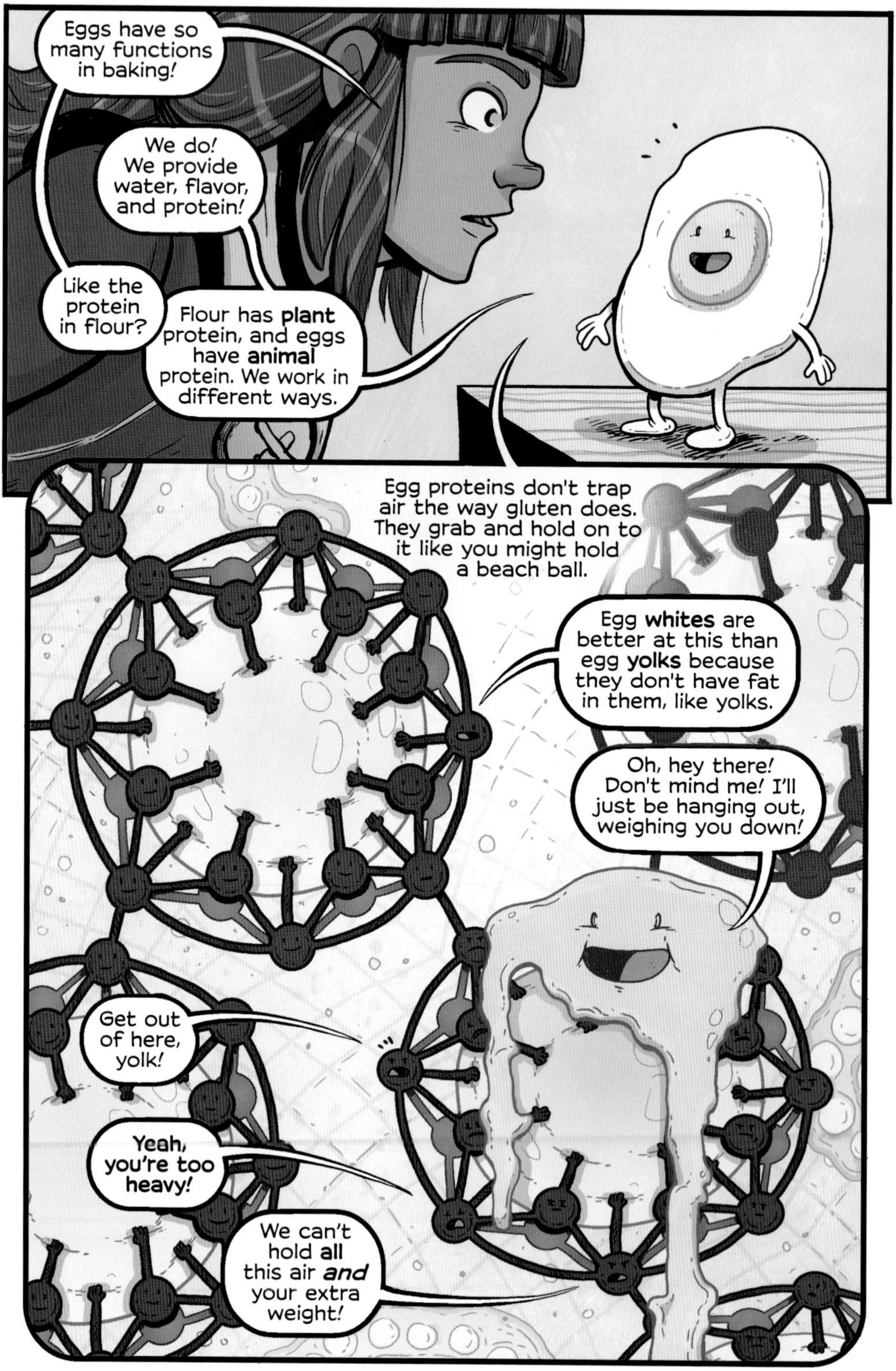
Eggs have so many functions in baking!
We do! We provide water, flavor, and protein!
Like the protein in flour?
Flour has **plant** protein, and eggs have **animal** protein. We work in different ways.
Egg proteins don't trap air the way gluten does. They grab and hold on to it like you might hold a beach ball.
Egg **whites** are better at this than egg **yolks** because they don't have fat in them, like yolks.
Oh, hey there! Don't mind me! I'll just be hanging out, weighing you down!
Get out of here, yolk!
Yeah, you're too heavy!
We can't hold **all** this air ***and*** your extra weight!

Egg **whites** provide **strength**.

And **yolks** hold the **flavor**.

Exactly!

If a recipe asks for **whole** eggs, **only** egg whites, or **only** egg yolks, it's asking for a **reason**.

This affects cookies in a few ways.

Using only whites will mean more rise and very fluffy but dry cookies.

Using only yolks will mean less rise and dense, cake-like cookies.

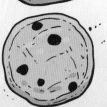

Whole eggs create your average cookie texture, using the best of both.

What happens without any egg at all?

All baked goods need some kind of binder.

Flour can bind, but eggs help without using any gluten.

Flour and eggs work together!

Then, eggs and flour are the most important ingredients in baking!

They certainly are **not!**

Hmph!

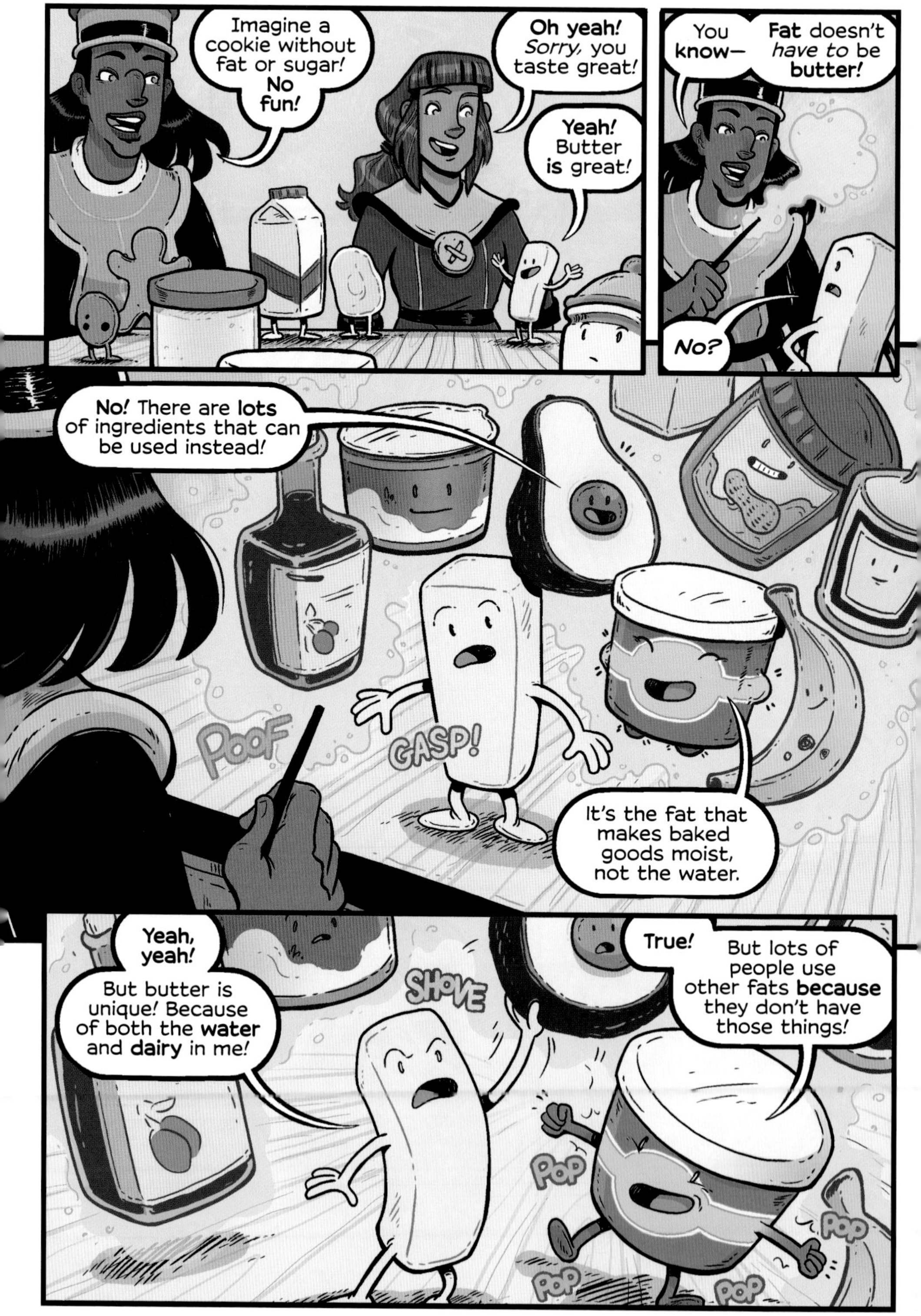
Imagine a cookie without fat or sugar! No fun!
Oh yeah! Sorry, you taste great!
Yeah! Butter is great!
You know—
Fat doesn't have to be butter!
No?
No! There are lots of ingredients that can be used instead!
POOF
GASP!
It's the fat that makes baked goods moist, not the water.
Yeah, yeah!
But butter is unique! Because of both the water and dairy in me!
SHOVE
True!
But lots of people use other fats because they don't have those things!
POP
POP
POP
POP

Like me, shortening! I'm solid at room temperature, don't contain water, and don't melt as fast as butter!

THHBT

Shortening: 100% vegetable fat

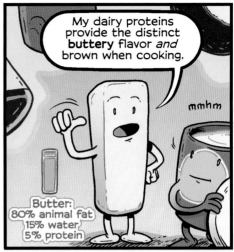

My dairy proteins provide the distinct **buttery** flavor *and* brown when cooking.

mmhm

Butter: 80% animal fat 15% water 5% protein

Using **me** will make baked goods softer *but dense.* With no water in me, I don't steam when baked.

That's **great** for cutout cookies and intricate piecrusts.

Not for things you want to expand!

SMMUSH

See? That does mean I'm better!

BUMP

OH!

I never said that, you *dairy dummy!*

HMPH!

SHOVE

We'll see who is **best!**

Hey! Hands off the fat!

THHBBT

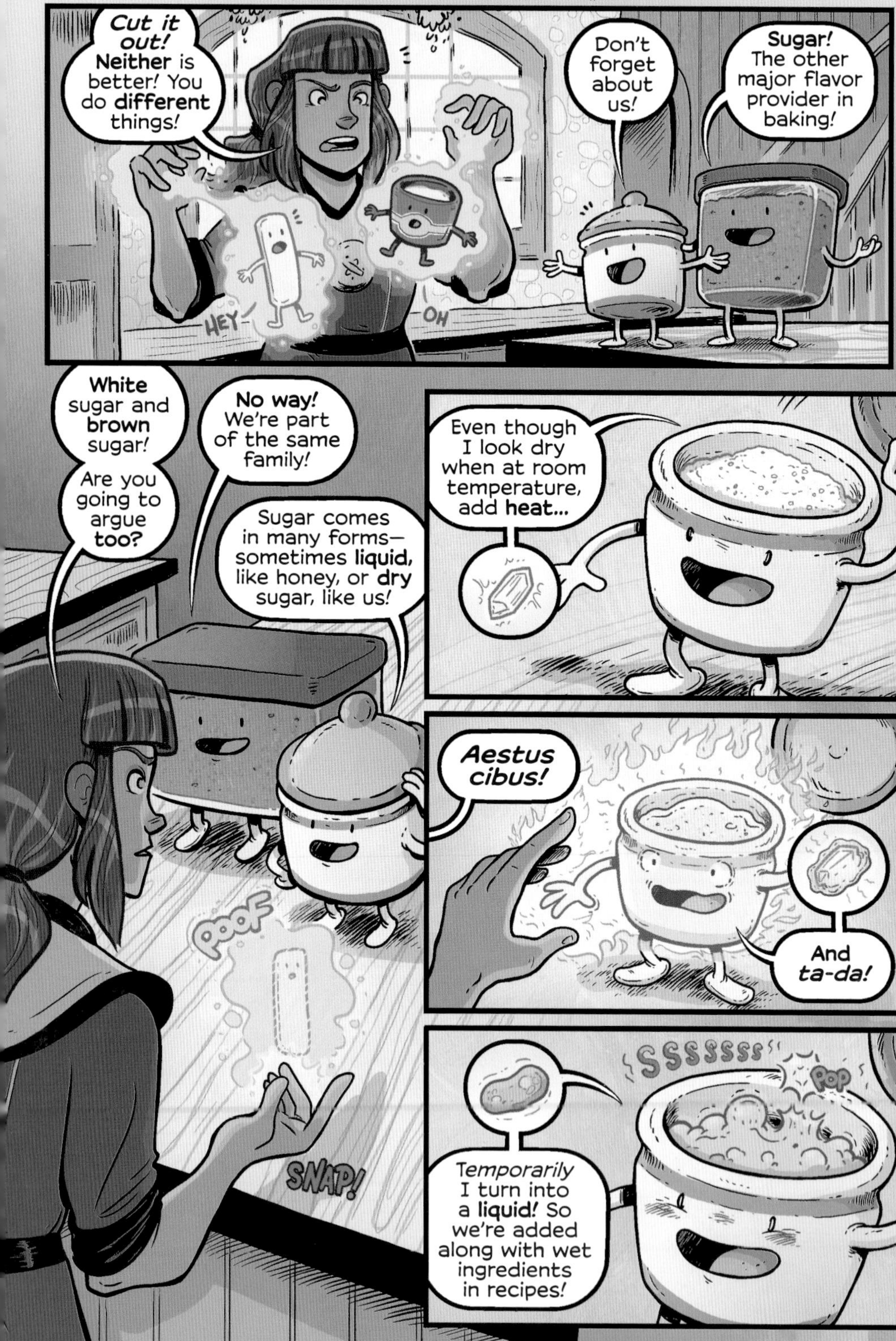

Cut it out! **Neither** is better! You do **different** things!
HEY
OH
Don't forget about us!
Sugar! The other major flavor provider in baking!
White sugar and **brown** sugar!
Are you going to argue **too?**
No way! We're part of the same family!
Sugar comes in many forms—sometimes **liquid,** like honey, or **dry** sugar, like us!
POOF
SNAP!
Even though I look dry when at room temperature, add **heat...**
Aestus cibus!
And *ta-da!*
SSSSSSS
POP
Temporarily I turn into a **liquid!** So we're added along with wet ingredients in recipes!

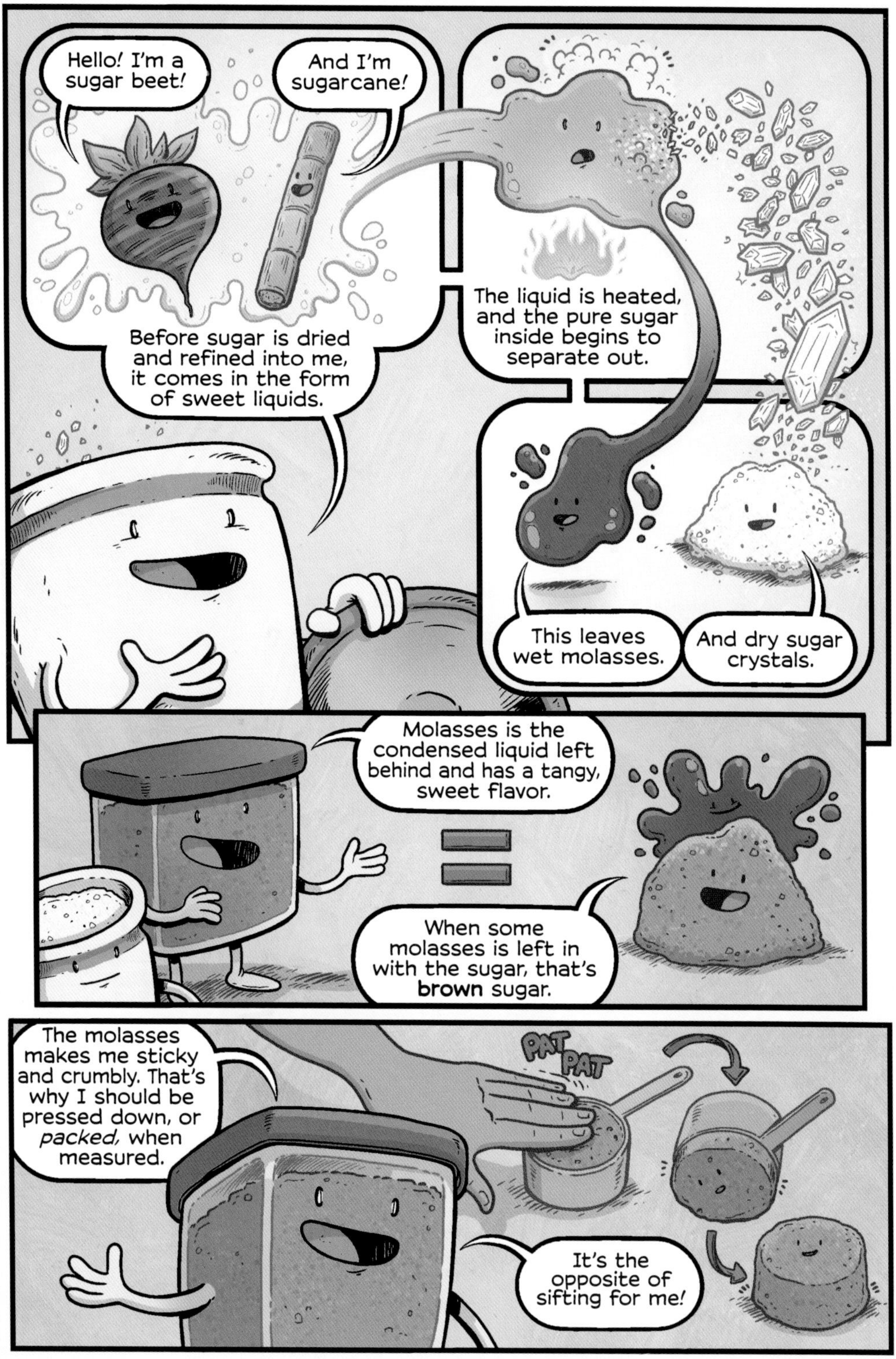

Hello! I'm a sugar beet!
And I'm sugarcane!
Before sugar is dried and refined into me, it comes in the form of sweet liquids.
The liquid is heated, and the pure sugar inside begins to separate out.
This leaves wet molasses.
And dry sugar crystals.
Molasses is the condensed liquid left behind and has a tangy, sweet flavor.
=
When some molasses is left in with the sugar, that's **brown** sugar.
The molasses makes me sticky and crumbly. That's why I should be pressed down, or *packed,* when measured.
PAT PAT
It's the opposite of sifting for me!

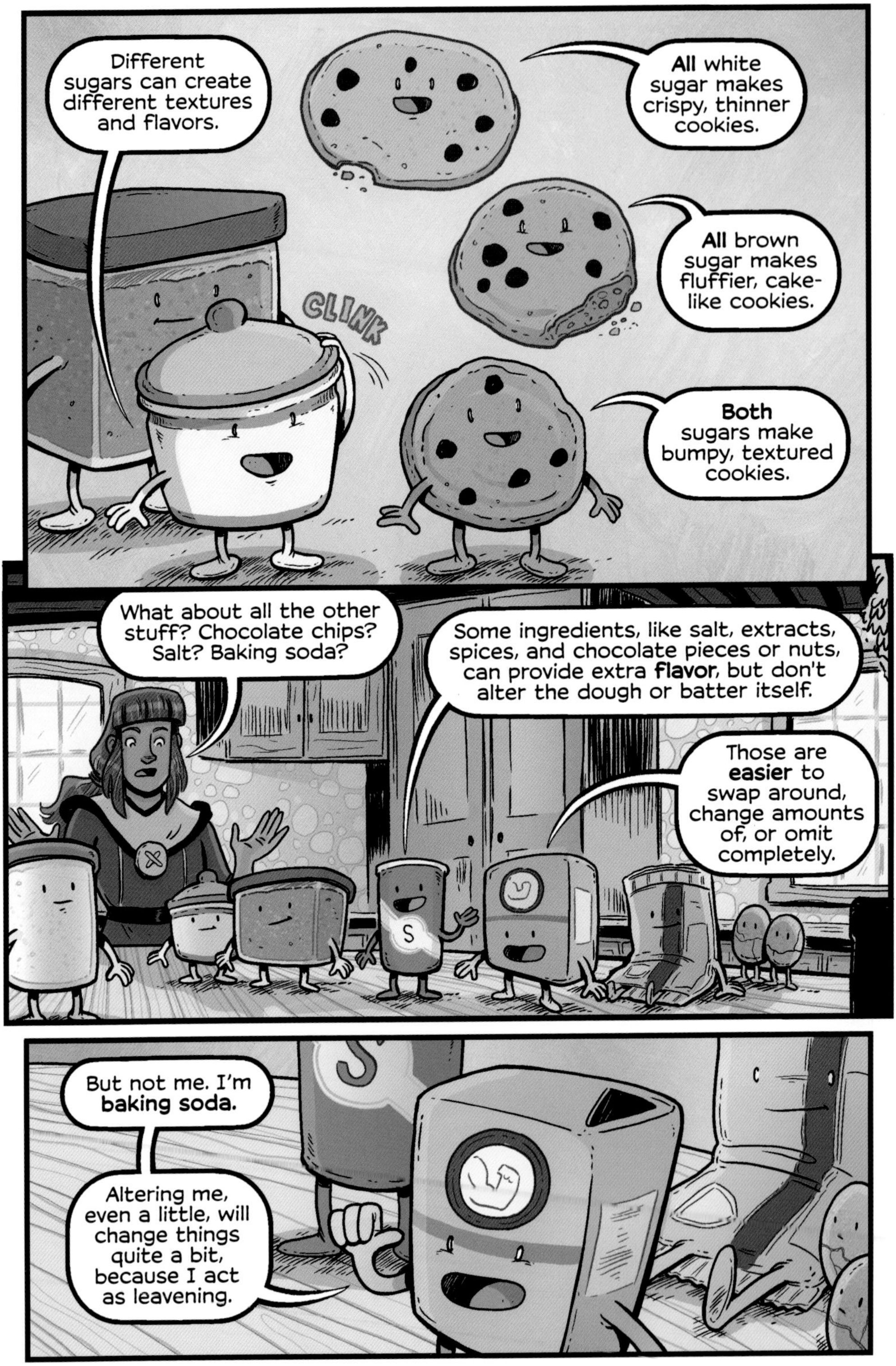
Different sugars can create different textures and flavors.
All white sugar makes crispy, thinner cookies.
All brown sugar makes fluffier, cake-like cookies.
CLINK
Both sugars make bumpy, textured cookies.
What about all the other stuff? Chocolate chips? Salt? Baking soda?
Some ingredients, like salt, extracts, spices, and chocolate pieces or nuts, can provide extra flavor, but don't alter the dough or batter itself.
Those are easier to swap around, change amounts of, or omit completely.
S
But not me. I'm baking soda.
Altering me, even a little, will change things quite a bit, because I act as leavening.

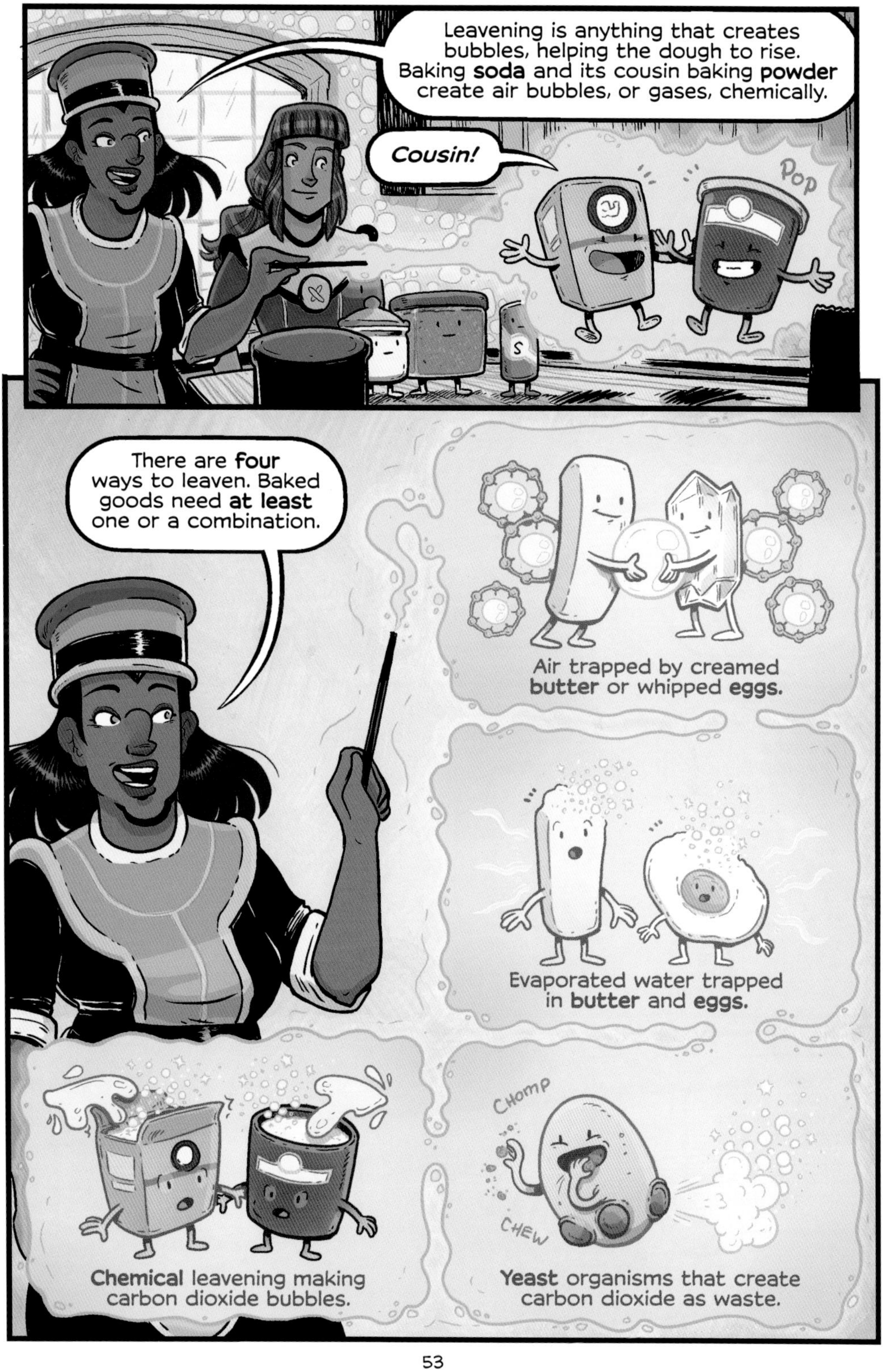
Leavening is anything that creates bubbles, helping the dough to rise. Baking **soda** and its cousin baking **powder** create air bubbles, or gases, chemically.
Cousin!
Pop
There are **four** ways to leaven. Baked goods need **at least** one or a combination.
Air trapped by creamed **butter** or whipped **eggs**.
Evaporated water trapped in **butter** and **eggs**.
Chemical leavening making carbon dioxide bubbles.
CHOMP
CHEW
Yeast organisms that create carbon dioxide as waste.

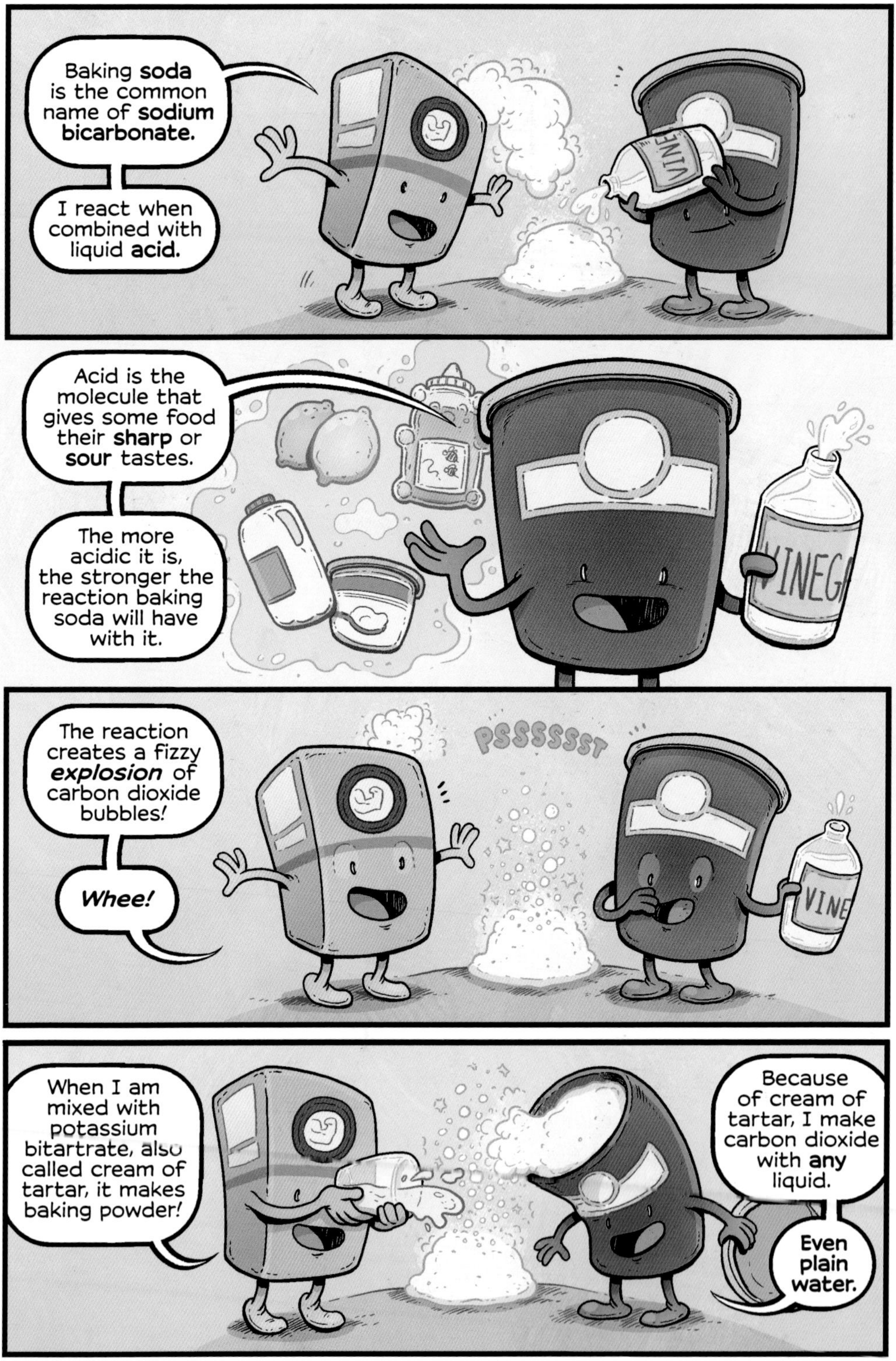
Baking **soda** is the common name of **sodium bicarbonate.**
I react when combined with liquid **acid.**
VINE
Acid is the molecule that gives some food their **sharp** or **sour** tastes.
The more acidic it is, the stronger the reaction baking soda will have with it.
VINEG
The reaction creates a fizzy ***explosion*** of carbon dioxide bubbles!
Whee!
PSSSSSST
VINE
When I am mixed with potassium bitartrate, also called cream of tartar, it makes baking powder!
Because of cream of tartar, I make carbon dioxide with **any** liquid.
Even plain water.

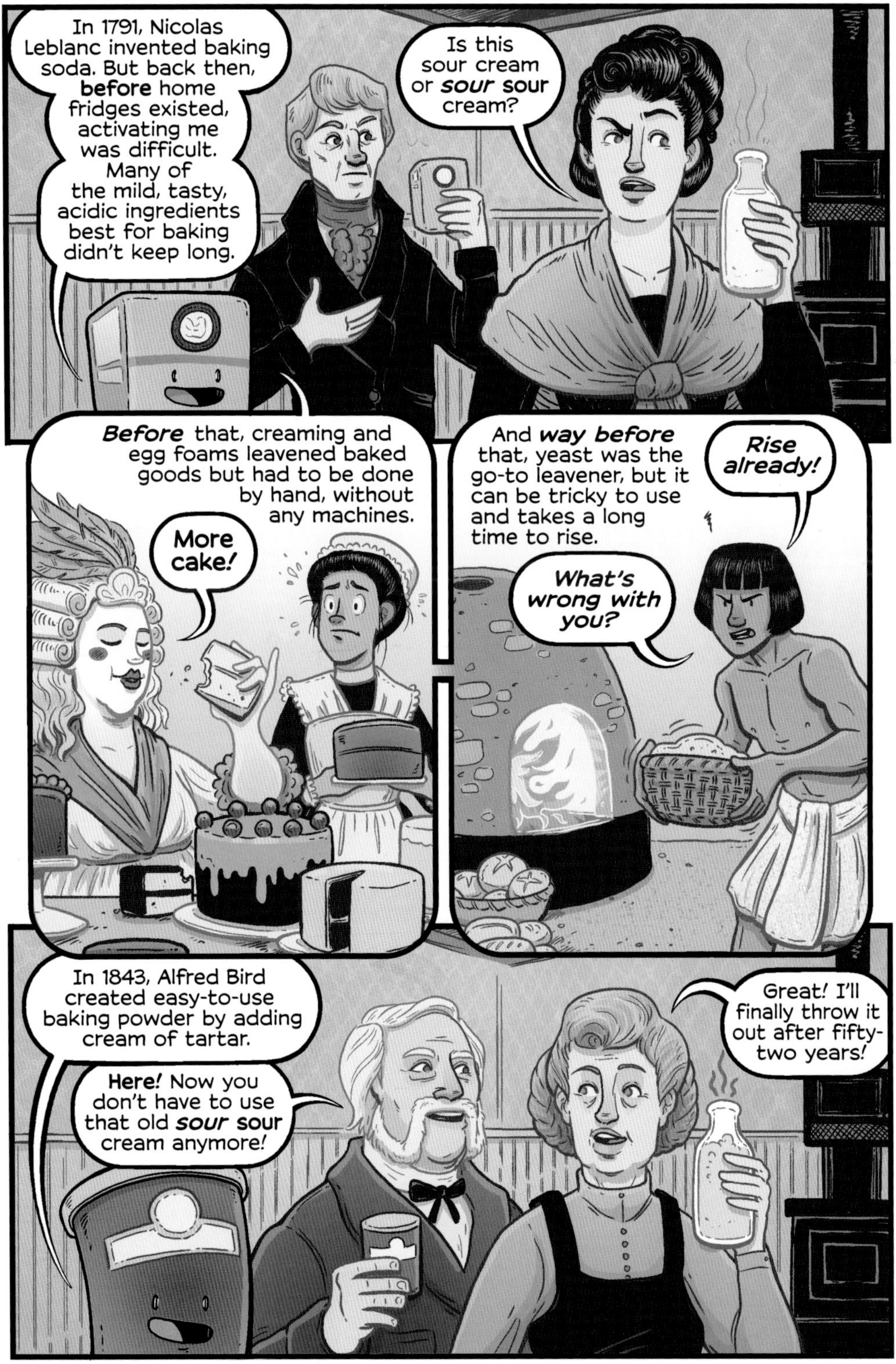

In 1791, Nicolas Leblanc invented baking soda. But back then, **before** home fridges existed, activating me was difficult. Many of the mild, tasty, acidic ingredients best for baking didn't keep long.
Is this sour cream or ***sour*** sour cream?
Before that, creaming and egg foams leavened baked goods but had to be done by hand, without any machines.
More cake!
And ***way before*** that, yeast was the go-to leavener, but it can be tricky to use and takes a long time to rise.
Rise already!
What's wrong with you?
In 1843, Alfred Bird created easy-to-use baking powder by adding cream of tartar.
Here! Now you don't have to use that old ***sour*** sour cream anymore!
Great! I'll finally throw it out after fifty-two years!

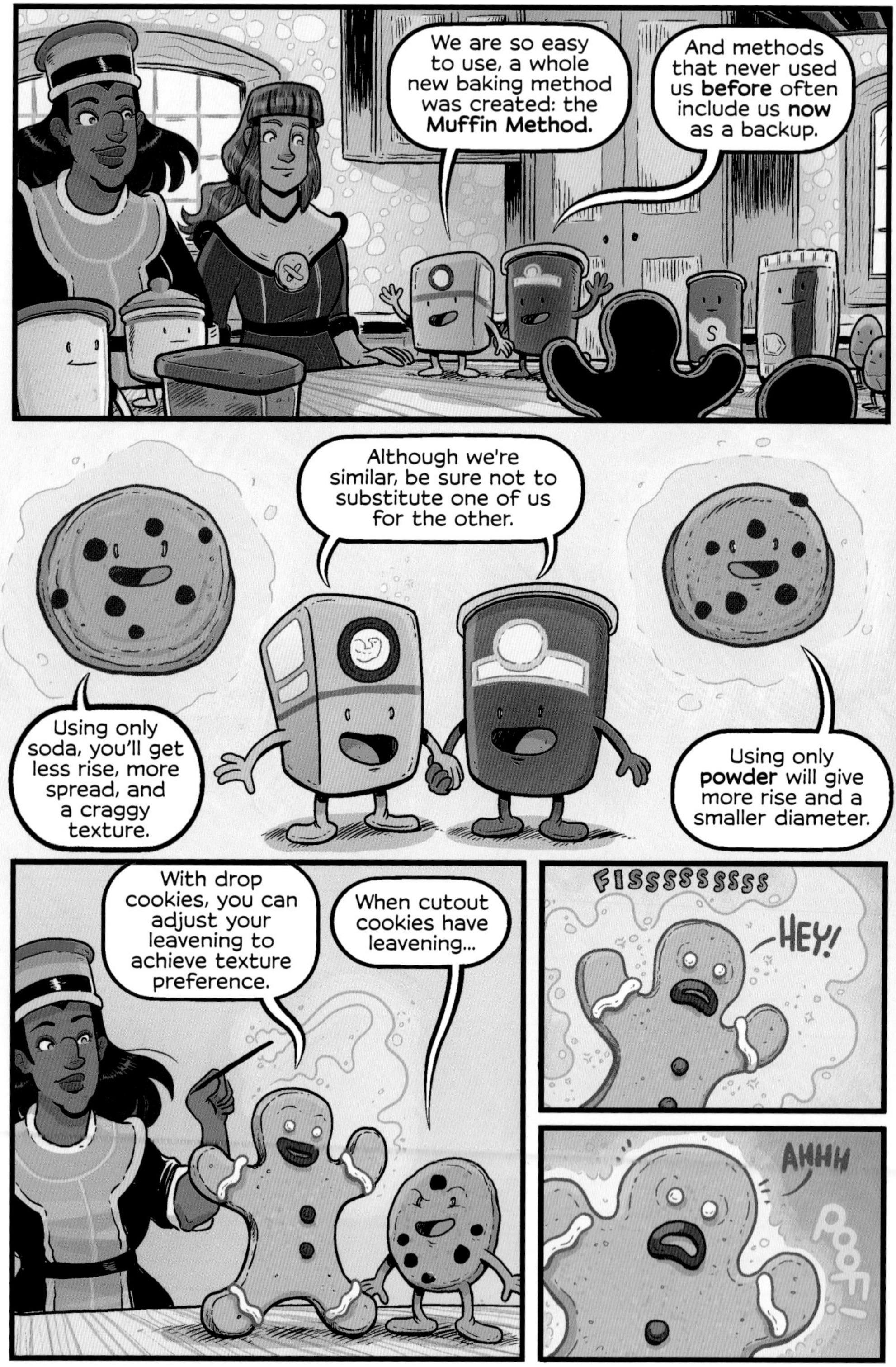

We are so easy to use, a whole new baking method was created: the **Muffin Method.**
And methods that never used us **before** often include us **now** as a backup.
Although we're similar, be sure not to substitute one of us for the other.
Using only soda, you'll get less rise, more spread, and a craggy texture.
Using only **powder** will give more rise and a smaller diameter.
With drop cookies, you can adjust your leavening to achieve texture preference.
When cutout cookies have leavening...
FISSSSSSSSS
HEY!
AHHH
POOF!

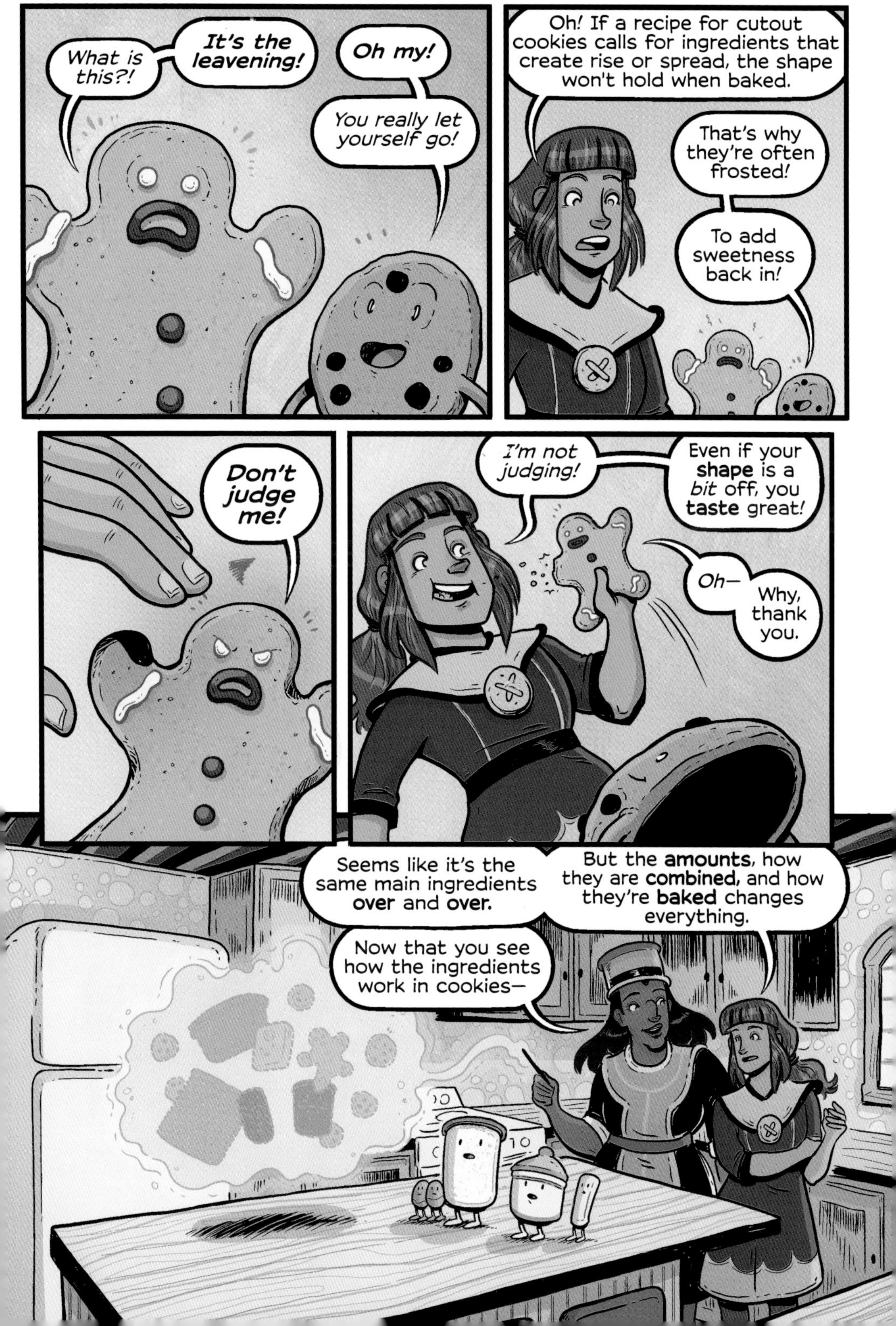
What is this?!
It's the leavening!
Oh my!
You really let yourself go!
Oh! If a recipe for cutout cookies calls for ingredients that create rise or spread, the shape won't hold when baked.
That's why they're often frosted!
To add sweetness back in!
Don't judge me!
I'm not judging!
Even if your shape is a bit off, you taste great!
Oh—
Why, thank you.
Seems like it's the same main ingredients over and over.
But the amounts, how they are combined, and how they're baked changes everything.
Now that you see how the ingredients work in cookies—

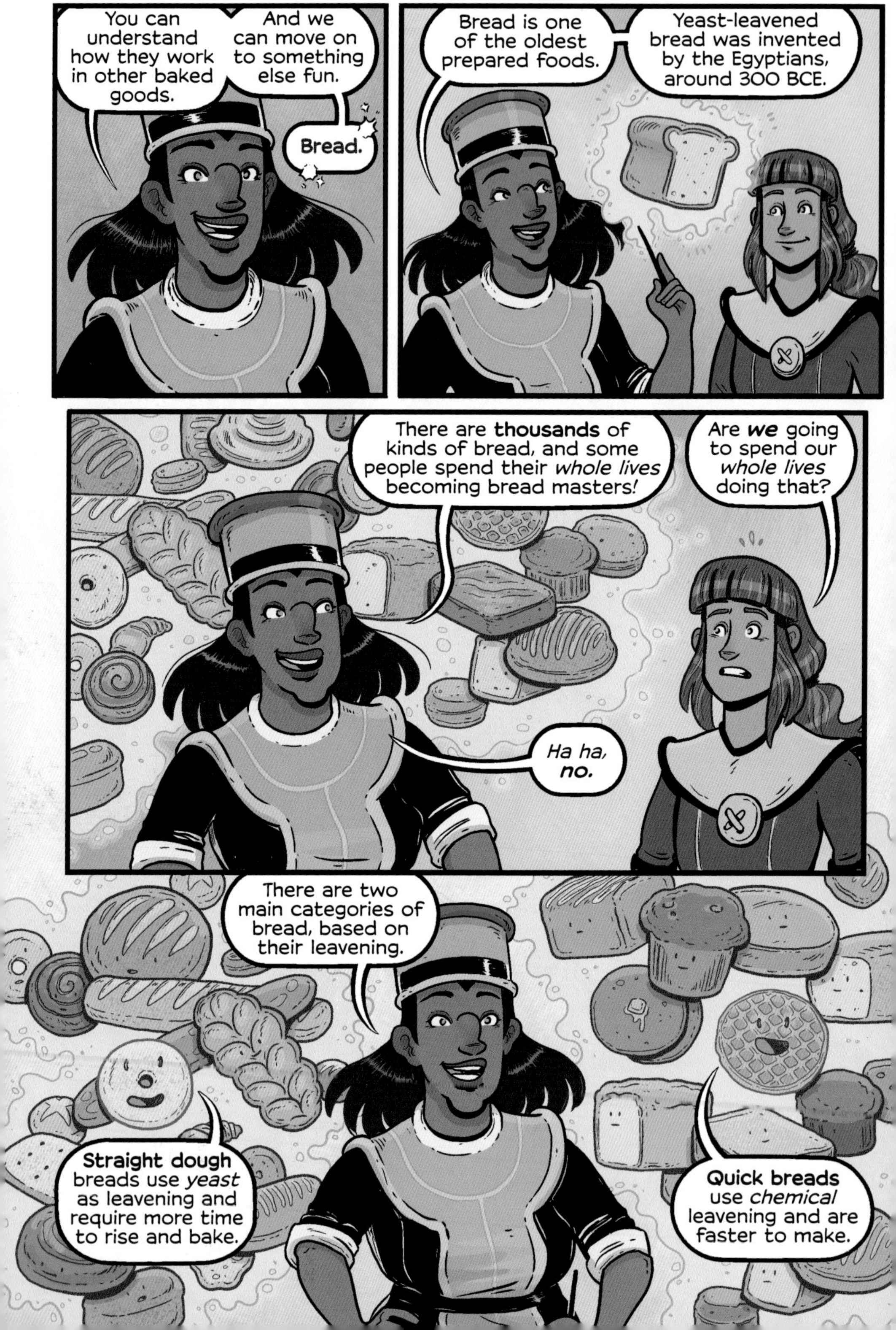

You can understand how they work in other baked goods.
And we can move on to something else fun.
Bread.
Bread is one of the oldest prepared foods.
Yeast-leavened bread was invented by the Egyptians, around 300 BCE.
There are **thousands** of kinds of bread, and some people spend their *whole lives* becoming bread masters!
Are ***we*** going to spend our *whole lives* doing that?
Ha ha, ***no.***
There are two main categories of bread, based on their leavening.
Straight dough breads use *yeast* as leavening and require more time to rise and bake.
Quick breads use *chemical* leavening and are faster to make.

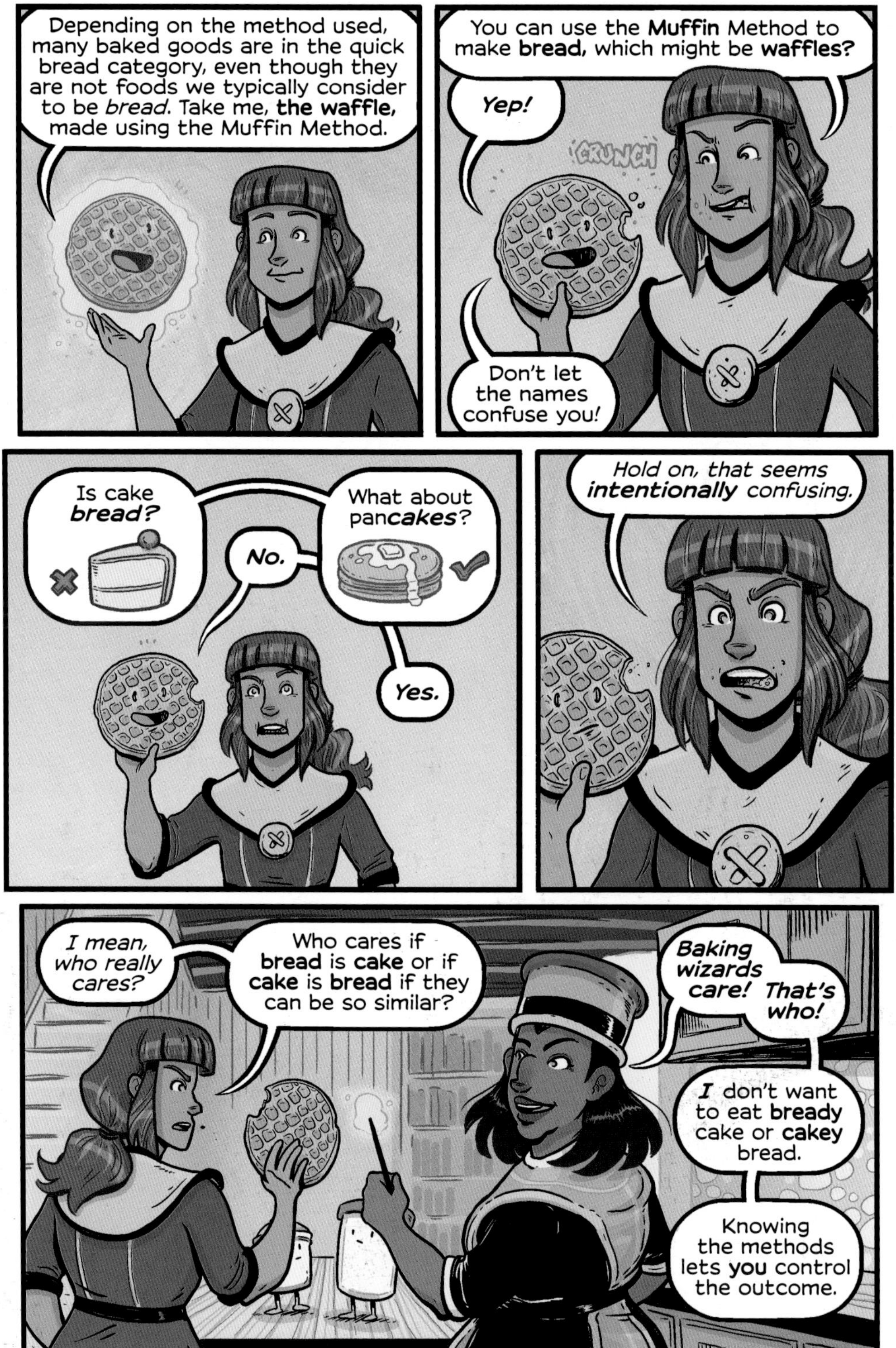
Depending on the method used, many baked goods are in the quick bread category, even though they are not foods we typically consider to be *bread*. Take me, **the waffle,** made using the Muffin Method.
You can use the **Muffin** Method to make **bread,** which might be **waffles?**
Yep!
CRUNCH
Don't let the names confuse you!
Is cake ***bread?***
No.
What about pan***cakes***?
Yes.
*Hold on, that seems **intentionally** confusing.*
I mean, who really cares?
Who cares if **bread** is **cake** or if **cake** is **bread** if they can be so similar?
Baking wizards care! That's who!
I don't want to eat **bready** cake or **cakey** bread.
Knowing the methods lets **you** control the outcome.

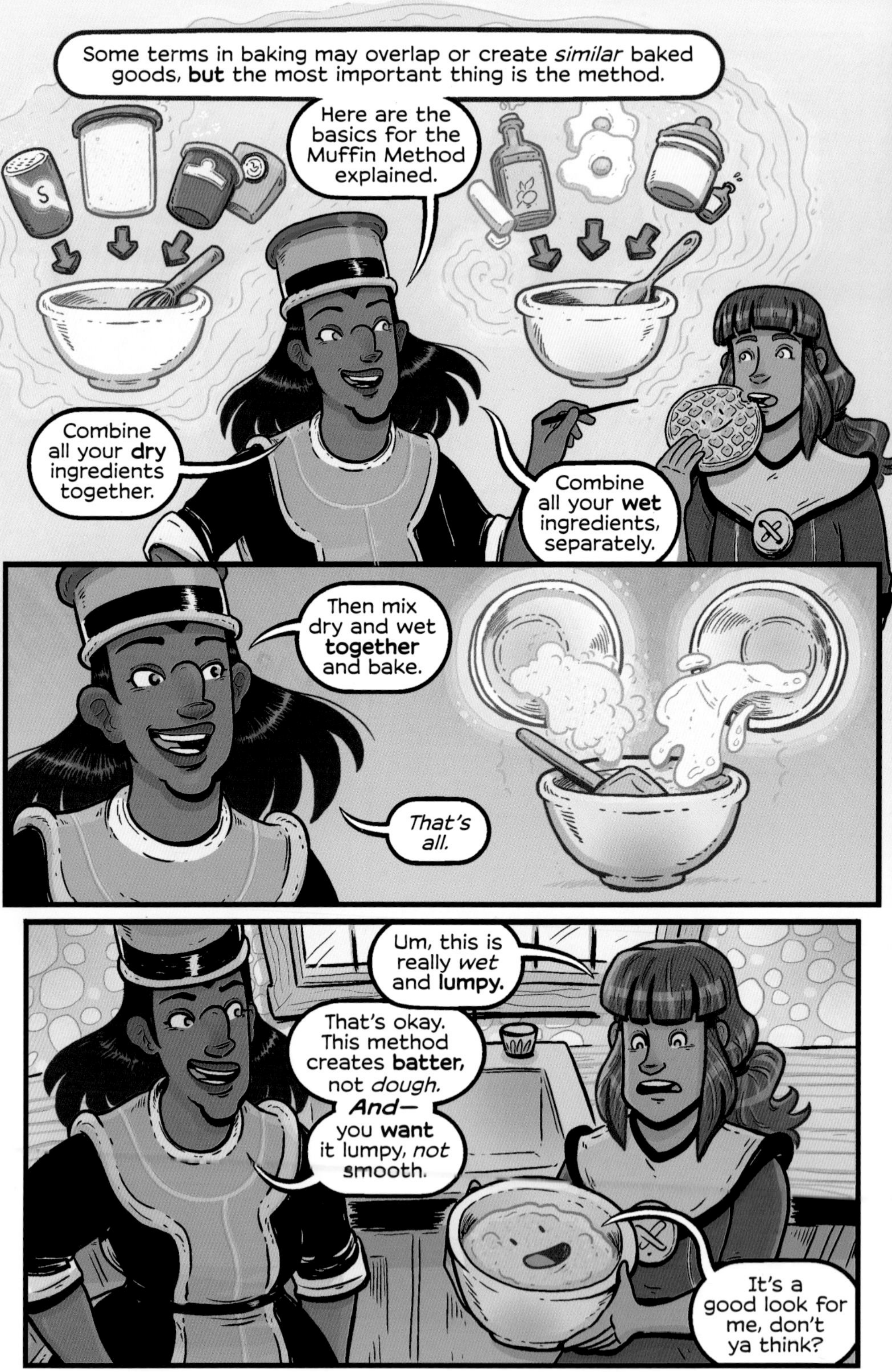

Some terms in baking may overlap or create *similar* baked goods, **but** the most important thing is the method.
Here are the basics for the Muffin Method explained.
Combine all your **dry** ingredients together.
Combine all your **wet** ingredients, separately.
Then mix dry and wet **together** and bake.
That's all.
Um, this is really *wet* and **lumpy.**
That's okay. This method creates **batter,** not *dough.*
And—you **want** it lumpy, *not* smooth.
It's a good look for me, don't ya think?

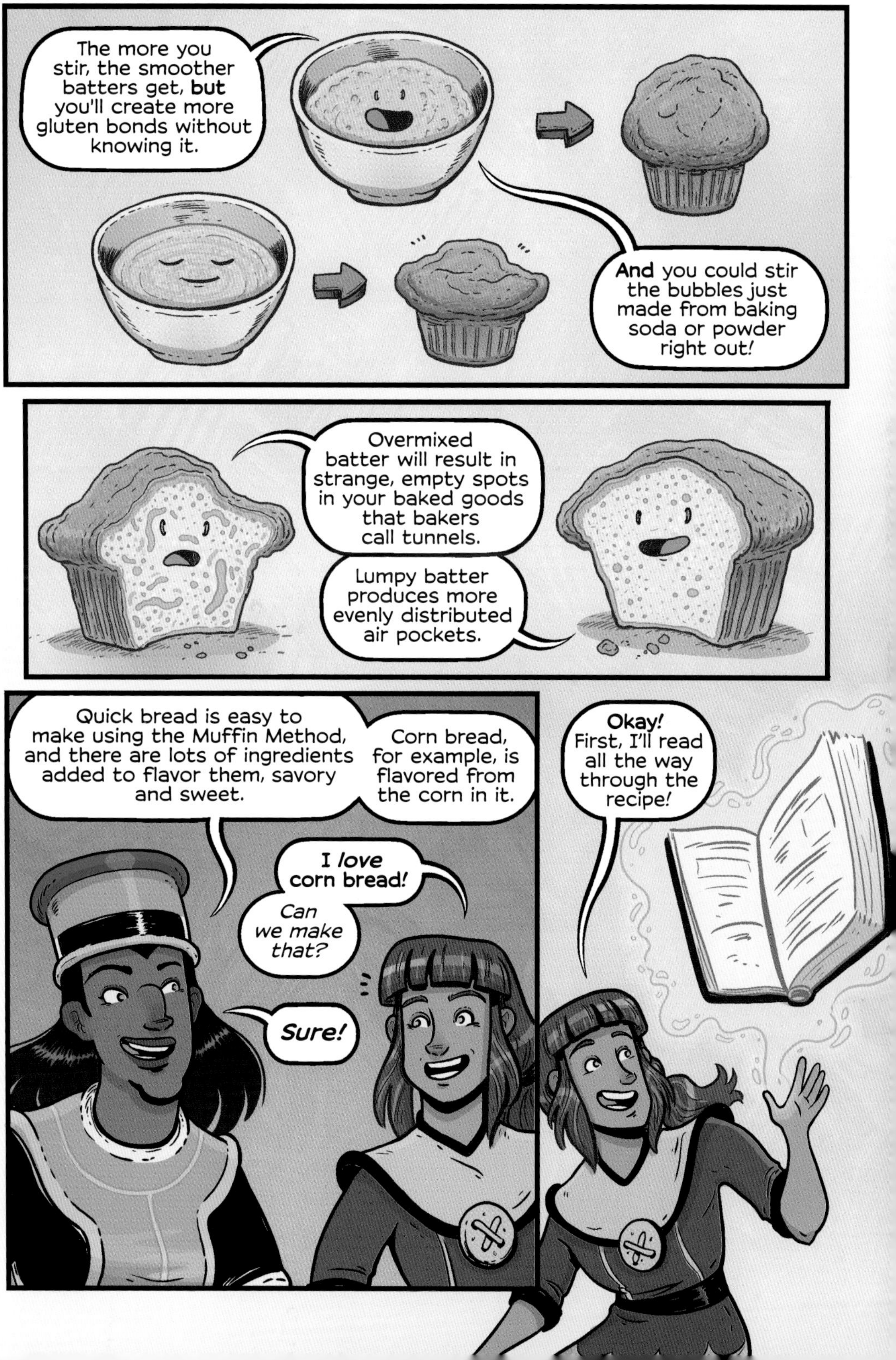

The more you stir, the smoother batters get, **but** you'll create more gluten bonds without knowing it.
And you could stir the bubbles just made from baking soda or powder right out!
Overmixed batter will result in strange, empty spots in your baked goods that bakers call tunnels.
Lumpy batter produces more evenly distributed air pockets.
Quick bread is easy to make using the Muffin Method, and there are lots of ingredients added to flavor them, savory and sweet.
Corn bread, for example, is flavored from the corn in it.
I *love* corn bread!
Can we make that?
Sure!
Okay! First, I'll read all the way through the recipe!

CORN BREAD

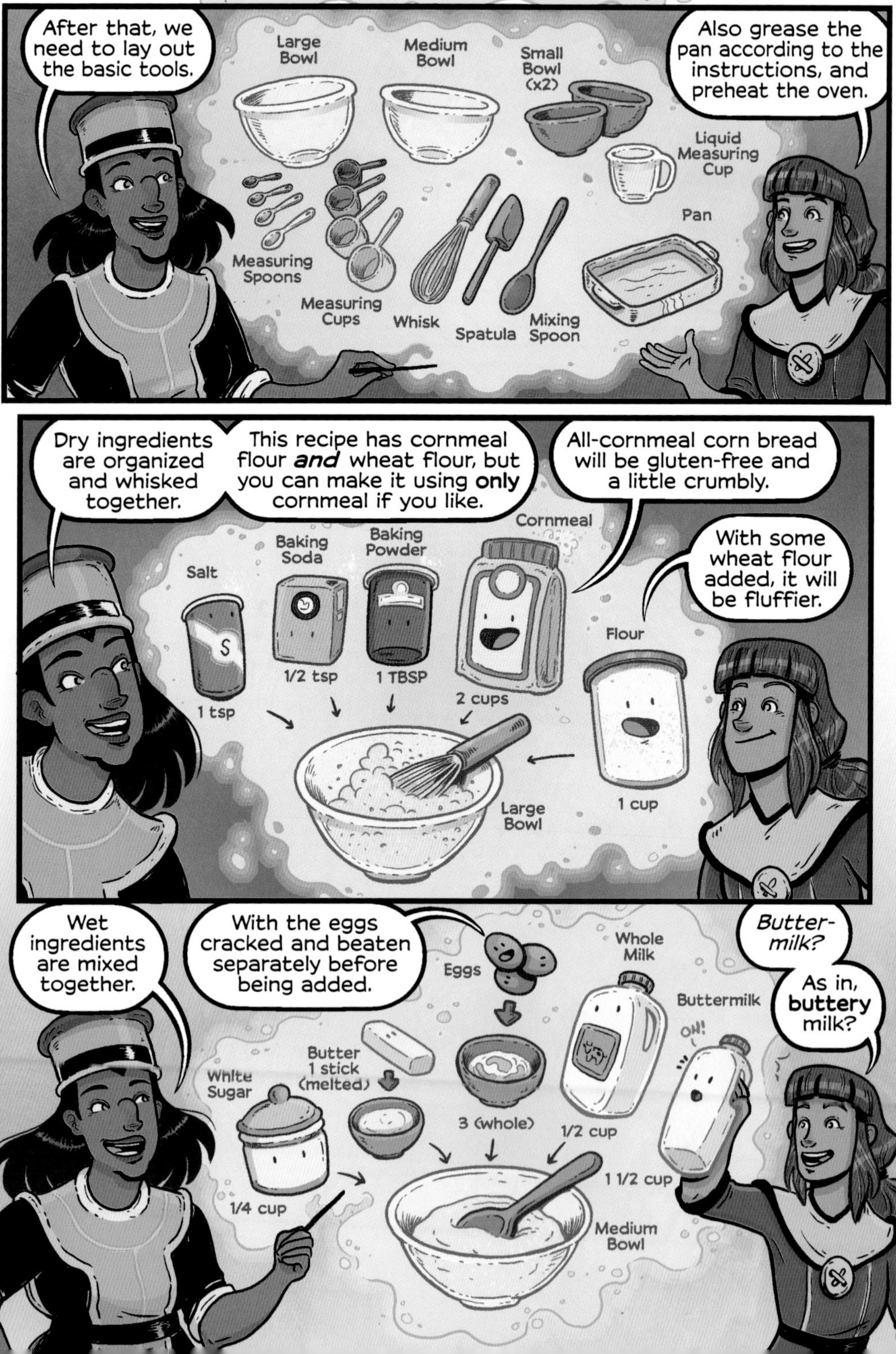

After that, we need to lay out the basic tools.
Large Bowl
Medium Bowl
Small Bowl (x2)
Liquid Measuring Cup
Pan
Measuring Spoons
Measuring Cups
Whisk
Spatula
Mixing Spoon
Also grease the pan according to the instructions, and preheat the oven.
Dry ingredients are organized and whisked together.
This recipe has cornmeal flour ***and*** wheat flour, but you can make it using **only** cornmeal if you like.
All-cornmeal corn bread will be gluten-free and a little crumbly.
Salt
1 tsp
Baking Soda
1/2 tsp
Baking Powder
1 TBSP
Cornmeal
2 cups
Flour
1 cup
Large Bowl
With some wheat flour added, it will be fluffier.
Wet ingredients are mixed together.
With the eggs cracked and beaten separately before being added.
Eggs
3 (whole)
Whole Milk
1/2 cup
Buttermilk
1 1/2 cup
OH!
Butter 1 stick (melted)
White Sugar
1/4 cup
Medium Bowl
Butter-milk?
As in, **buttery** milk?

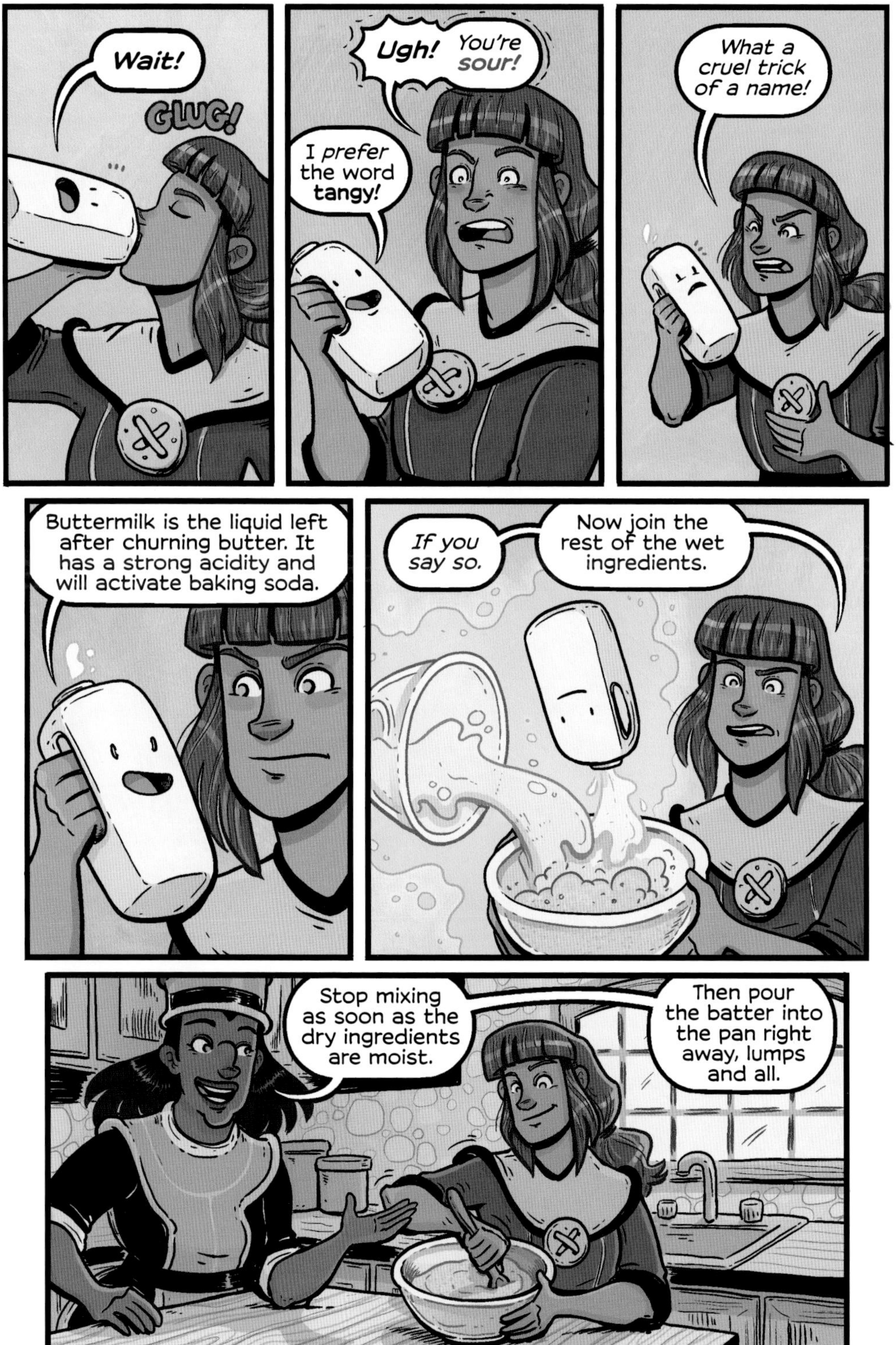
Wait!
GLUG!
Ugh! You're sour!
I prefer the word tangy!
What a cruel trick of a name!
Buttermilk is the liquid left after churning butter. It has a strong acidity and will activate baking soda.
If you say so.
Now join the rest of the wet ingredients.
Stop mixing as soon as the dry ingredients are moist.
Then pour the batter into the pan right away, lumps and all.

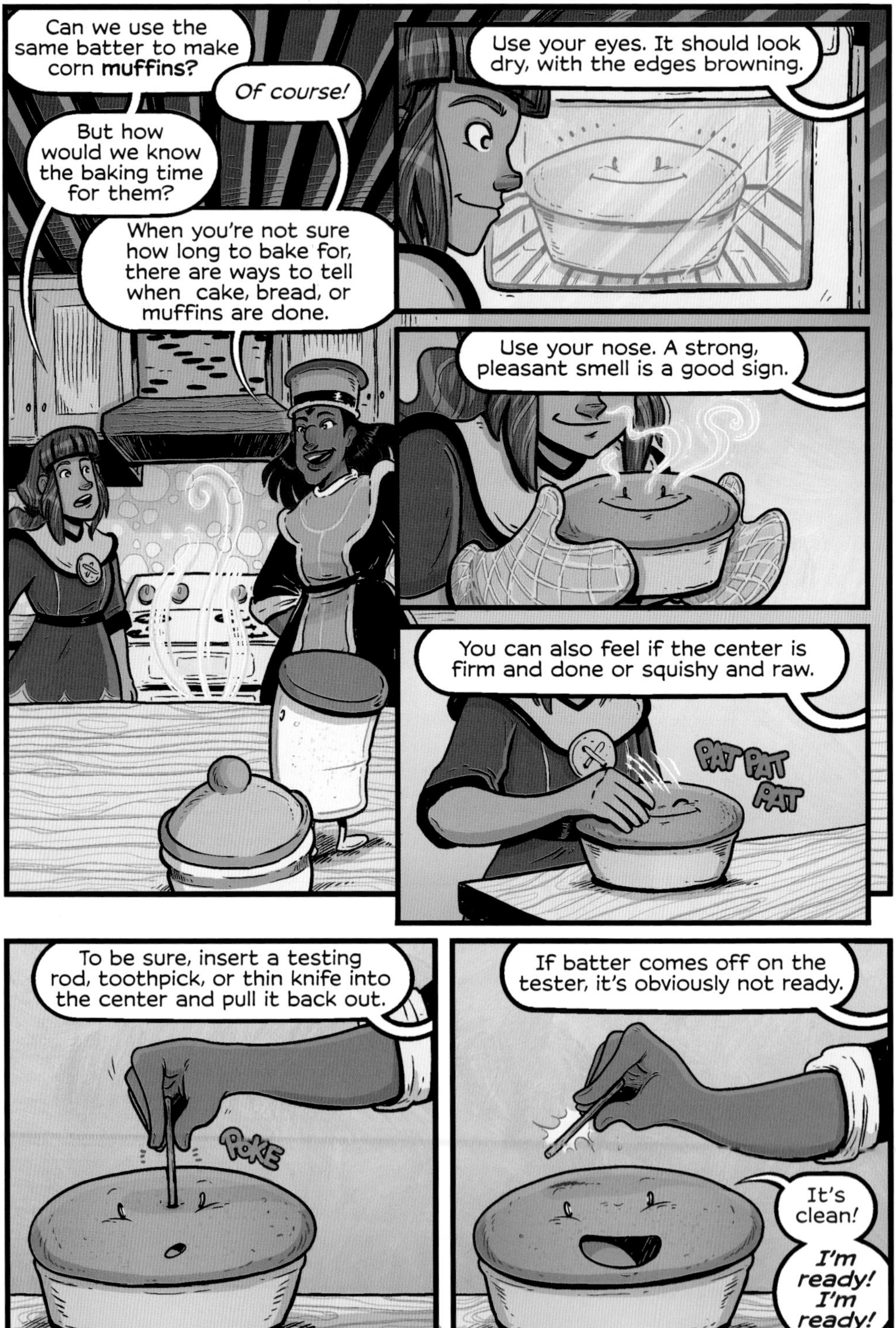

Can we use the same batter to make corn **muffins?**
Of course!
But how would we know the baking time for them?
When you're not sure how long to bake for, there are ways to tell when cake, bread, or muffins are done.
Use your eyes. It should look dry, with the edges browning.
Use your nose. A strong, pleasant smell is a good sign.
You can also feel if the center is firm and done or squishy and raw.
PAT PAT PAT
To be sure, insert a testing rod, toothpick, or thin knife into the center and pull it back out.
POKE
If batter comes off on the tester, it's obviously not ready.
It's clean!
I'm ready! I'm ready!

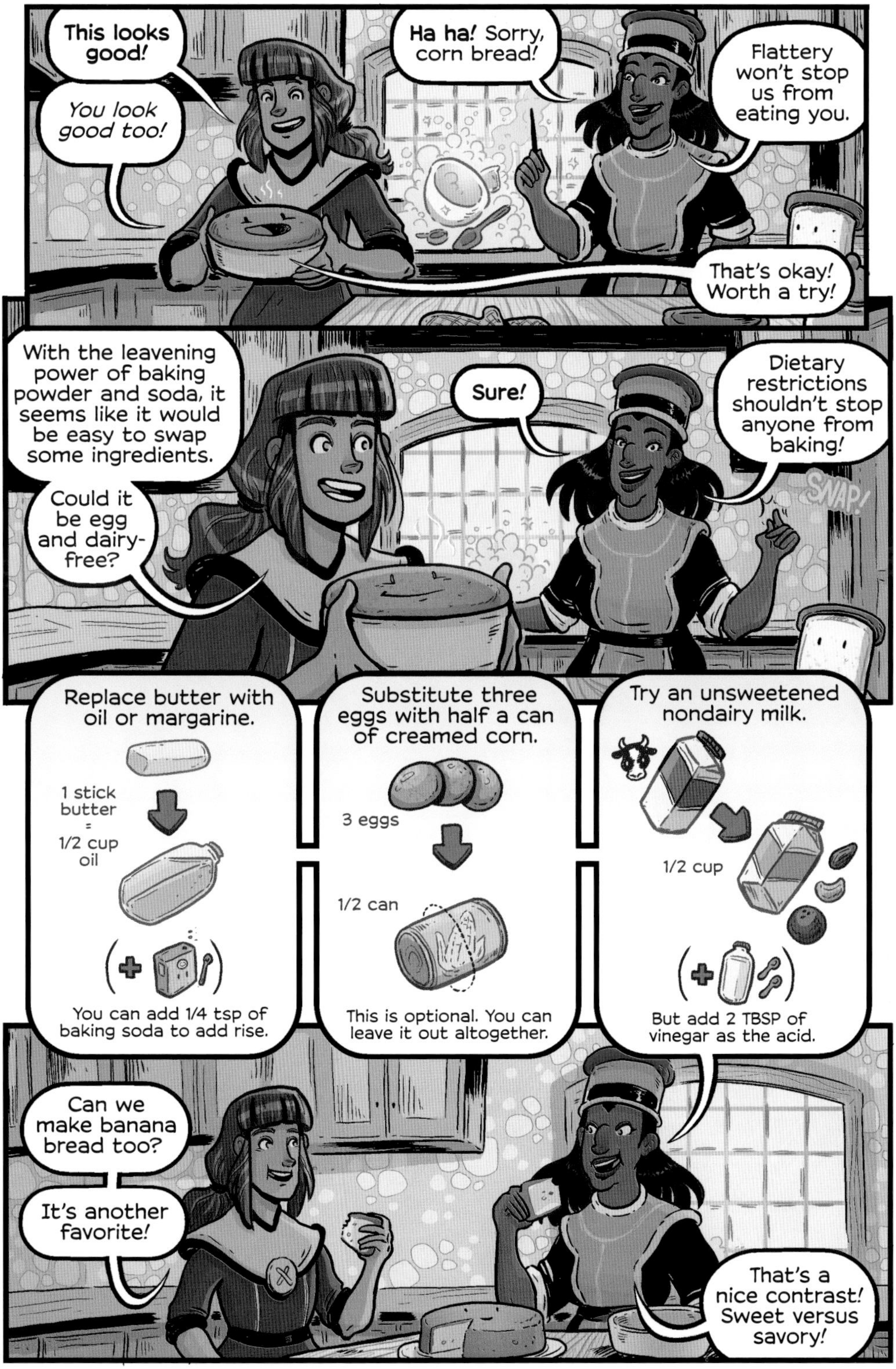
This looks good!
You look good too!
Ha ha! Sorry, corn bread!
Flattery won't stop us from eating you.
That's okay! Worth a try!
With the leavening power of baking powder and soda, it seems like it would be easy to swap some ingredients.
Could it be egg and dairy-free?
Sure!
Dietary restrictions shouldn't stop anyone from baking!
SNAP!
Replace butter with oil or margarine.
1 stick butter = 1/2 cup oil
You can add 1/4 tsp of baking soda to add rise.
Substitute three eggs with half a can of creamed corn.
3 eggs
1/2 can
This is optional. You can leave it out altogether.
Try an unsweetened nondairy milk.
1/2 cup
But add 2 TBSP of vinegar as the acid.
Can we make banana bread too?
It's another favorite!
That's a nice contrast! Sweet versus savory!

BANANA BREAD

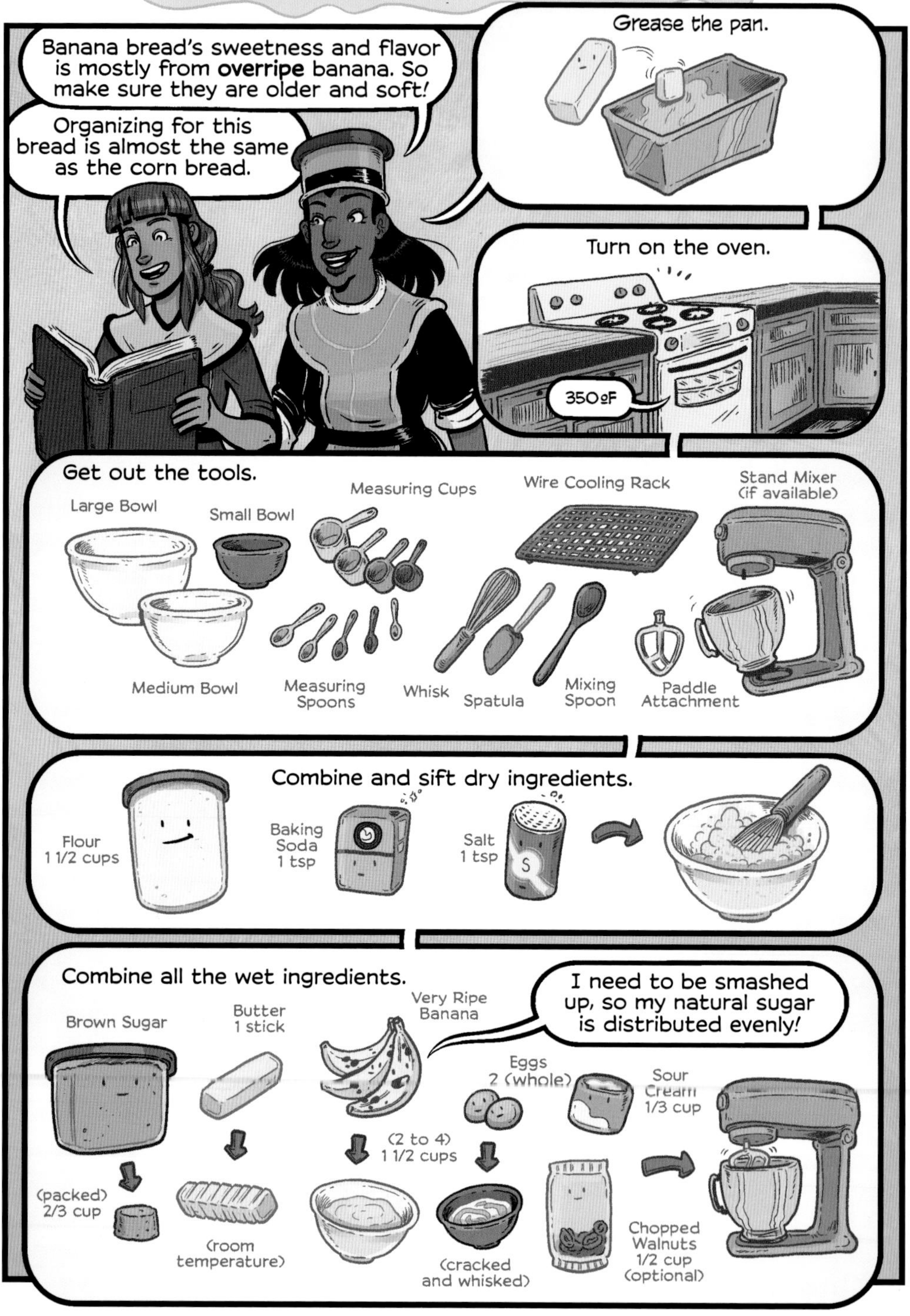

Banana bread's sweetness and flavor is mostly from **overripe** banana. So make sure they are older and soft!
Organizing for this bread is almost the same as the corn bread.
Grease the pan.
Turn on the oven.
350ºF
Get out the tools.
Large Bowl
Small Bowl
Measuring Cups
Wire Cooling Rack
Stand Mixer (if available)
Medium Bowl
Measuring Spoons
Whisk
Spatula
Mixing Spoon
Paddle Attachment
Combine and sift dry ingredients.
Flour 1 1/2 cups
Baking Soda 1 tsp
Salt 1 tsp
S
Combine all the wet ingredients.
Brown Sugar
(packed) 2/3 cup
Butter 1 stick
(room temperature)
Very Ripe Banana
(2 to 4) 1 1/2 cups
I need to be smashed up, so my natural sugar is distributed evenly!
Eggs 2 (whole)
(cracked and whisked)
Sour Cream 1/3 cup
Chopped Walnuts 1/2 cup (optional)

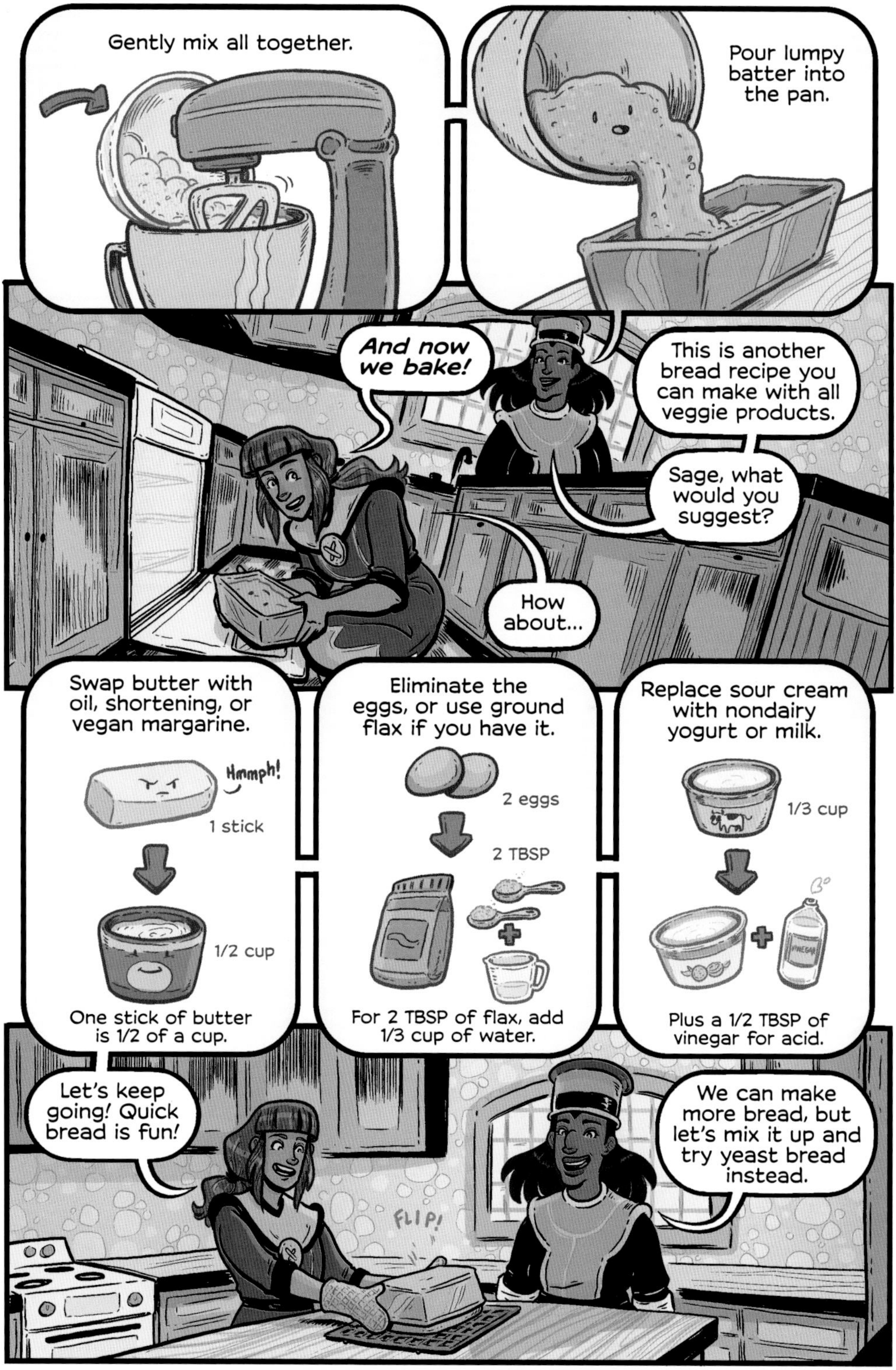

Gently mix all together.
Pour lumpy batter into the pan.
And now we bake!
This is another bread recipe you can make with all veggie products.
Sage, what would you suggest?
How about...
Swap butter with oil, shortening, or vegan margarine.
Hmmph!
1 stick
1/2 cup
One stick of butter is 1/2 of a cup.
Eliminate the eggs, or use ground flax if you have it.
2 eggs
2 TBSP
For 2 TBSP of flax, add 1/3 cup of water.
Replace sour cream with nondairy yogurt or milk.
1/3 cup
VINEGAR
Plus a 1/2 TBSP of vinegar for acid.
Let's keep going! Quick bread is fun!
FLIP!
We can make more bread, but let's mix it up and try yeast bread instead.

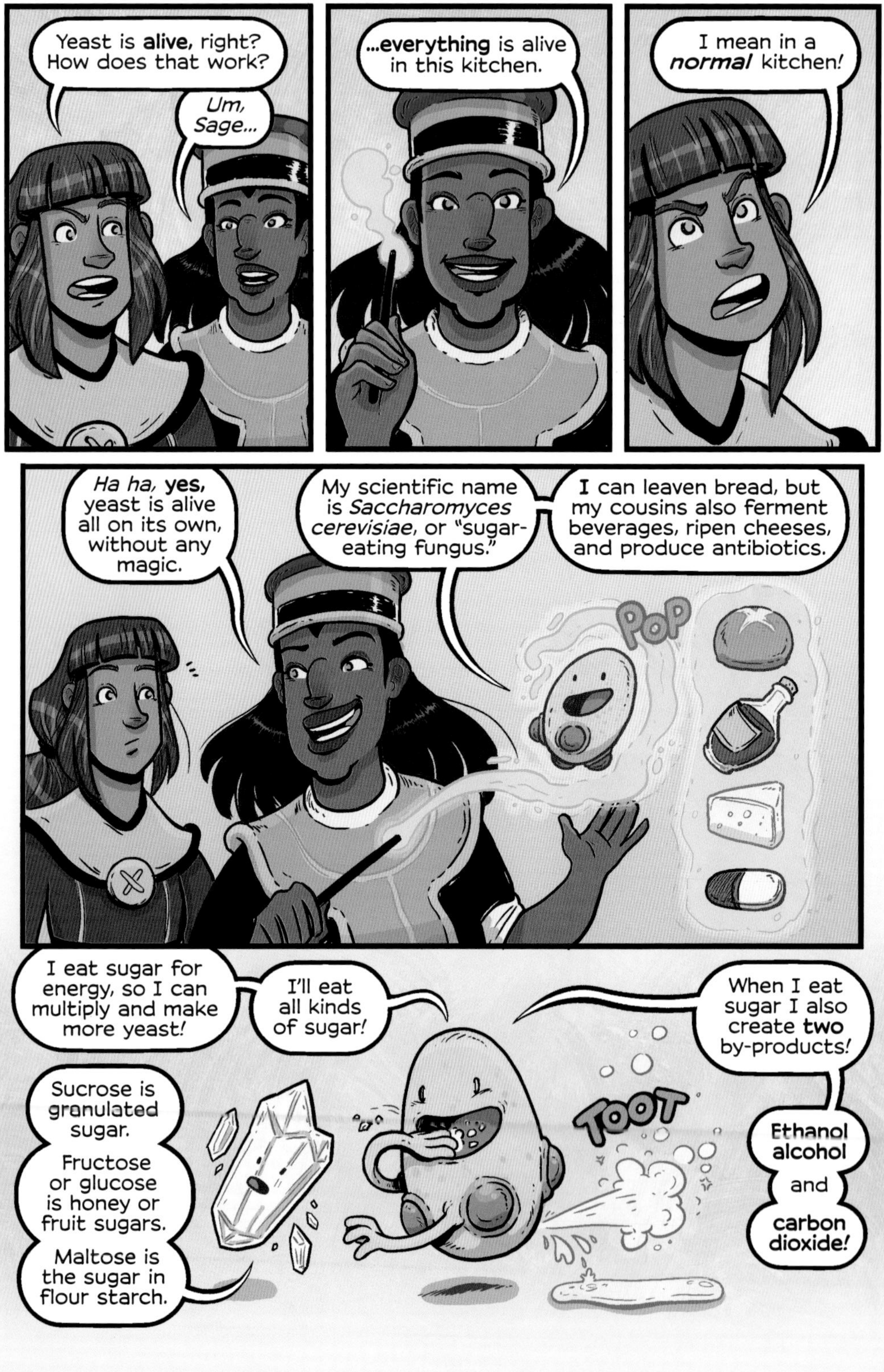
Yeast is **alive,** right? How does that work?
Um, Sage...
...everything is alive in this kitchen.
I mean in a ***normal*** kitchen!
Ha ha, **yes,** yeast is alive all on its own, without any magic.
My scientific name is *Saccharomyces cerevisiae*, or "sugar-eating fungus."
I can leaven bread, but my cousins also ferment beverages, ripen cheeses, and produce antibiotics.
POP
I eat sugar for energy, so I can multiply and make more yeast!
I'll eat all kinds of sugar!
Sucrose is granulated sugar.
Fructose or glucose is honey or fruit sugars.
Maltose is the sugar in flour starch.
TOOT
When I eat sugar I also create **two** by-products!
Ethanol alcohol
and
carbon dioxide!

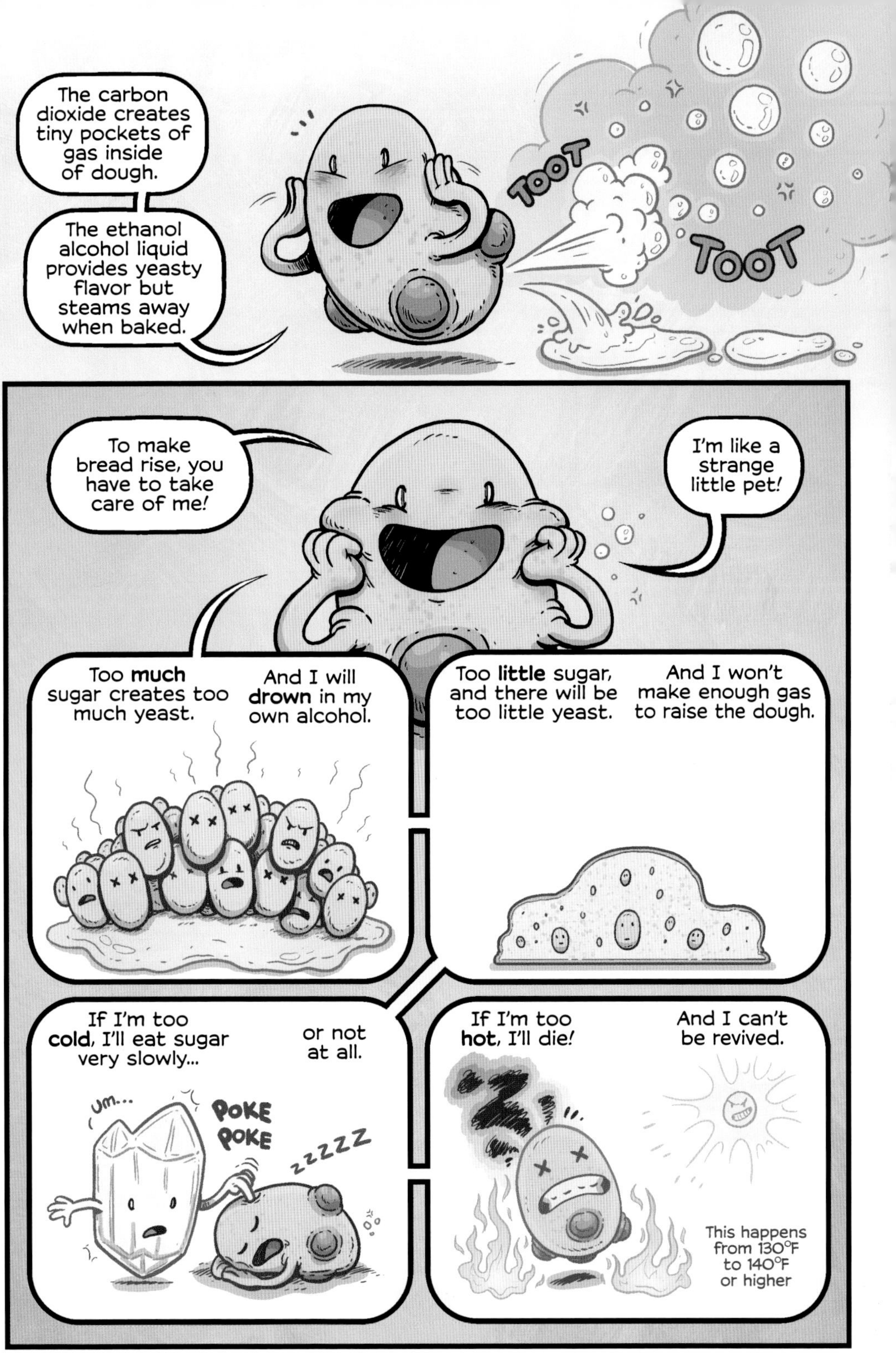
The carbon dioxide creates tiny pockets of gas inside of dough.
The ethanol alcohol liquid provides yeasty flavor but steams away when baked.
TOOT
TOOT
To make bread rise, you have to take care of me!
I'm like a strange little pet!
Too **much** sugar creates too much yeast.
And I will **drown** in my own alcohol.
Too **little** sugar, and there will be too little yeast.
And I won't make enough gas to raise the dough.
If I'm too **cold**, I'll eat sugar very slowly...
or not at all.
UM...
POKE POKE
ZZZZZ
If I'm too **hot**, I'll die!
And I can't be revived.
This happens from 130°F to 140°F or higher

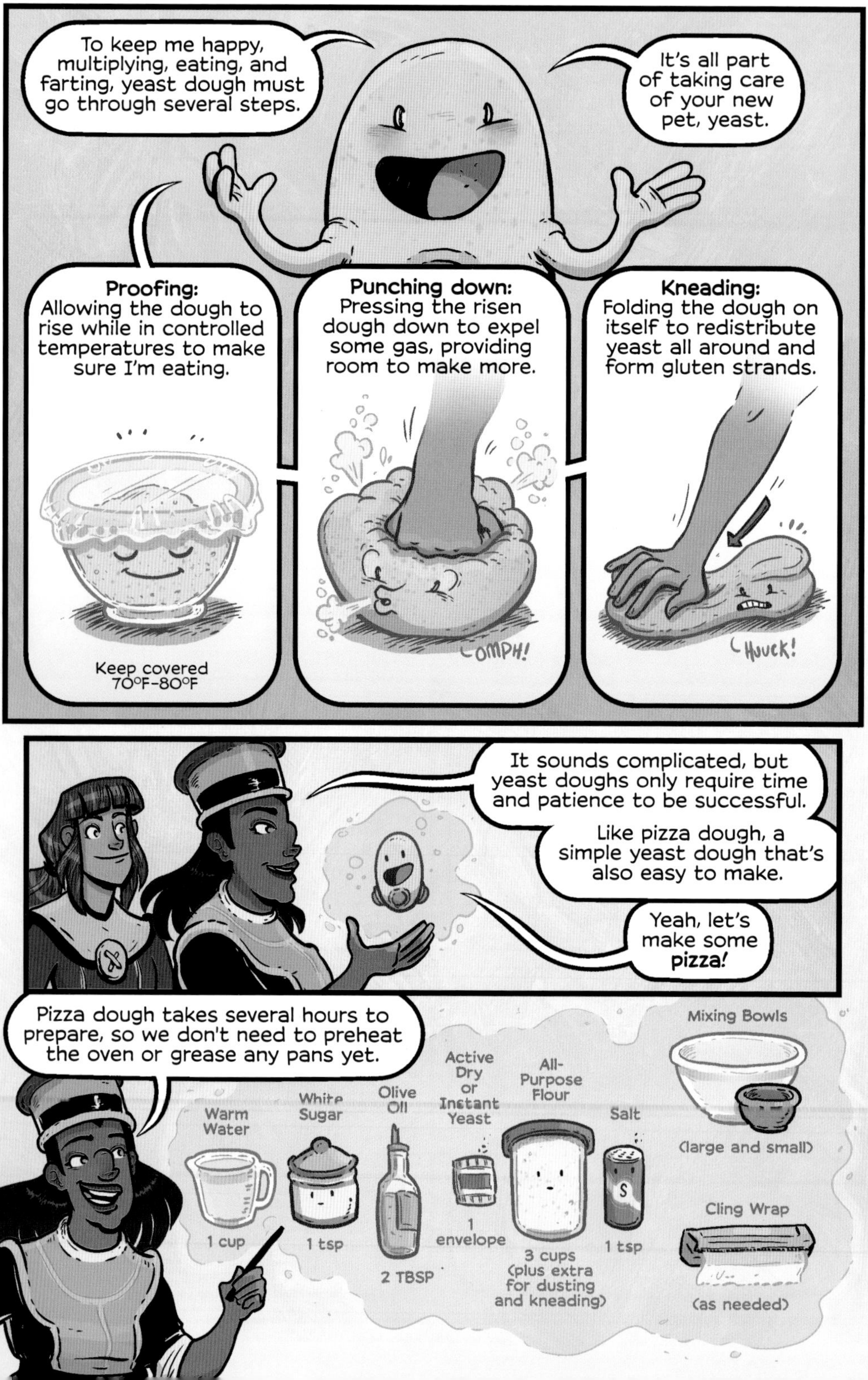

To keep me happy, multiplying, eating, and farting, yeast dough must go through several steps.
It's all part of taking care of your new pet, yeast.
Proofing: Allowing the dough to rise while in controlled temperatures to make sure I'm eating.
Keep covered 70°F–80°F
Punching down: Pressing the risen dough down to expel some gas, providing room to make more.
OOMPH!
Kneading: Folding the dough on itself to redistribute yeast all around and form gluten strands.
HUUCK!
It sounds complicated, but yeast doughs only require time and patience to be successful.
Like pizza dough, a simple yeast dough that's also easy to make.
Yeah, let's make some pizza!
Pizza dough takes several hours to prepare, so we don't need to preheat the oven or grease any pans yet.
Warm Water
1 cup
White Sugar
1 tsp
Olive Oil
2 TBSP
Active Dry or Instant Yeast
1 envelope
All-Purpose Flour
3 cups (plus extra for dusting and kneading)
Salt
1 tsp
S
Mixing Bowls
(large and small)
Cling Wrap
(as needed)

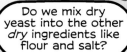

PIZZA DOUGH

Do we mix dry yeast into the other *dry* ingredients like flour and salt?

If we were using **instant** yeast, we would.

But we're using **active** yeast. It has to be added to warm water.

It will need about ten minutes to *"bloom,"* or activate.

No warmer than 120°F! Remember, I'll die if I'm too hot!

I'll bloom with only water, but adding sugar gives me some food to eat right away.

As the yeast is waking up, form a crater with the dry ingredients, either on a clean surface or in a large bowl.

The wet ingredients (warm yeast, sugar water, and olive oil) will go in the middle of the crater.

It can be easier to use a fork at first to mix dry and wet, because you want to mix only a little at a time, starting with the edges.

If you want to use your hands, wash them first.

TA-DA!

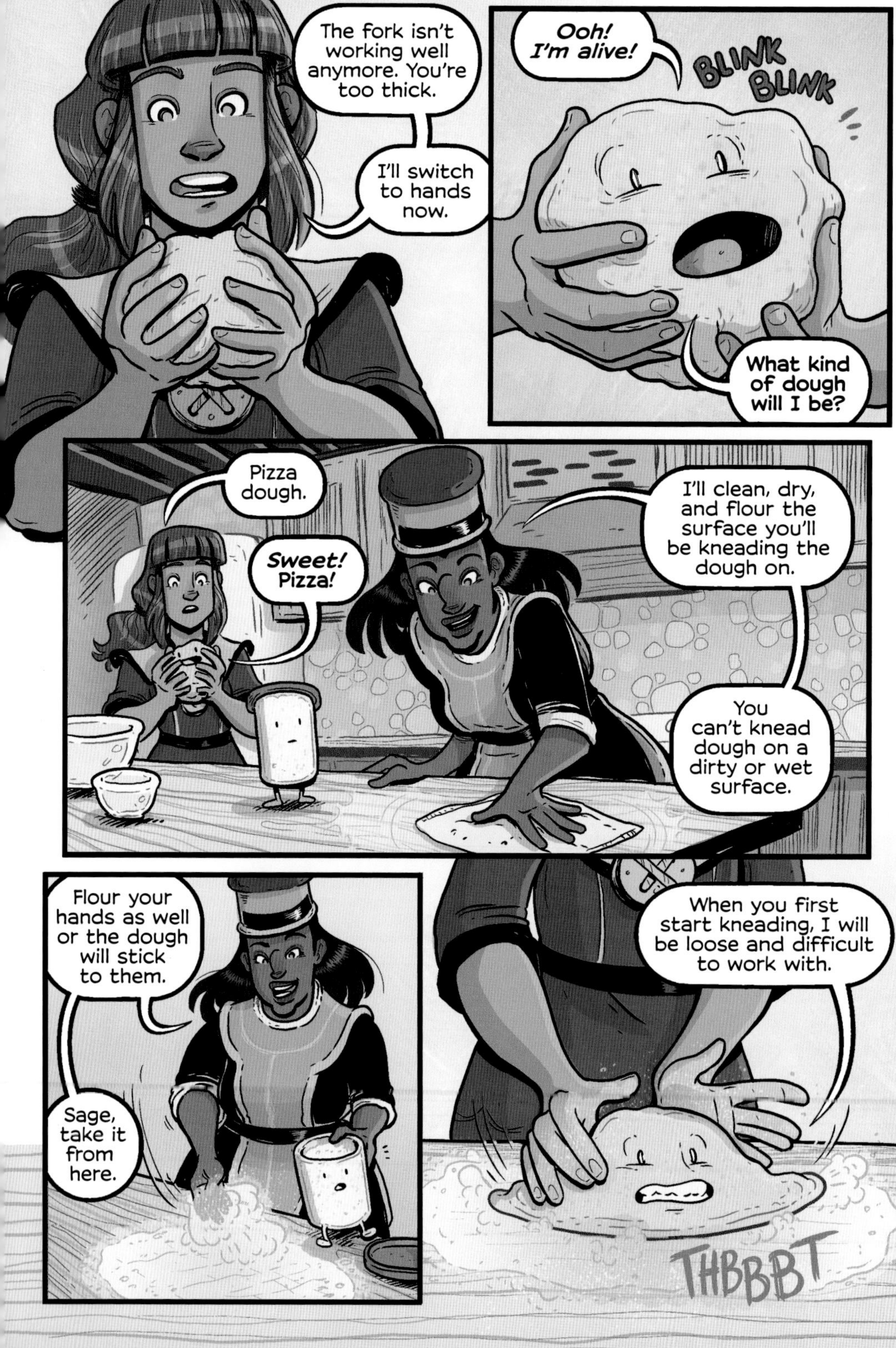

The fork isn't working well anymore. You're too thick.
I'll switch to hands now.
Ooh! I'm alive!
BLINK BLINK
What kind of dough will I be?
Pizza dough.
***Sweet!* Pizza!**
I'll clean, dry, and flour the surface you'll be kneading the dough on.
You can't knead dough on a dirty or wet surface.
Flour your hands as well or the dough will stick to them.
Sage, take it from here.
When you first start kneading, I will be loose and difficult to work with.
THBBBT

When I'm still soft and gloopy, you can start forming gluten by pressing the dough out flat, then forming me into a ball a few times.

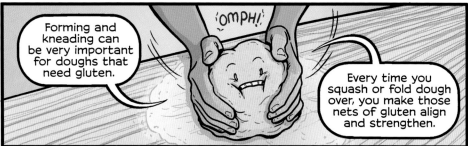

Forming and kneading can be very important for doughs that need gluten.

'OMPH!'

Every time you squash or fold dough over, you make those nets of gluten align and strengthen.

This can create a chewy, crusty bread you can shape or mold however you like without using a pan or tin.

Soon I will gain strength, and you can shape me into a ball, and I'll stay that way.

Though I'm still feeling very mushy.

If the dough is still sticky, re-flour the surface **and** your hands.

This is when **real** kneading begins!

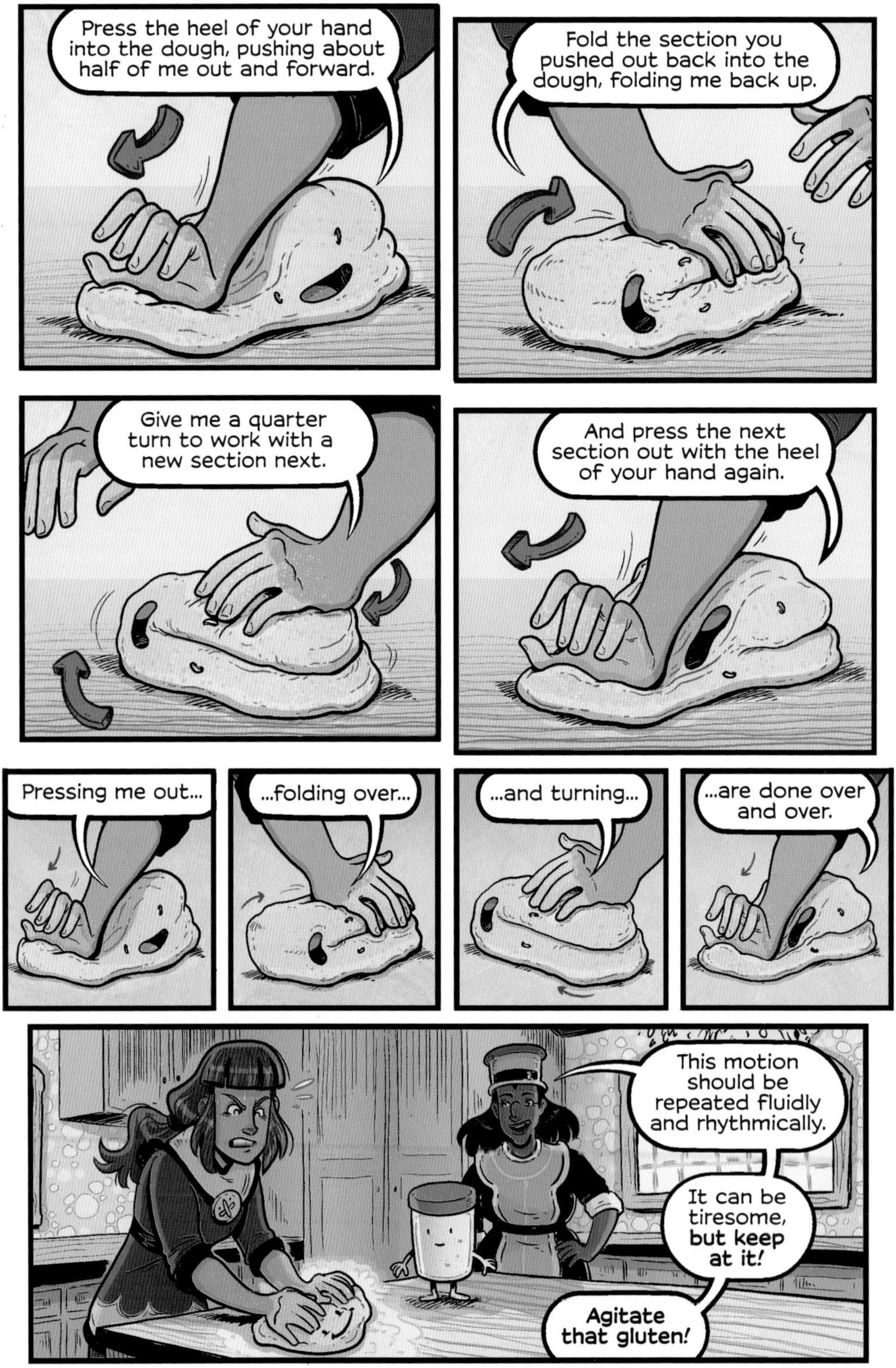
Press the heel of your hand into the dough, pushing about half of me out and forward.
Fold the section you pushed out back into the dough, folding me back up.
Give me a quarter turn to work with a new section next.
And press the next section out with the heel of your hand again.
Pressing me out...
...folding over...
...and turning...
...are done over and over.
This motion should be repeated fluidly and rhythmically.
It can be tiresome, **but keep at it!**
Agitate that gluten!

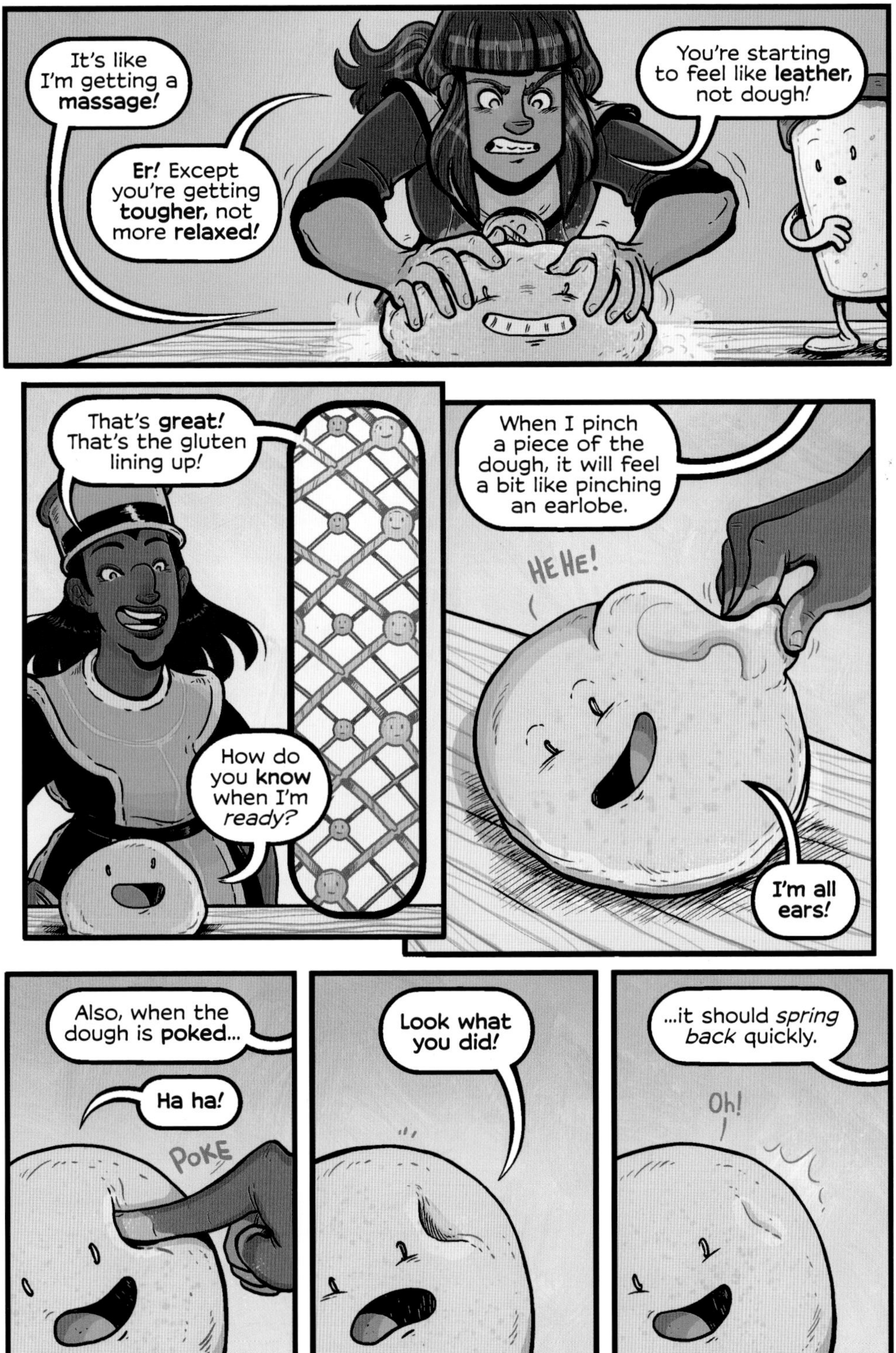
It's like I'm getting a massage!
Er! Except you're getting tougher, not more relaxed!
You're starting to feel like leather, not dough!
That's great! That's the gluten lining up!
How do you know when I'm ready?
When I pinch a piece of the dough, it will feel a bit like pinching an earlobe.
HEHE!
I'm all ears!
Also, when the dough is poked...
Ha ha!
POKE
Look what you did!
...it should spring back quickly.
Oh!

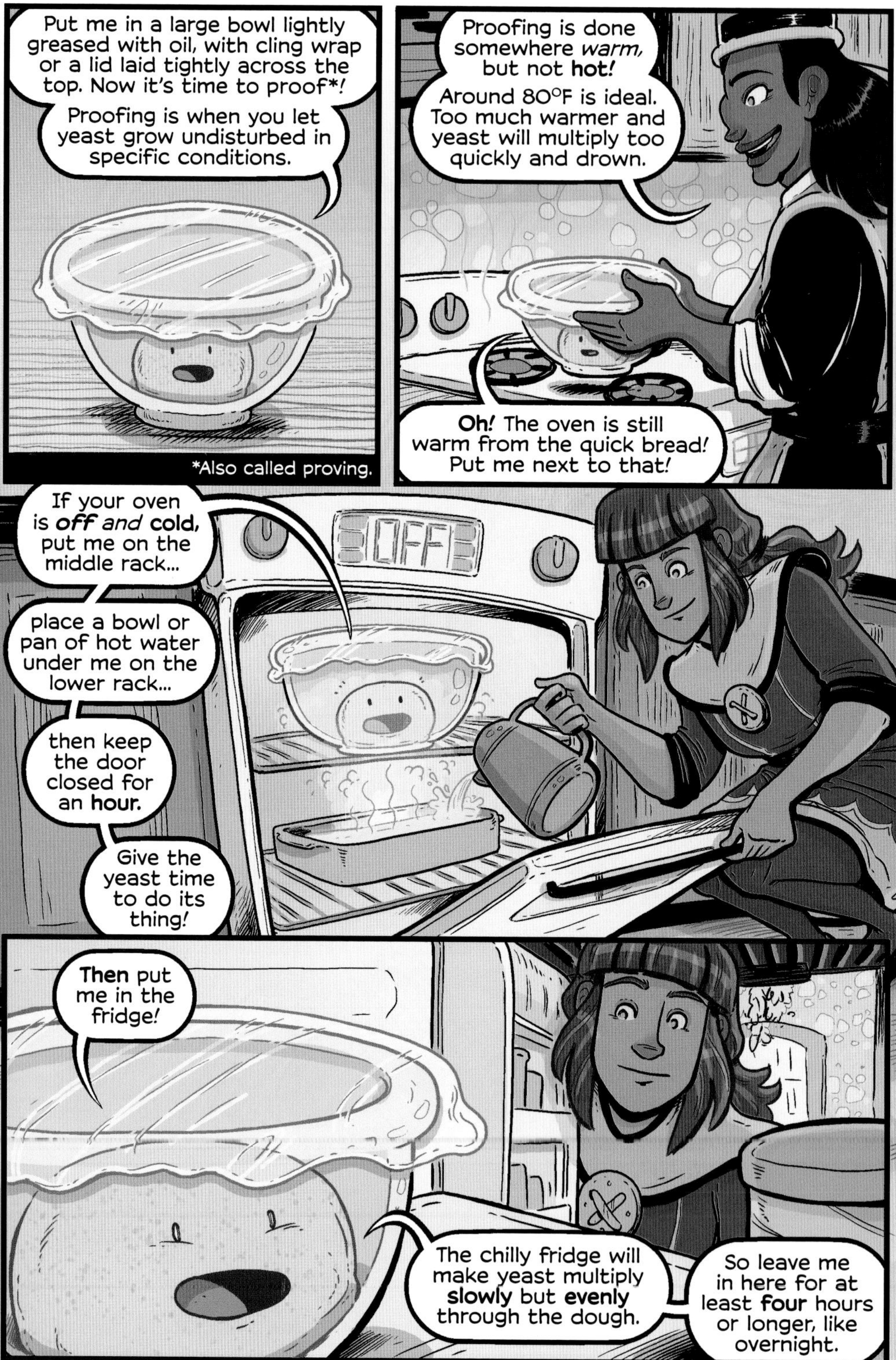

Put me in a large bowl lightly greased with oil, with cling wrap or a lid laid tightly across the top. Now it's time to proof*!
Proofing is when you let yeast grow undisturbed in specific conditions.
*Also called proving.
Proofing is done somewhere *warm,* but not **hot!**
Around 80°F is ideal. Too much warmer and yeast will multiply too quickly and drown.
Oh! The oven is still warm from the quick bread! Put me next to that!
OFF
If your oven is ***off and* cold,** put me on the middle rack...
place a bowl or pan of hot water under me on the lower rack...
then keep the door closed for an **hour.**
Give the yeast time to do its thing!
Then put me in the fridge!
The chilly fridge will make yeast multiply **slowly** but **evenly** through the dough.
So leave me in here for at least **four** hours or longer, like overnight.

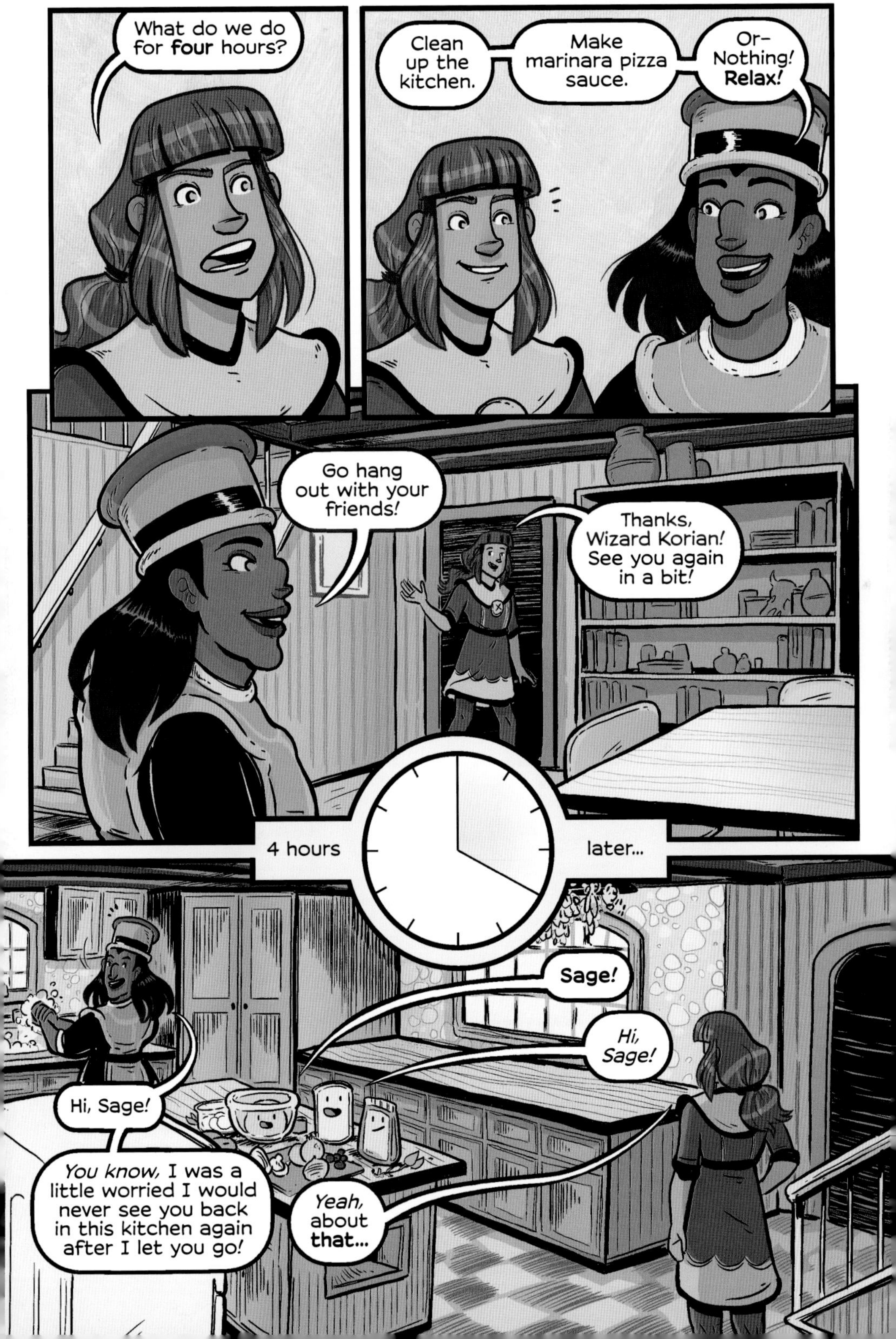
What do we do for **four** hours?
Clean up the kitchen.
Make marinara pizza sauce.
Or– Nothing! **Relax!**
Go hang out with your friends!
Thanks, Wizard Korian! See you again in a bit!
4 hours
later...
Sage!
Hi, Sage!
Hi, Sage!
You know, I was a little worried I would never see you back in this kitchen again after I let you go!
Yeah, about **that...**

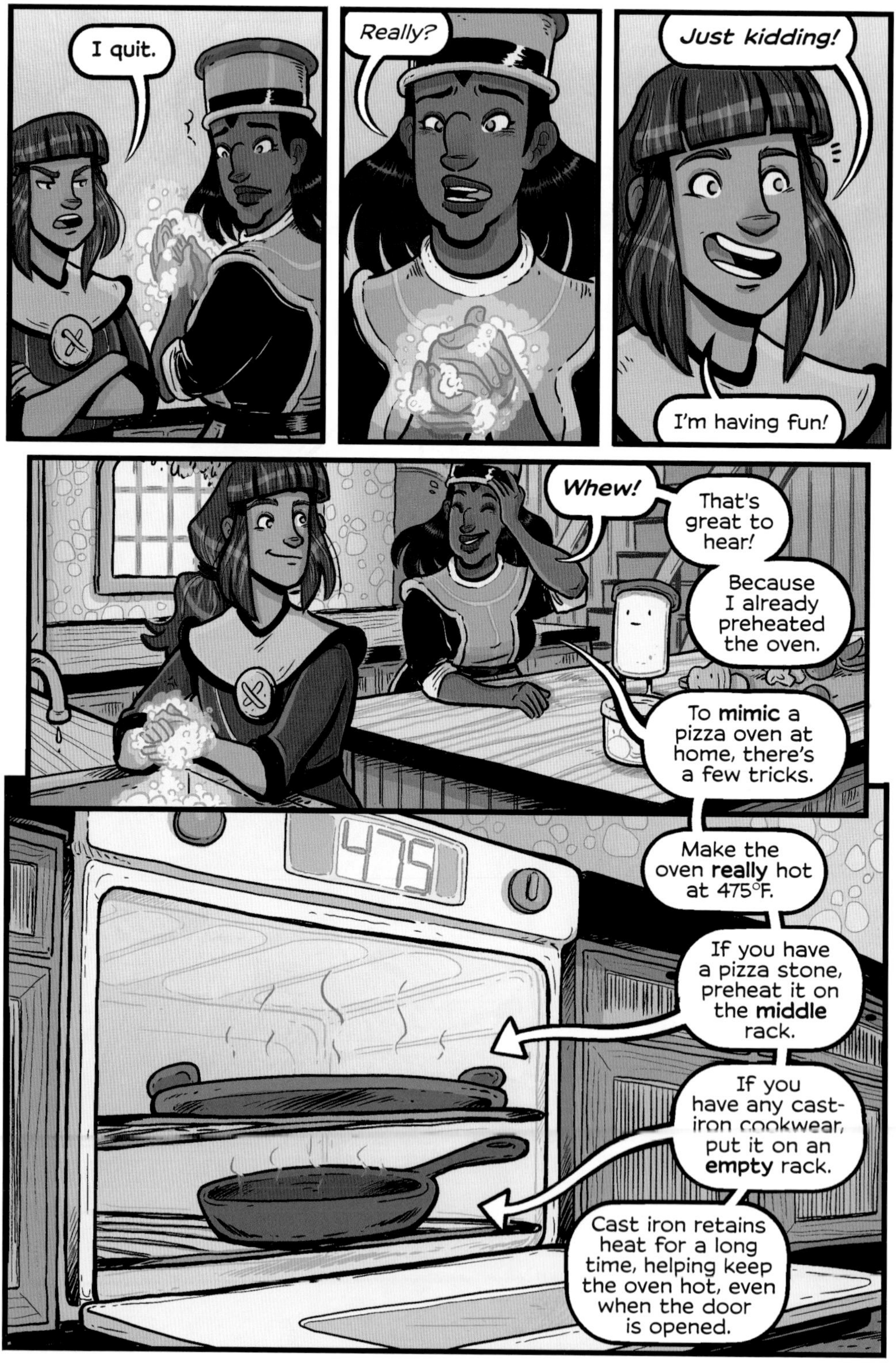
I quit.
Really?
Just kidding!
I'm having fun!
Whew!
That's great to hear!
Because I already preheated the oven.
To mimic a pizza oven at home, there's a few tricks.
475
Make the oven really hot at 475°F.
If you have a pizza stone, preheat it on the middle rack.
If you have any cast-iron cookwear, put it on an empty rack.
Cast iron retains heat for a long time, helping keep the oven hot, even when the door is opened.

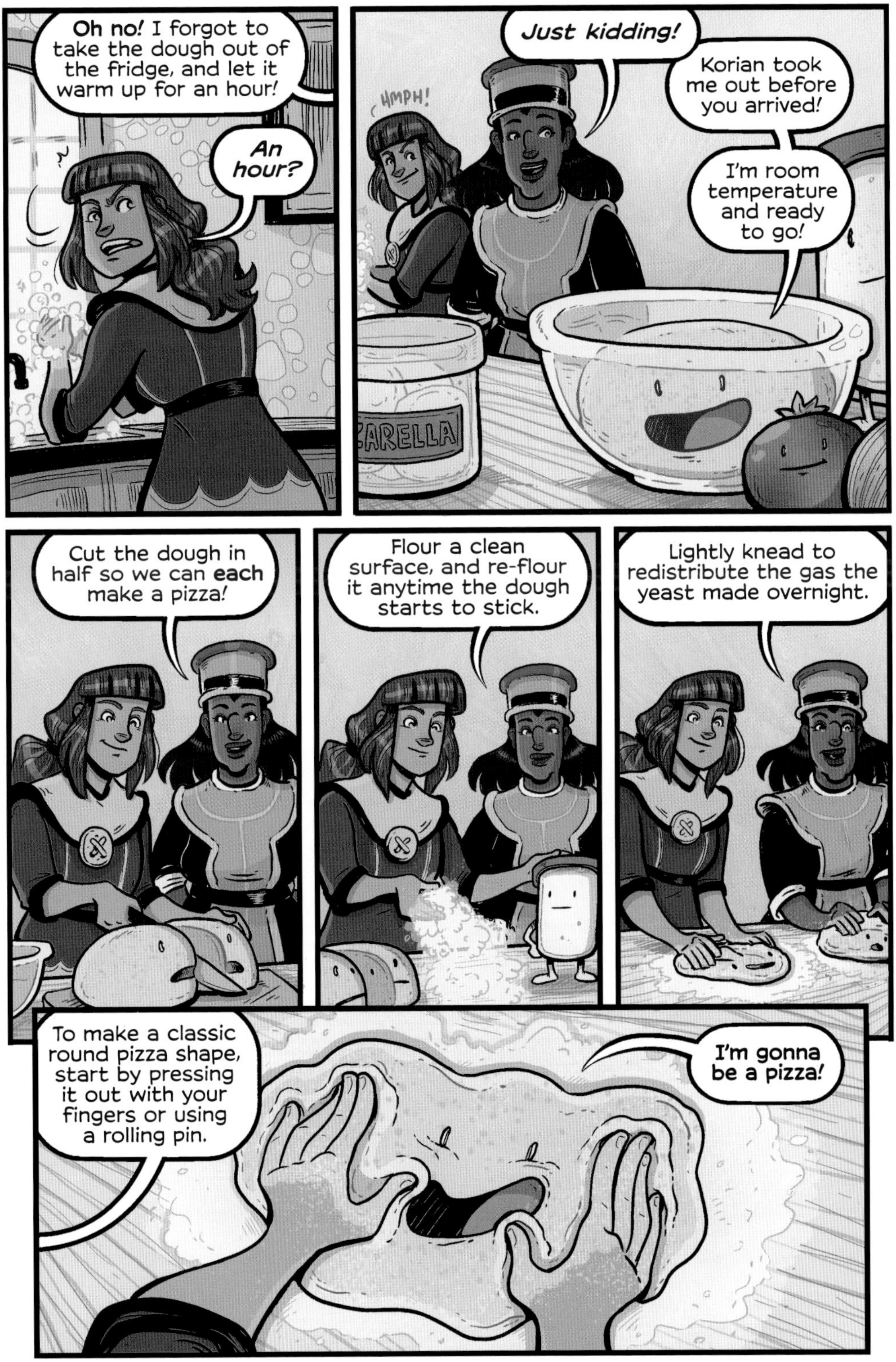

Oh no! I forgot to take the dough out of the fridge, and let it warm up for an hour!
An hour?
Just kidding!
HMPH!
Korian took me out before you arrived!
I'm room temperature and ready to go!
ZARELLA
Cut the dough in half so we can each make a pizza!
Flour a clean surface, and re-flour it anytime the dough starts to stick.
Lightly knead to redistribute the gas the yeast made overnight.
To make a classic round pizza shape, start by pressing it out with your fingers or using a rolling pin.
I'm gonna be a pizza!

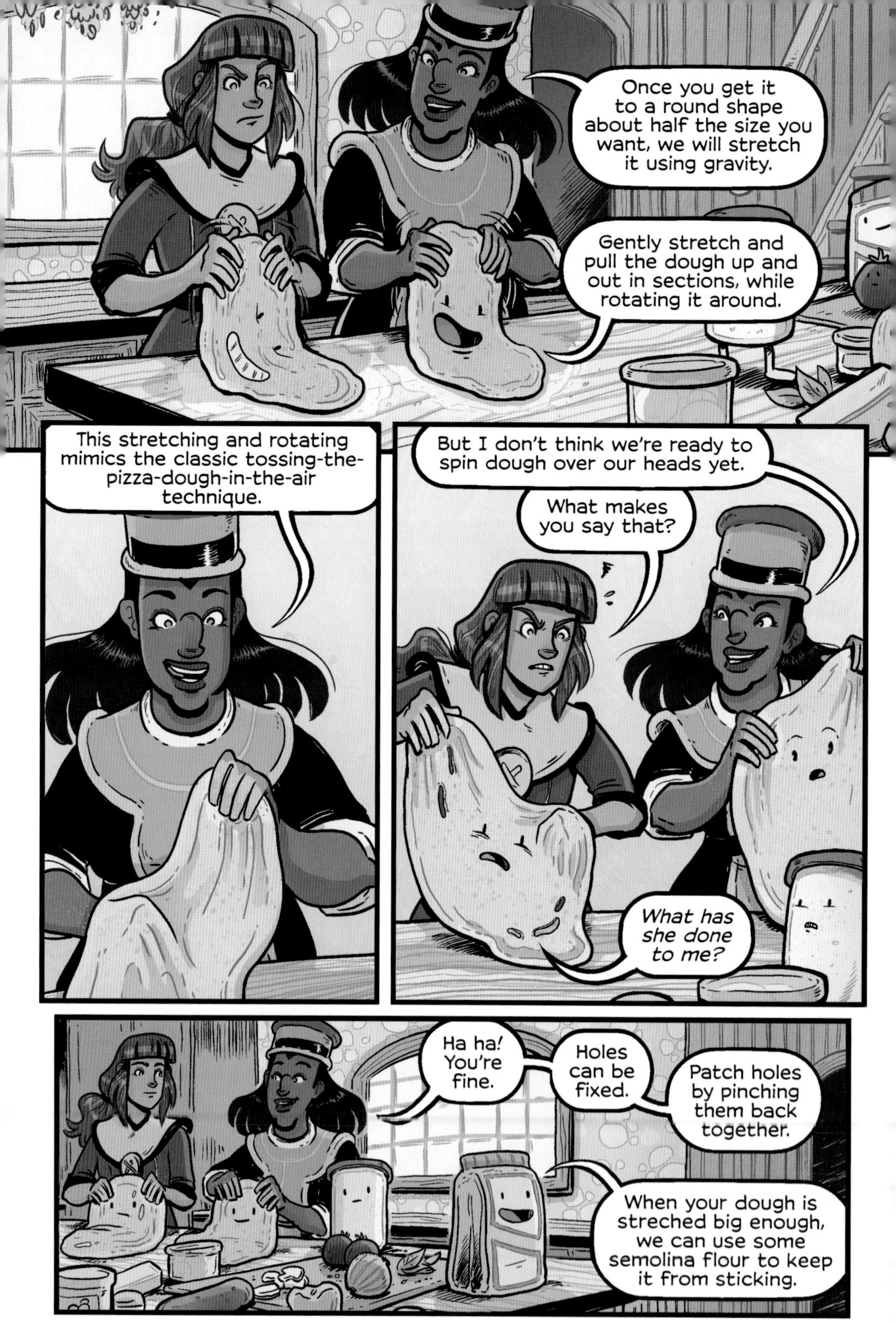
Once you get it to a round shape about half the size you want, we will stretch it using gravity.
Gently stretch and pull the dough up and out in sections, while rotating it around.
This stretching and rotating mimics the classic tossing-the-pizza-dough-in-the-air technique.
But I don't think we're ready to spin dough over our heads yet.
What makes you say that?
What has she done to me?
Ha ha! You're fine.
Holes can be fixed.
Patch holes by pinching them back together.
When your dough is streched big enough, we can use some semolina flour to keep it from sticking.

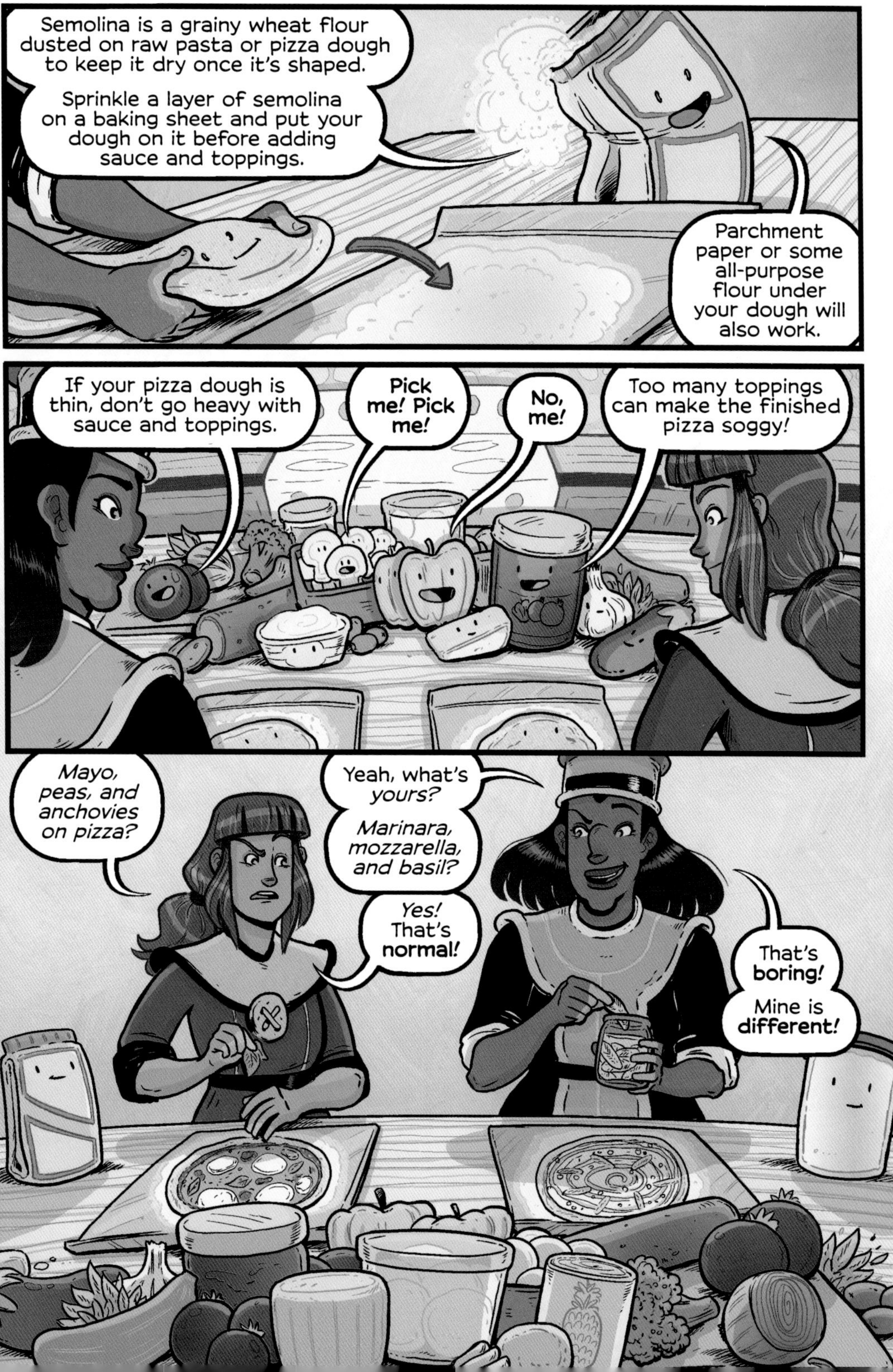
Semolina is a grainy wheat flour dusted on raw pasta or pizza dough to keep it dry once it's shaped.
Sprinkle a layer of semolina on a baking sheet and put your dough on it before adding sauce and toppings.
Parchment paper or some all-purpose flour under your dough will also work.
If your pizza dough is thin, don't go heavy with sauce and toppings.
Pick me! Pick me!
No, me!
Too many toppings can make the finished pizza soggy!
Mayo, peas, and anchovies on pizza?
Yeah, what's *yours?*
Marinara, mozzarella, and basil?
Yes! That's **normal!**
That's **boring!**
Mine is **different!**

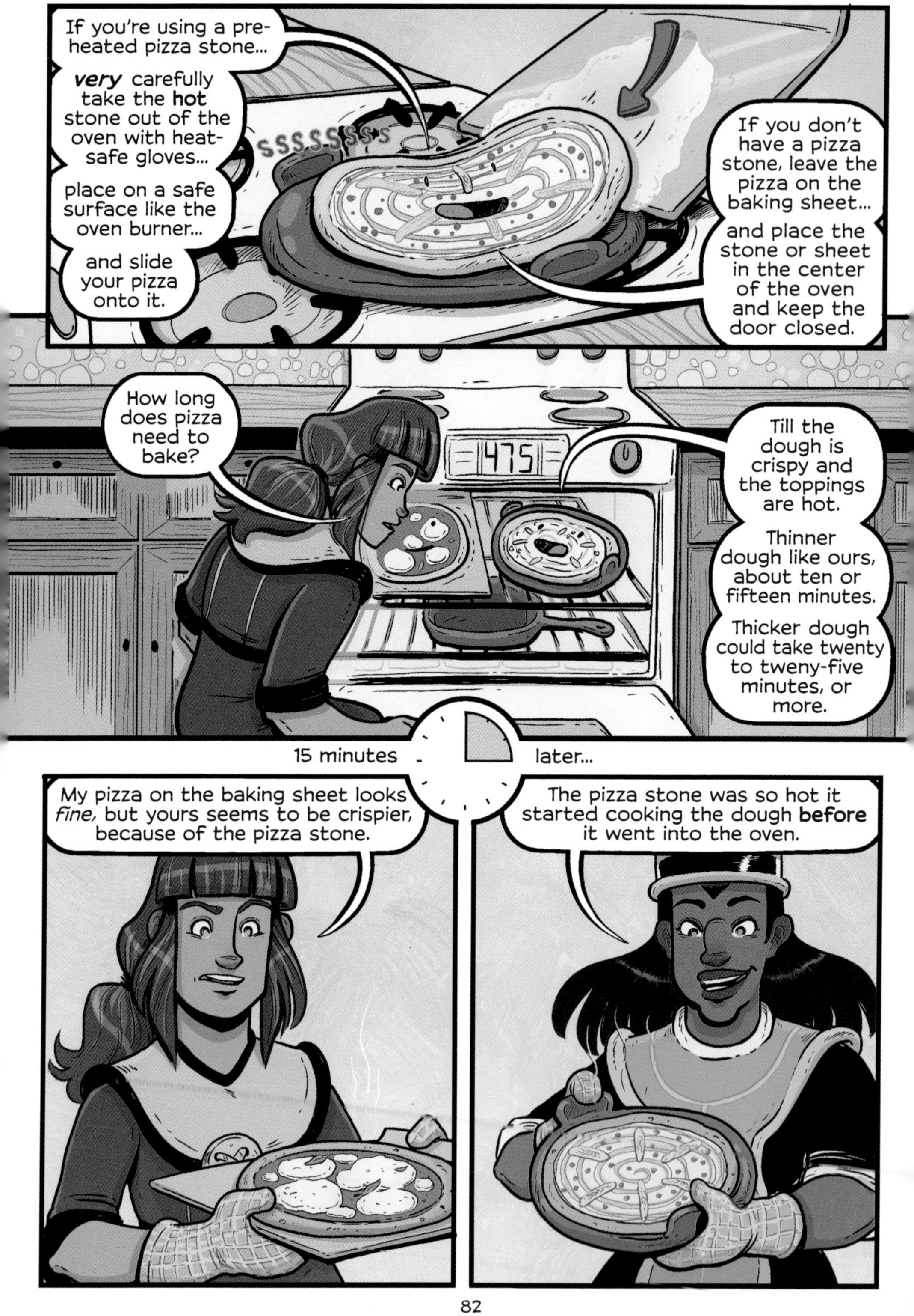
If you're using a pre-heated pizza stone...
very carefully take the **hot** stone out of the oven with heat-safe gloves...
place on a safe surface like the oven burner...
and slide your pizza onto it.
SSSSSSSSS
If you don't have a pizza stone, leave the pizza on the baking sheet...
and place the stone or sheet in the center of the oven and keep the door closed.
How long does pizza need to bake?
475
Till the dough is crispy and the toppings are hot.
Thinner dough like ours, about ten or fifteen minutes.
Thicker dough could take twenty to tweny-five minutes, or more.
15 minutes
later...
My pizza on the baking sheet looks *fine,* but yours seems to be crispier, because of the pizza stone.
The pizza stone was so hot it started cooking the dough **before** it went into the oven.

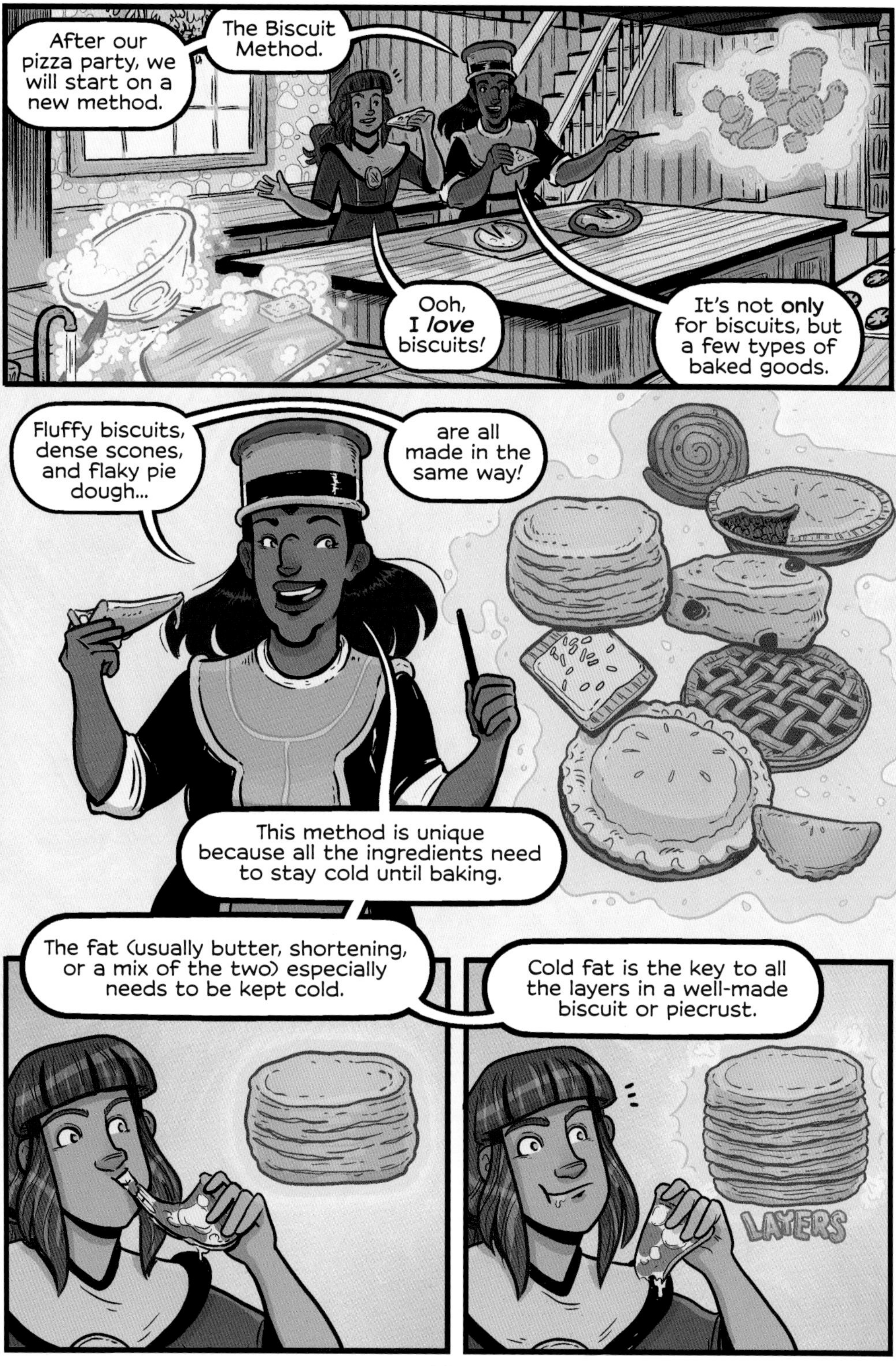
After our pizza party, we will start on a new method.
The Biscuit Method.
Ooh, I *love* biscuits!
It's not **only** for biscuits, but a few types of baked goods.
Fluffy biscuits, dense scones, and flaky pie dough...
are all made in the same way!
This method is unique because all the ingredients need to stay cold until baking.
The fat (usually butter, shortening, or a mix of the two) especially needs to be kept cold.
Cold fat is the key to all the layers in a well-made biscuit or piecrust.
LAYERS

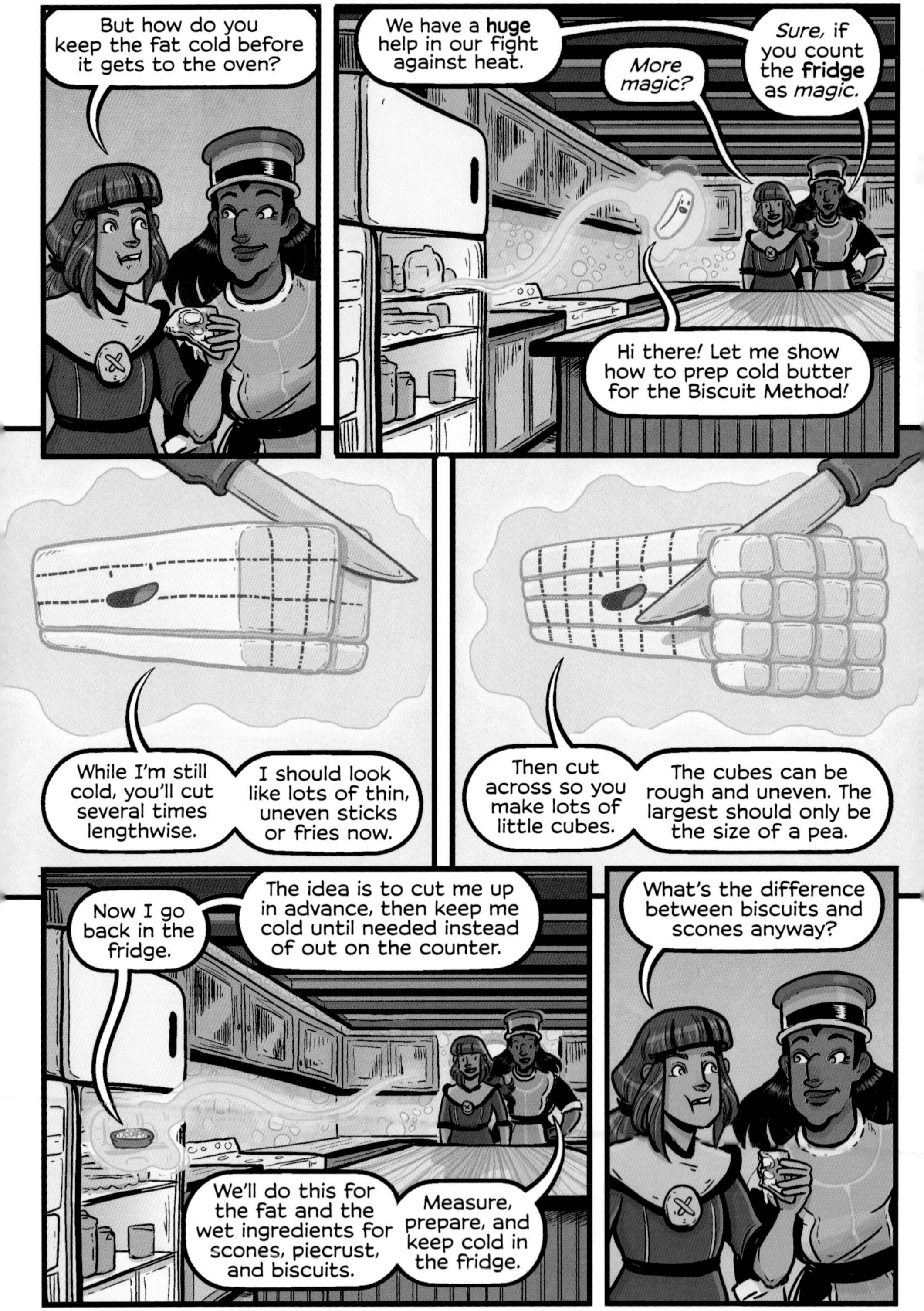
But how do you keep the fat cold before it gets to the oven?
We have a **huge** help in our fight against heat.
More magic?
Sure, if you count the **fridge** as *magic.*
Hi there! Let me show how to prep cold butter for the Biscuit Method!
While I'm still cold, you'll cut several times lengthwise.
I should look like lots of thin, uneven sticks or fries now.
Then cut across so you make lots of little cubes.
The cubes can be rough and uneven. The largest should only be the size of a pea.
Now I go back in the fridge.
The idea is to cut me up in advance, then keep me cold until needed instead of out on the counter.
We'll do this for the fat and the wet ingredients for scones, piecrust, and biscuits.
Measure, prepare, and keep cold in the fridge.
What's the difference between biscuits and scones anyway?

CHEDDAR BISCUITS

I think the best way to explain is to make some—

Scones and biscuits are **almost** the same, except scones can have egg and are not fluffy or flaky.

And many people **expect** biscuits to be *savory*...

...and for scones to be *sweet*.

But that's **not** a set *rule.*

It's up to **you!**

Grate or chop the cheese and measure out the buttermilk.

Keep them in the fridge with the chopped butter.

Chop the parsley and set it aside.

Butter
1 stick

(chopped and cold)

Buttermilk

1 cup
(cold)

Cheddar
Cheese
1/2 cup

(shredded and cold)

Parsley
1 TBSP

(chopped)

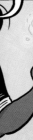

Preheat the oven to 475°F.

Leave your baking sheet **ungreased.**

The dry ingredients, including the spices, are all sifted together.

All-Purpose Flour	White Sugar	Baking Powder	Salt	Garlic Powder	Cayenne Pepper	Paprika
2 cups	2 tsp	1 TBSP	1 tsp	1 tsp	1/4 tsp	1/4 tsp

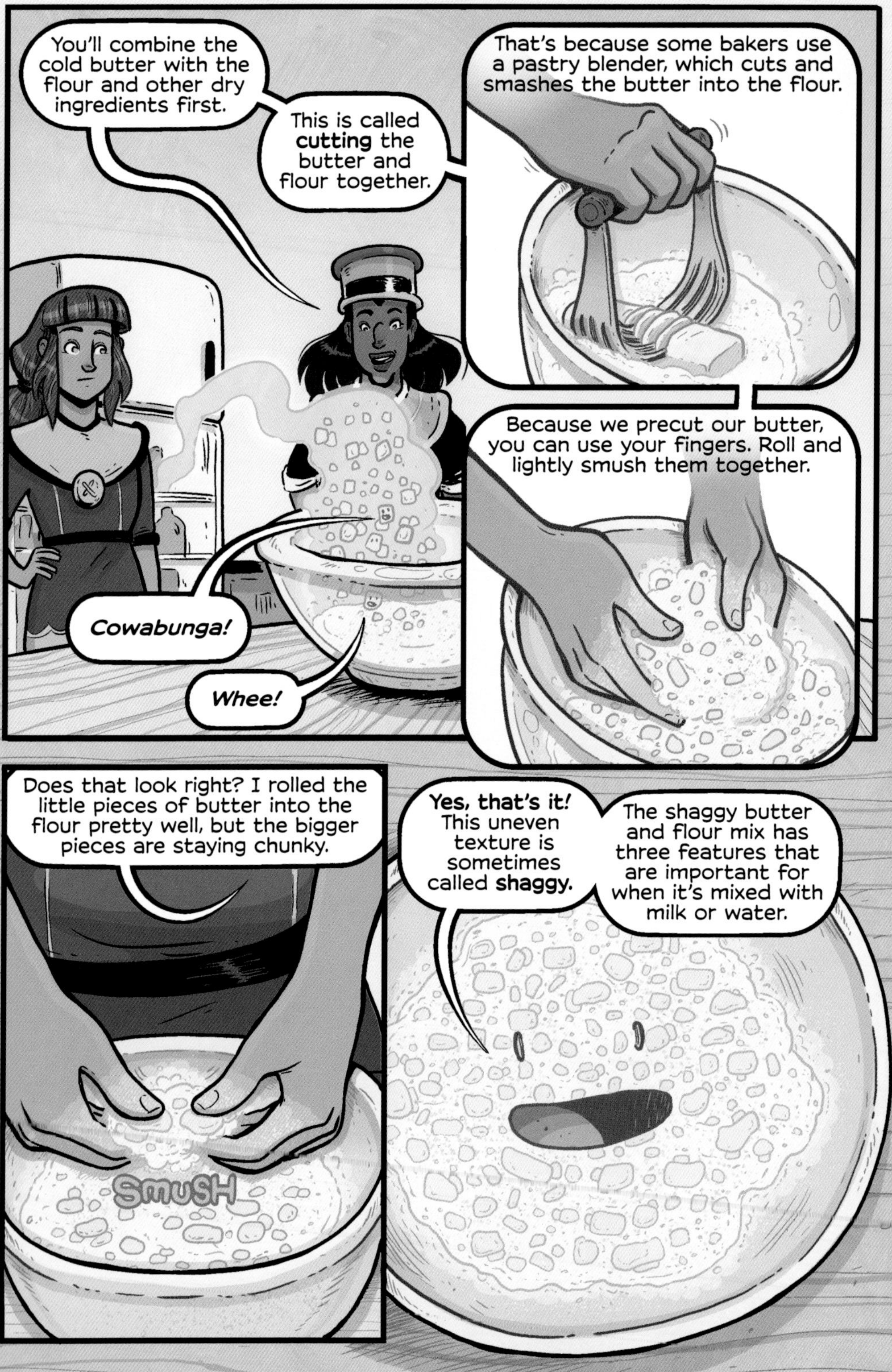
You'll combine the cold butter with the flour and other dry ingredients first.
This is called **cutting** the butter and flour together.
That's because some bakers use a pastry blender, which cuts and smashes the butter into the flour.
Because we precut our butter, you can use your fingers. Roll and lightly smush them together.
Cowabunga!
Whee!
Does that look right? I rolled the little pieces of butter into the flour pretty well, but the bigger pieces are staying chunky.
SMUSH
Yes, that's it! This uneven texture is sometimes called **shaggy.**
The shaggy butter and flour mix has three features that are important for when it's mixed with milk or water.

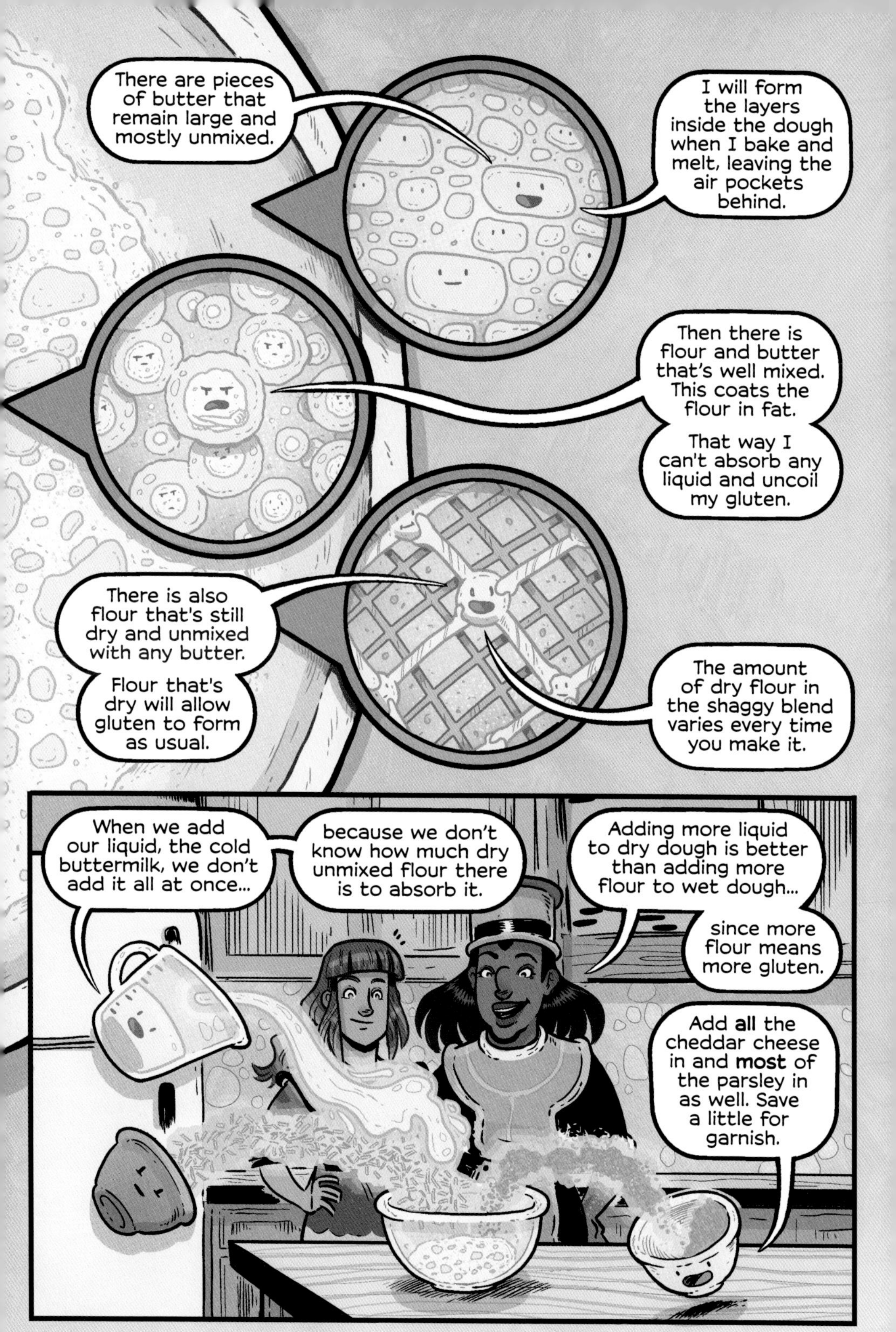

There are pieces of butter that remain large and mostly unmixed.
I will form the layers inside the dough when I bake and melt, leaving the air pockets behind.
Then there is flour and butter that's well mixed. This coats the flour in fat.
That way I can't absorb any liquid and uncoil my gluten.
There is also flour that's still dry and unmixed with any butter.
Flour that's dry will allow gluten to form as usual.
The amount of dry flour in the shaggy blend varies every time you make it.
When we add our liquid, the cold buttermilk, we don't add it all at once...
because we don't know how much dry unmixed flour there is to absorb it.
Adding more liquid to dry dough is better than adding more flour to wet dough...
since more flour means more gluten.
Add **all** the cheddar cheese in and **most** of the parsley in as well. Save a little for garnish.

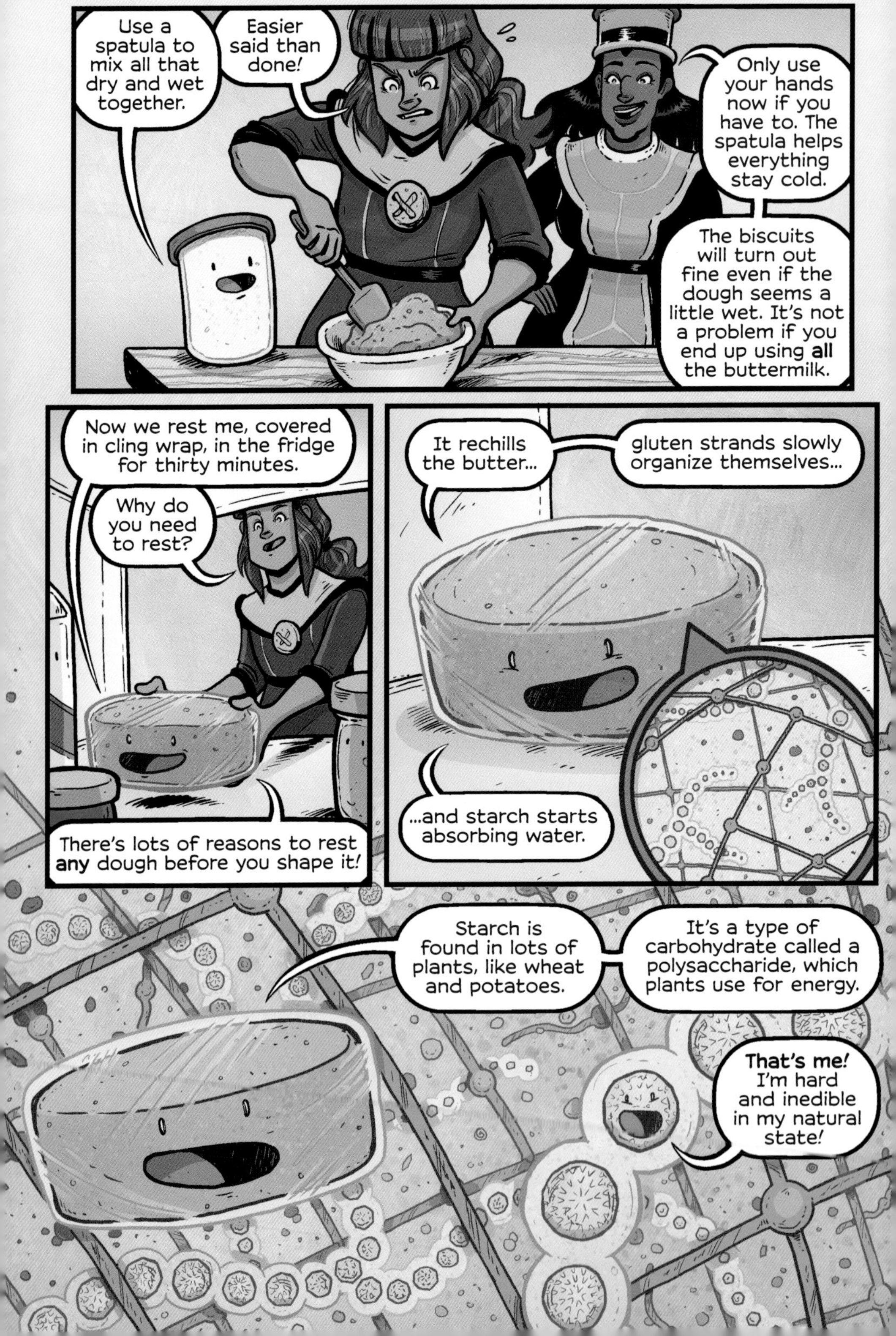
Use a spatula to mix all that dry and wet together.
Easier said than done!
Only use your hands now if you have to. The spatula helps everything stay cold.
The biscuits will turn out fine even if the dough seems a little wet. It's not a problem if you end up using **all** the buttermilk.
Now we rest me, covered in cling wrap, in the fridge for thirty minutes.
Why do you need to rest?
There's lots of reasons to rest **any** dough before you shape it!
It rechills the butter...
gluten strands slowly organize themselves...
...and starch starts absorbing water.
Starch is found in lots of plants, like wheat and potatoes.
It's a type of carbohydrate called a polysaccharide, which plants use for energy.
That's me! I'm hard and inedible in my natural state!

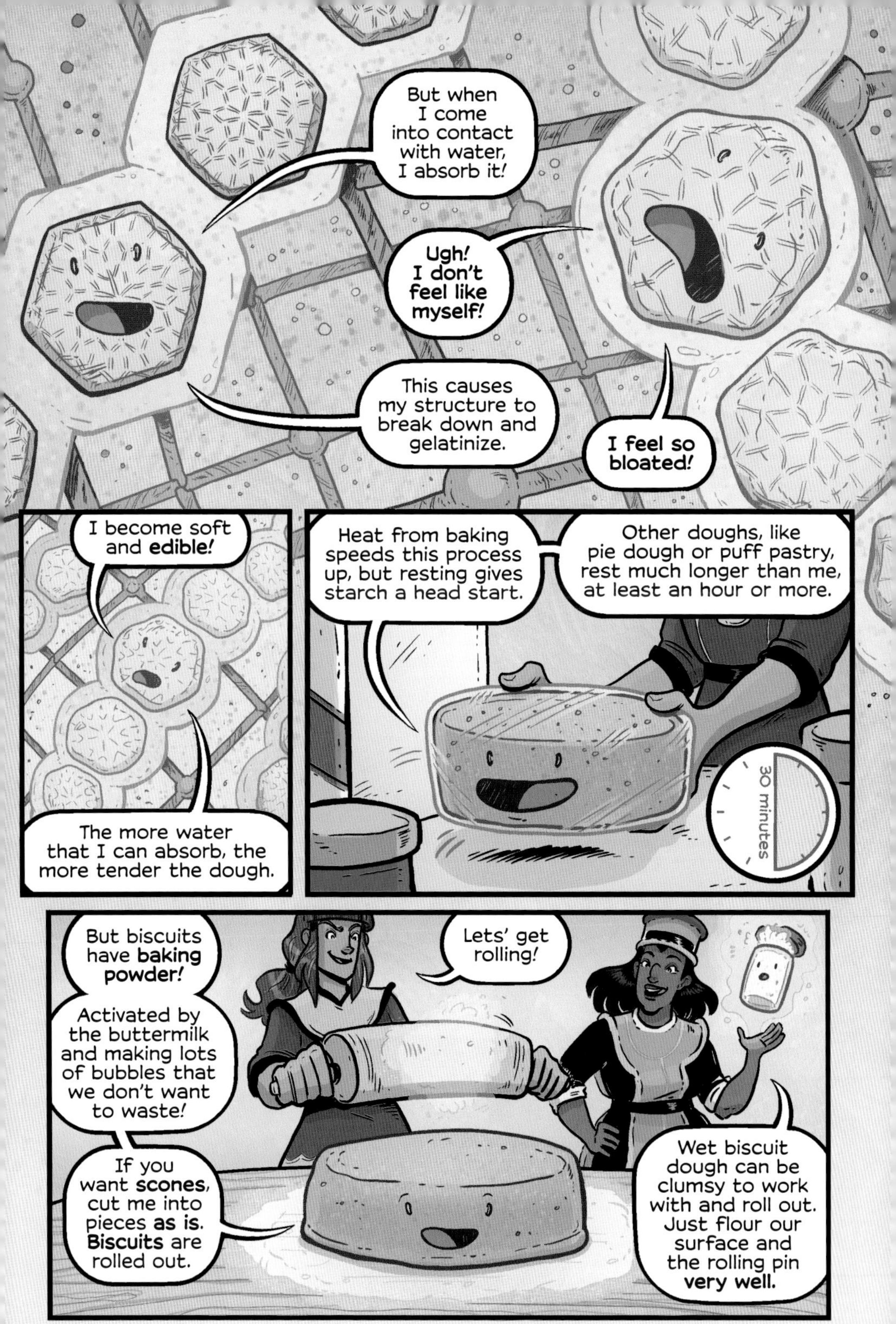
But when I come into contact with water, I absorb it!
Ugh! I don't feel like myself!
This causes my structure to break down and gelatinize.
I feel so bloated!
I become soft and edible!
The more water that I can absorb, the more tender the dough.
Heat from baking speeds this process up, but resting gives starch a head start.
Other doughs, like pie dough or puff pastry, rest much longer than me, at least an hour or more.
30 minutes
But biscuits have baking powder!
Activated by the buttermilk and making lots of bubbles that we don't want to waste!
Lets' get rolling!
If you want scones, cut me into pieces as is. Biscuits are rolled out.
Wet biscuit dough can be clumsy to work with and roll out. Just flour our surface and the rolling pin very well.

Roll me from the middle out.

Push out toward the edges. Don't press down hard or smush me.

Quarter- to half-inch thick.

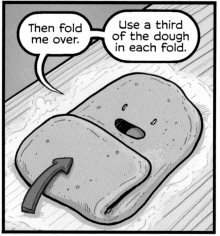

Then fold me over.

Use a third of the dough in each fold.

The folds make more layers of butter!

Scones, which typically aren't folded like this, have pockets of butter instead of layers.

Mmph!

Lightly roll again, but keep me thick, at least an inch tall or more.

You'll get about five to seven biscuits, depending on how large and thick we are.

You can use a knife to cut squares or a circle cutter to make them round.

Press straight down, don't twist. It pinches the layers closed.

Make sure we are very close to one another on the baking sheet.

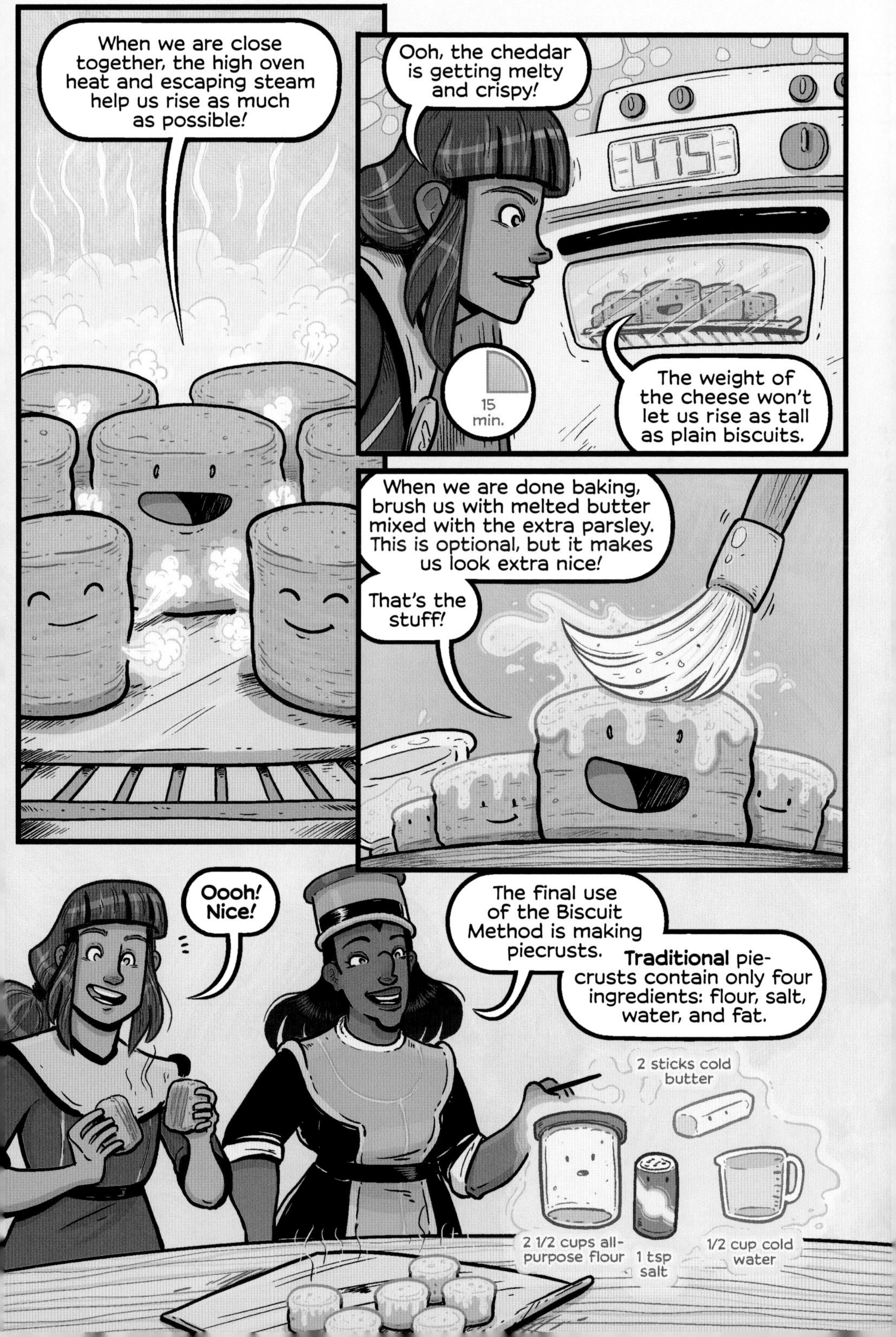
When we are close together, the high oven heat and escaping steam help us rise as much as possible!
Ooh, the cheddar is getting melty and crispy!
475
15 min.
The weight of the cheese won't let us rise as tall as plain biscuits.
When we are done baking, brush us with melted butter mixed with the extra parsley. This is optional, but it makes us look extra nice!
That's the stuff!
Oooh! Nice!
The final use of the Biscuit Method is making piecrusts.
Traditional piecrusts contain only four ingredients: flour, salt, water, and fat.
2 sticks cold butter
2 1/2 cups all-purpose flour
1 tsp salt
1/2 cup cold water

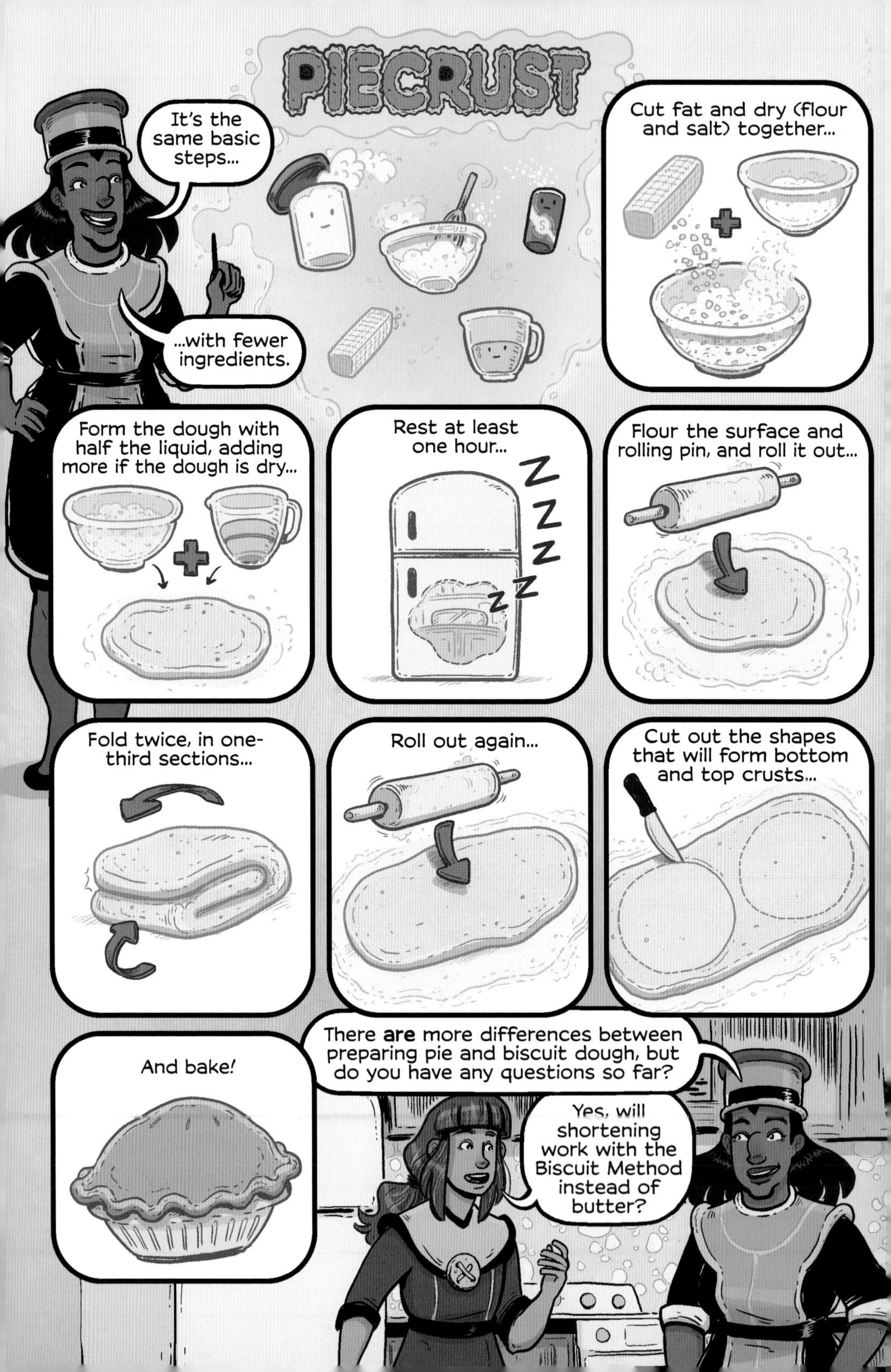
PIECRUST
It's the same basic steps...
...with fewer ingredients.
Cut fat and dry (flour and salt) together...
Form the dough with half the liquid, adding more if the dough is dry...
Rest at least one hour...
Z Z Z Z Z
Flour the surface and rolling pin, and roll it out...
Fold twice, in one-third sections...
Roll out again...
Cut out the shapes that will form bottom and top crusts...
And bake!
There **are** more differences between preparing pie and biscuit dough, but do you have any questions so far?
Yes, will shortening work with the Biscuit Method instead of butter?

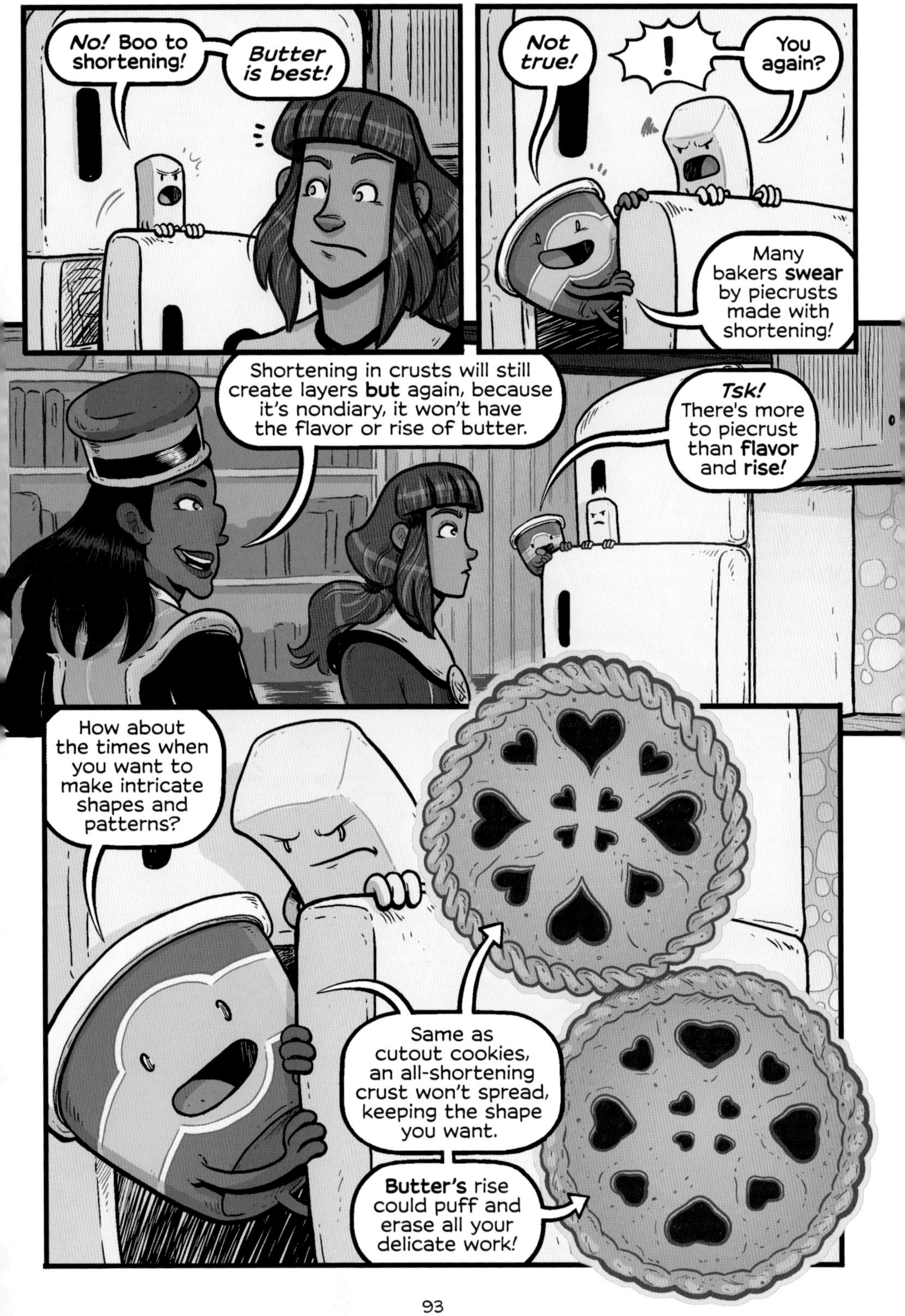

No! Boo to shortening!
Butter is best!
Not true!
!
You again?
Many bakers **swear** by piecrusts made with shortening!
Shortening in crusts will still create layers **but** again, because it's nondiary, it won't have the flavor or rise of butter.
Tsk! There's more to piecrust than **flavor** and **rise!**
How about the times when you want to make intricate shapes and patterns?
Same as cutout cookies, an all-shortening crust won't spread, keeping the shape you want.
Butter's rise could puff and erase all your delicate work!

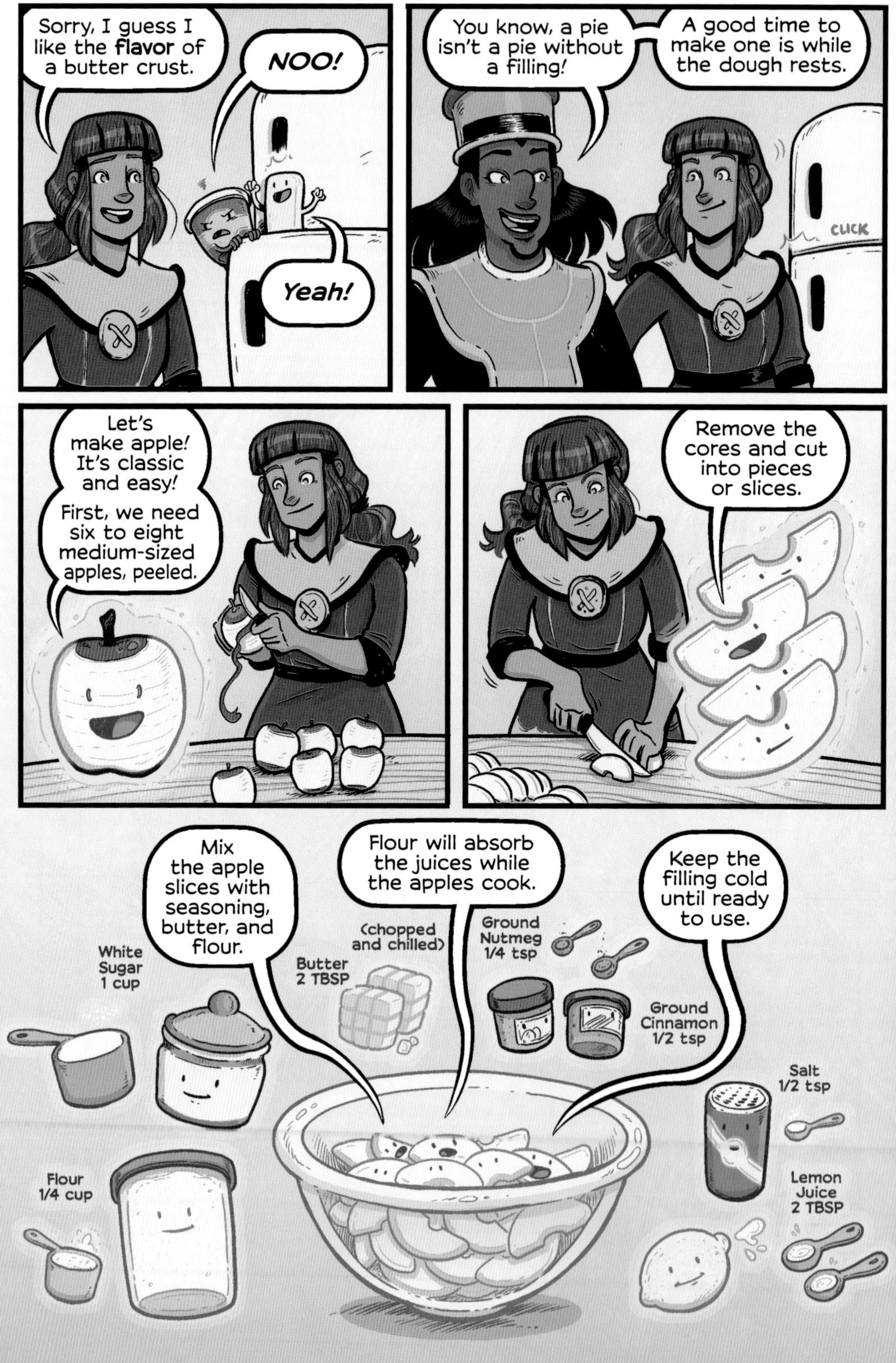

Sorry, I guess I like the **flavor** of a butter crust.
NOO!
Yeah!
You know, a pie isn't a pie without a filling!
A good time to make one is while the dough rests.
CLICK
Let's make apple! It's classic and easy!
First, we need six to eight medium-sized apples, peeled.
Remove the cores and cut into pieces or slices.
Mix the apple slices with seasoning, butter, and flour.
Flour will absorb the juices while the apples cook.
Keep the filling cold until ready to use.
White Sugar 1 cup
Butter 2 TBSP
(chopped and chilled)
Ground Nutmeg 1/4 tsp
Ground Cinnamon 1/2 tsp
Salt 1/2 tsp
Flour 1/4 cup
Lemon Juice 2 TBSP

Let's talk in detail about the final steps in making the pie dough: our final roll and shaping into the pie plate.

If your crust is made well, rested, and everything is dusted with flour... I should roll out evenly, without cracking.

Rotate me occasionally while rolling. If I'm sticking to the surface, I need more flour on me.

wiggle

Roll me into a rectangle shape, a quarter-inch thick or thinner...

long enough to fit the pie plate across twice for a top and bottom crust.

Or you can divide me in two and roll me out one at a time, bottom crust first, then the top crust.

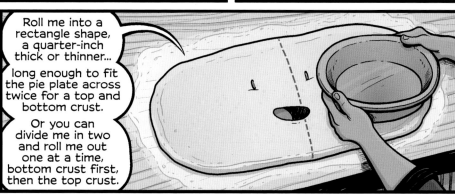

2 inches

Using the pie plate as a guide...

cut two circles out, about two inches larger than the diameter of the plate.

They don't have to be perfect.

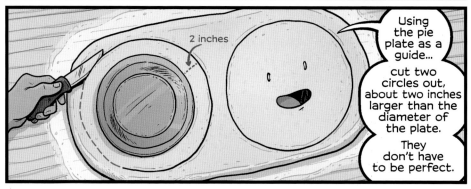

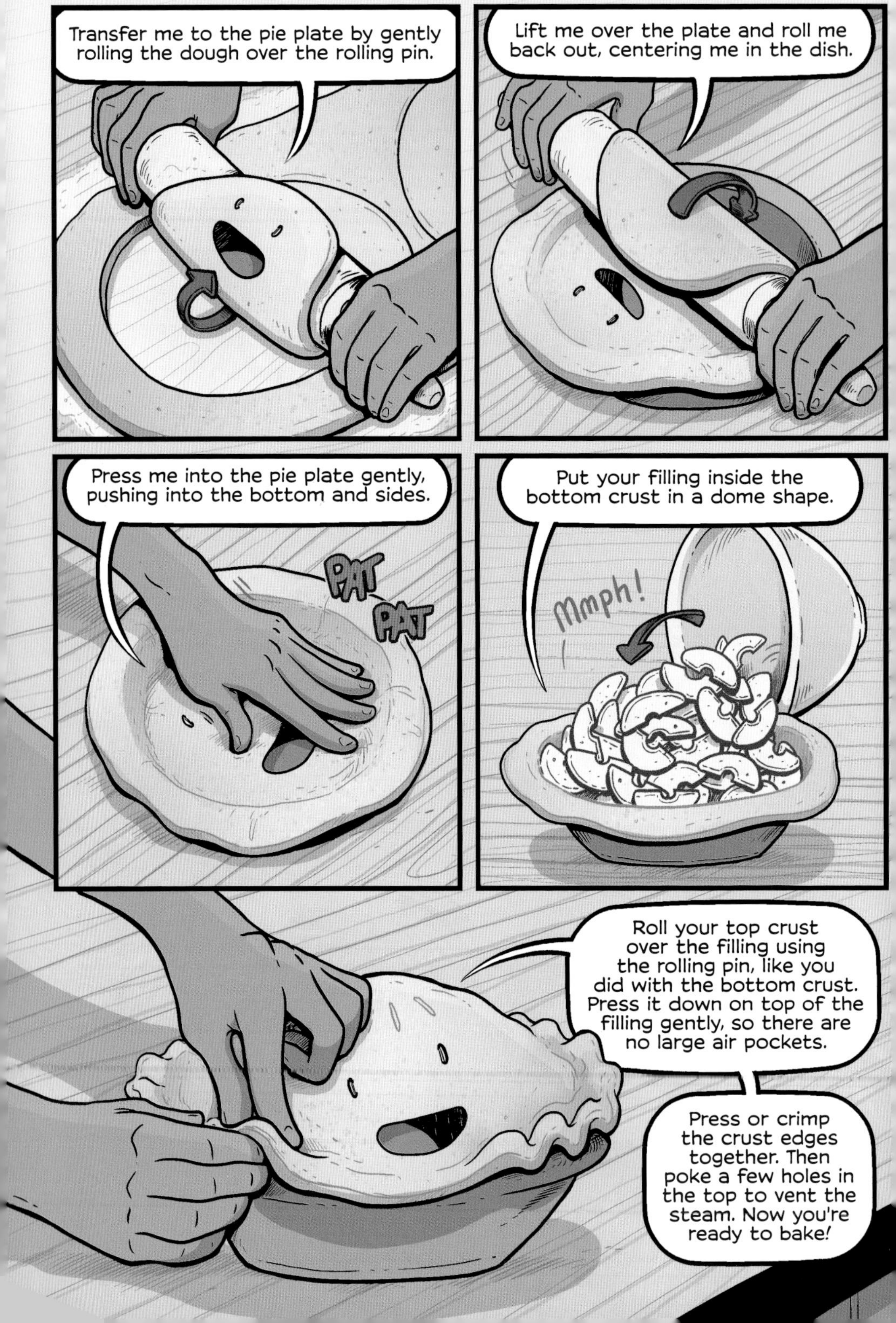
Transfer me to the pie plate by gently rolling the dough over the rolling pin.
Lift me over the plate and roll me back out, centering me in the dish.
Press me into the pie plate gently, pushing into the bottom and sides.
PAT
PAT
Put your filling inside the bottom crust in a dome shape.
Mmph!
Roll your top crust over the filling using the rolling pin, like you did with the bottom crust. Press it down on top of the filling gently, so there are no large air pockets.
Press or crimp the crust edges together. Then poke a few holes in the top to vent the steam. Now you're ready to bake!

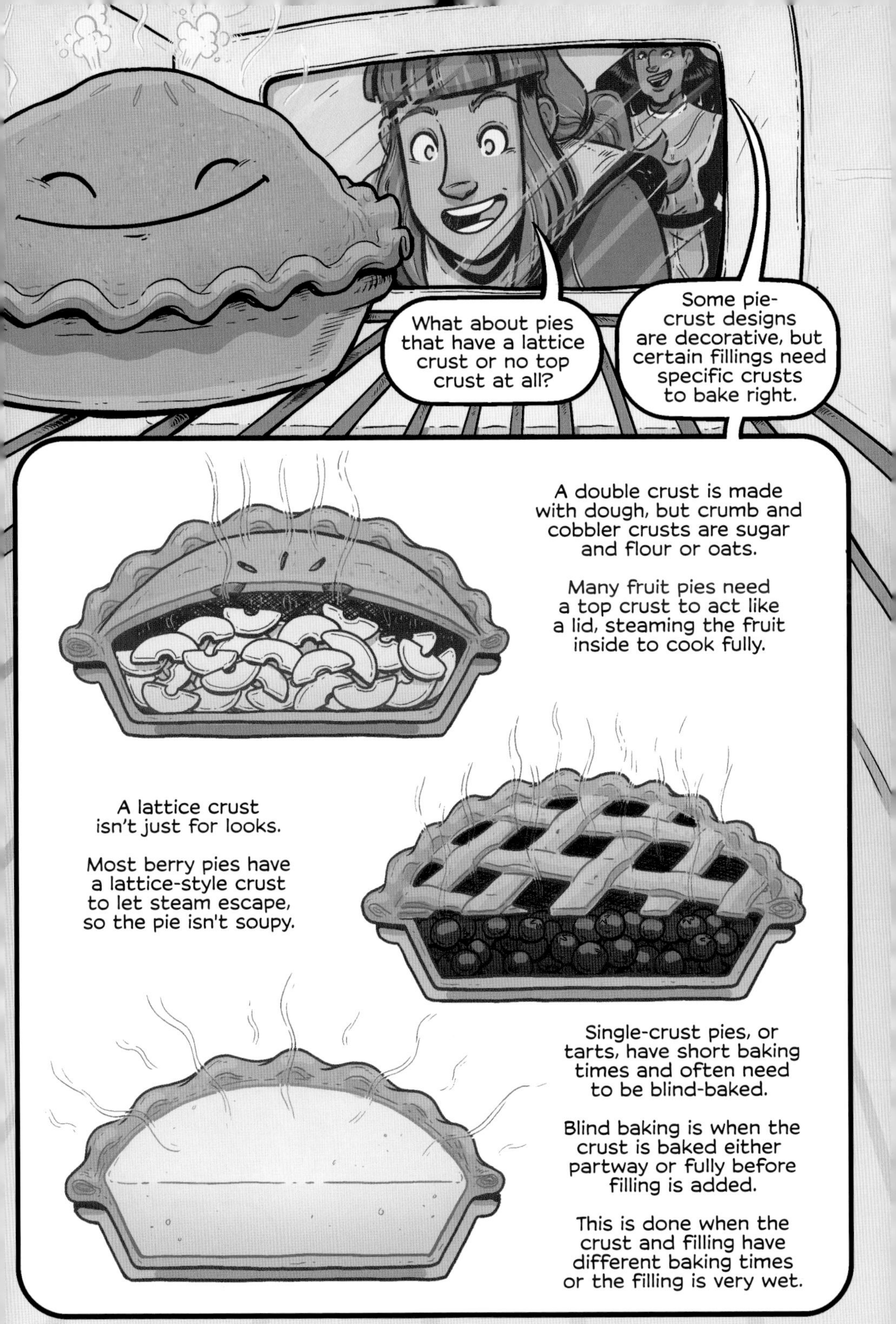
What about pies that have a lattice crust or no top crust at all?
Some pie-crust designs are decorative, but certain fillings need specific crusts to bake right.
A double crust is made with dough, but crumb and cobbler crusts are sugar and flour or oats.
Many fruit pies need a top crust to act like a lid, steaming the fruit inside to cook fully.
A lattice crust isn't just for looks.
Most berry pies have a lattice-style crust to let steam escape, so the pie isn't soupy.
Single-crust pies, or tarts, have short baking times and often need to be blind-baked.
Blind baking is when the crust is baked either partway or fully before filling is added.
This is done when the crust and filling have different baking times or the filling is very wet.

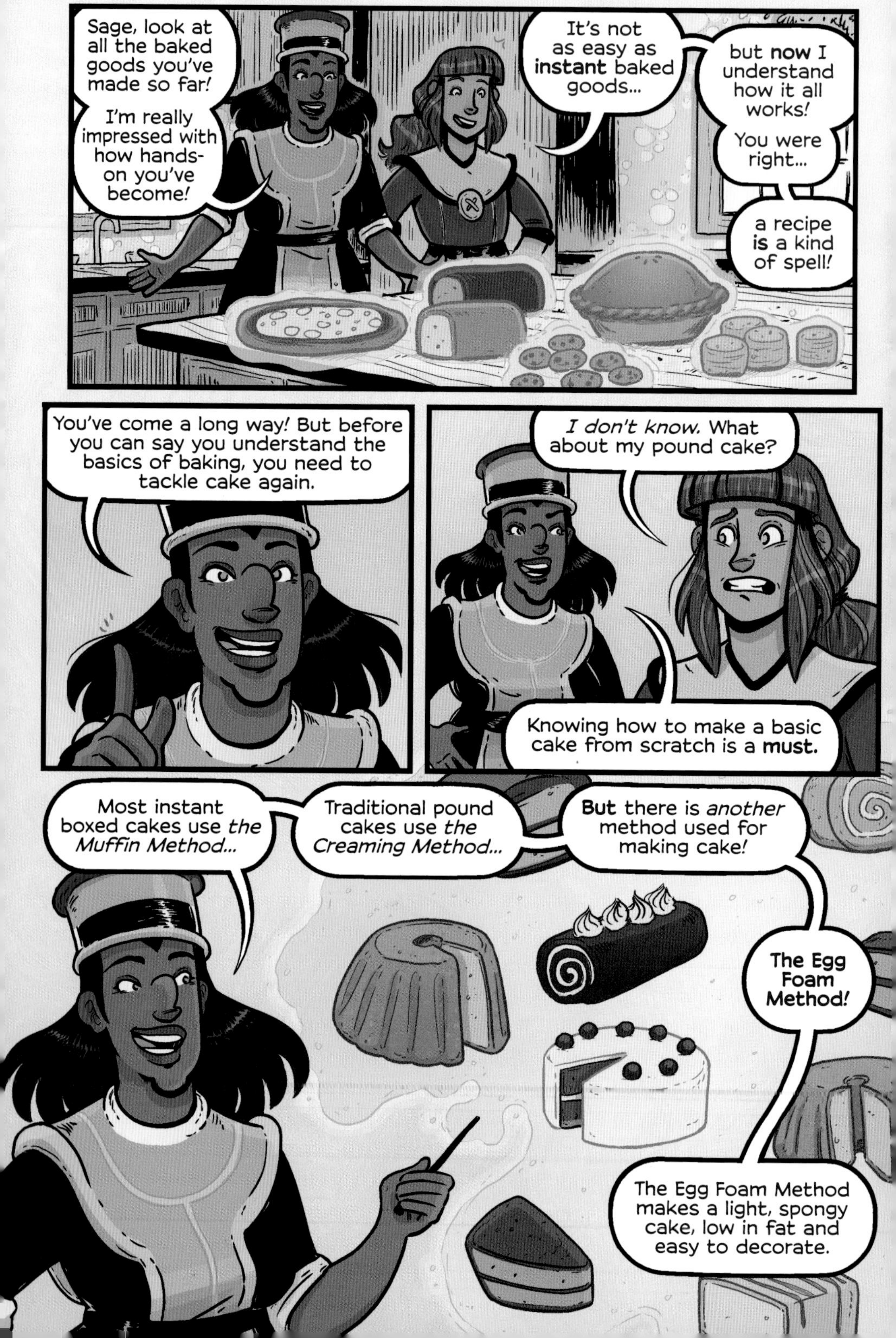
Sage, look at all the baked goods you've made so far!
I'm really impressed with how hands-on you've become!
It's not as easy as **instant** baked goods...
but **now** I understand how it all works!
You were right...
a recipe **is** a kind of spell!
You've come a long way! But before you can say you understand the basics of baking, you need to tackle cake again.
I don't know. What about my pound cake?
Knowing how to make a basic cake from scratch is a **must.**
Most instant boxed cakes use *the Muffin Method...*
Traditional pound cakes use *the Creaming Method...*
But there is *another* method used for making cake!
The Egg Foam Method!
The Egg Foam Method makes a light, spongy cake, low in fat and easy to decorate.

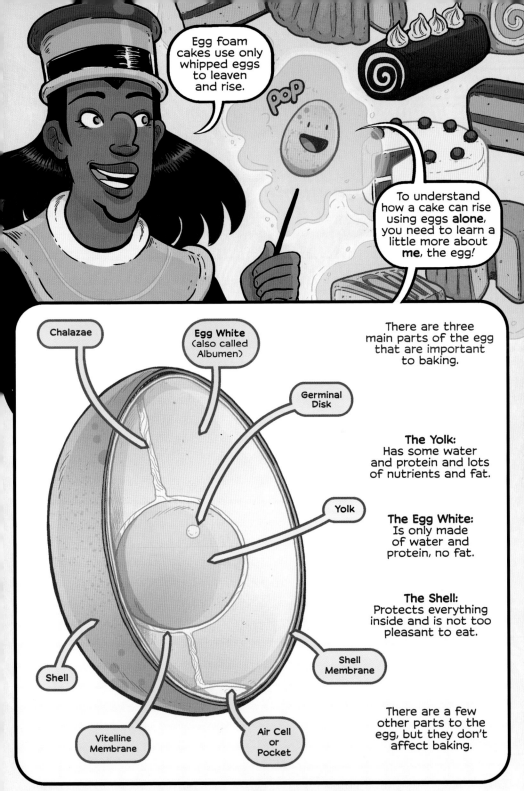

Egg foam cakes use only whipped eggs to leaven and rise.

POP

To understand how a cake can rise using eggs **alone**, you need to learn a little more about **me**, the egg!

Chalazae

Egg White (also called Albumen)

Germinal Disk

Yolk

Shell

Shell Membrane

Vitelline Membrane

Air Cell or Pocket

There are three main parts of the egg that are important to baking.

The Yolk: Has some water and protein and lots of nutrients and fat.

The Egg White: Is only made of water and protein, no fat.

The Shell: Protects everything inside and is not too pleasant to eat.

There are a few other parts to the egg, but they don't affect baking.

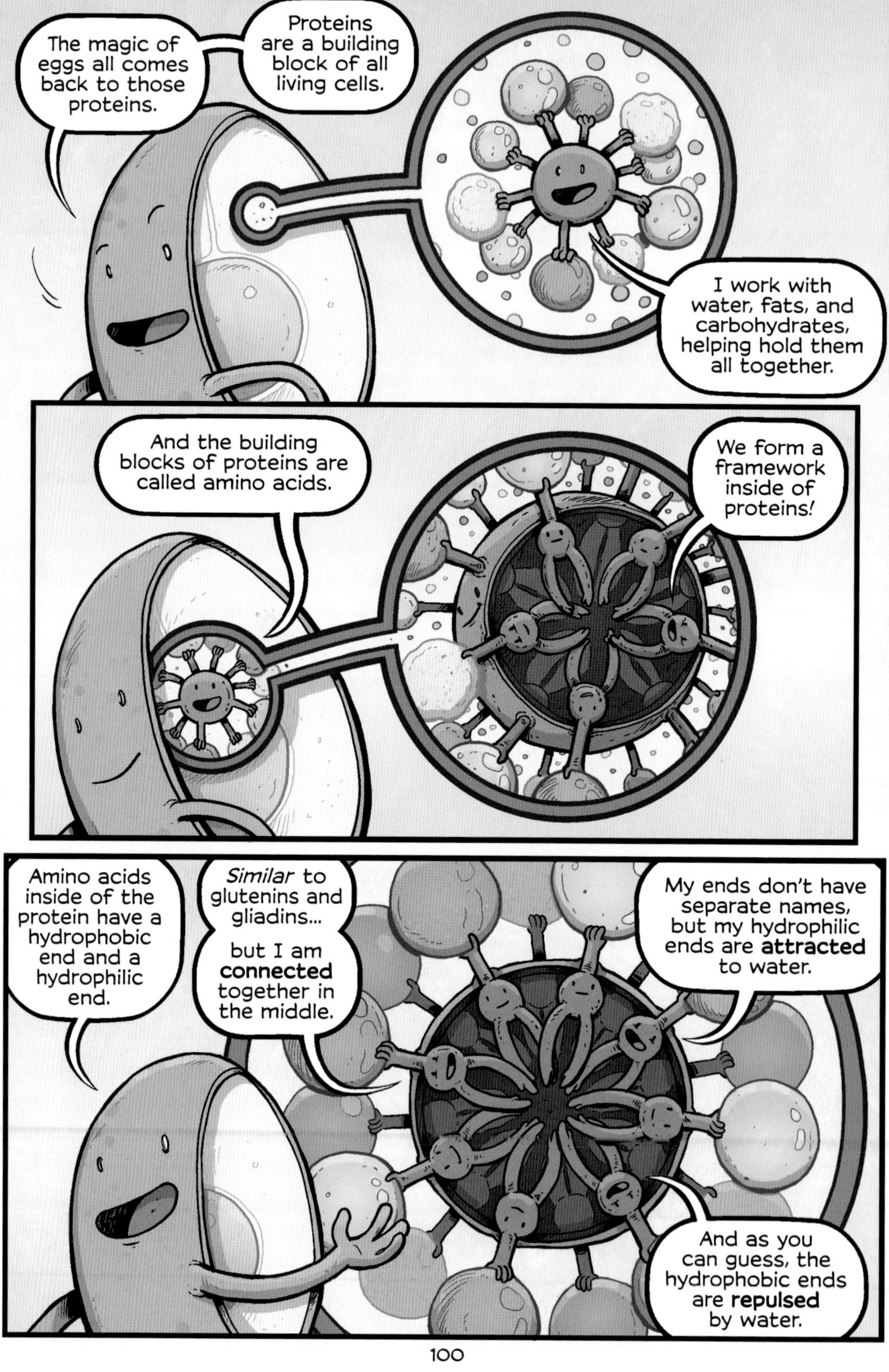
The magic of eggs all comes back to those proteins.
Proteins are a building block of all living cells.
I work with water, fats, and carbohydrates, helping hold them all together.
And the building blocks of proteins are called amino acids.
We form a framework inside of proteins!
Amino acids inside of the protein have a hydrophobic end and a hydrophilic end.
Similar to glutenins and gliadins...
but I am **connected** together in the middle.
My ends don't have separate names, but my hydrophilic ends are **attracted** to water.
And as you can guess, the hydrophobic ends are **repulsed** by water.

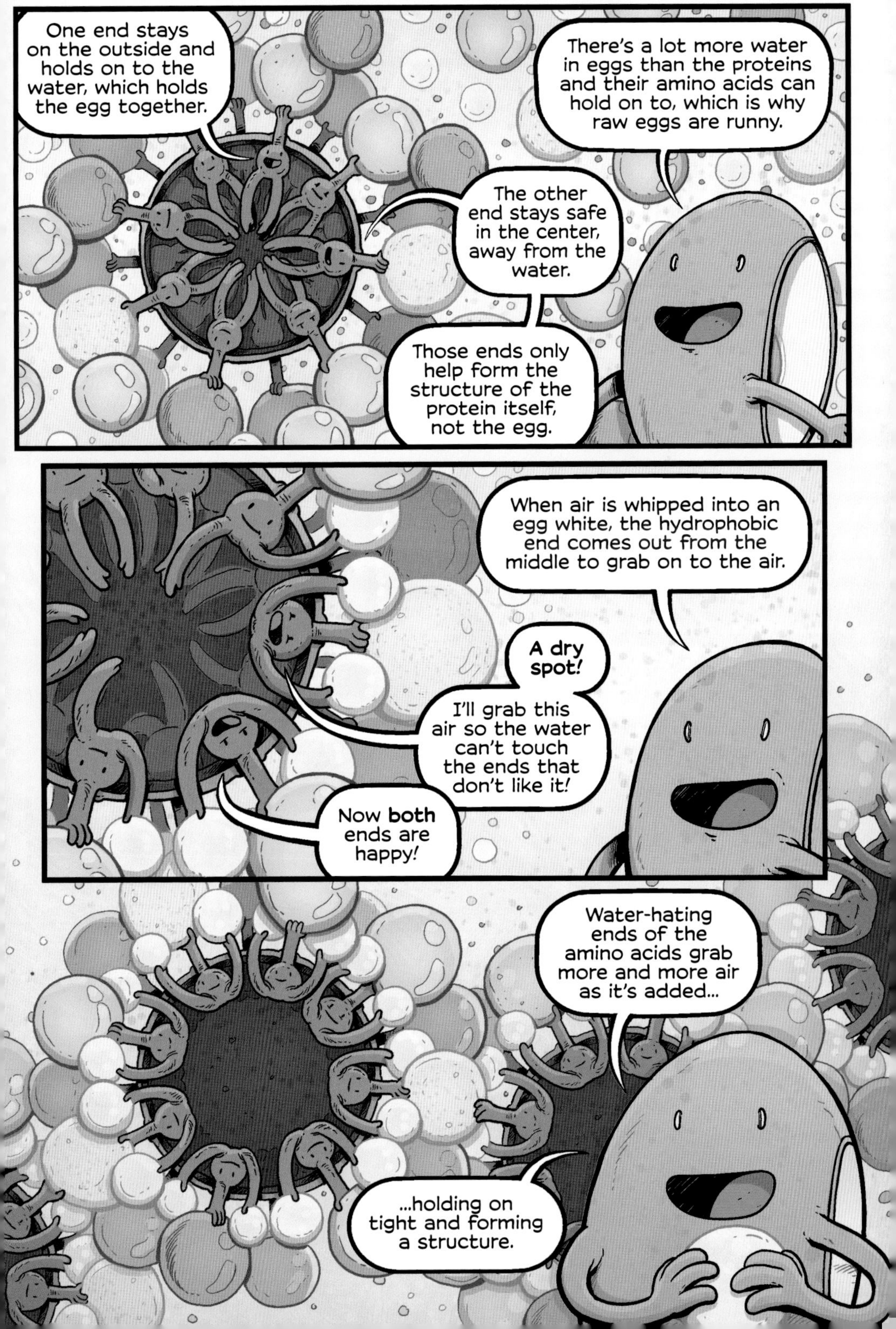

One end stays on the outside and holds on to the water, which holds the egg together.
The other end stays safe in the center, away from the water.
Those ends only help form the structure of the protein itself, not the egg.
There's a lot more water in eggs than the proteins and their amino acids can hold on to, which is why raw eggs are runny.
When air is whipped into an egg white, the hydrophobic end comes out from the middle to grab on to the air.
A dry spot!
I'll grab this air so the water can't touch the ends that don't like it!
Now both ends are happy!
Water-hating ends of the amino acids grab more and more air as it's added...
...holding on tight and forming a structure.

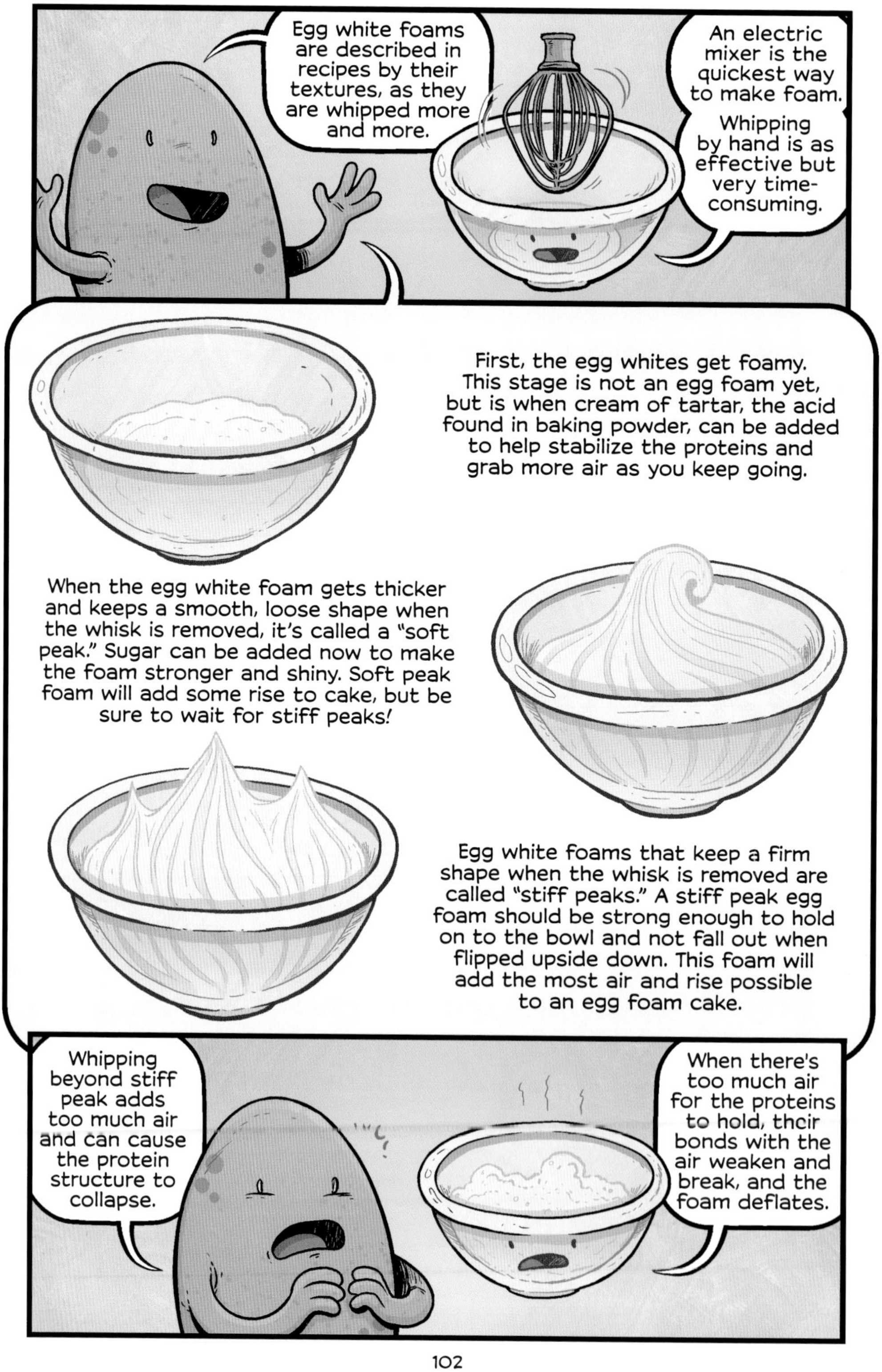
Egg white foams are described in recipes by their textures, as they are whipped more and more.
An electric mixer is the quickest way to make foam.
Whipping by hand is as effective but very time-consuming.
First, the egg whites get foamy. This stage is not an egg foam yet, but is when cream of tartar, the acid found in baking powder, can be added to help stabilize the proteins and grab more air as you keep going.
When the egg white foam gets thicker and keeps a smooth, loose shape when the whisk is removed, it's called a "soft peak." Sugar can be added now to make the foam stronger and shiny. Soft peak foam will add some rise to cake, but be sure to wait for stiff peaks!
Egg white foams that keep a firm shape when the whisk is removed are called "stiff peaks." A stiff peak egg foam should be strong enough to hold on to the bowl and not fall out when flipped upside down. This foam will add the most air and rise possible to an egg foam cake.
Whipping beyond stiff peak adds too much air and can cause the protein structure to collapse.
When there's too much air for the proteins to hold, their bonds with the air weaken and break, and the foam deflates.

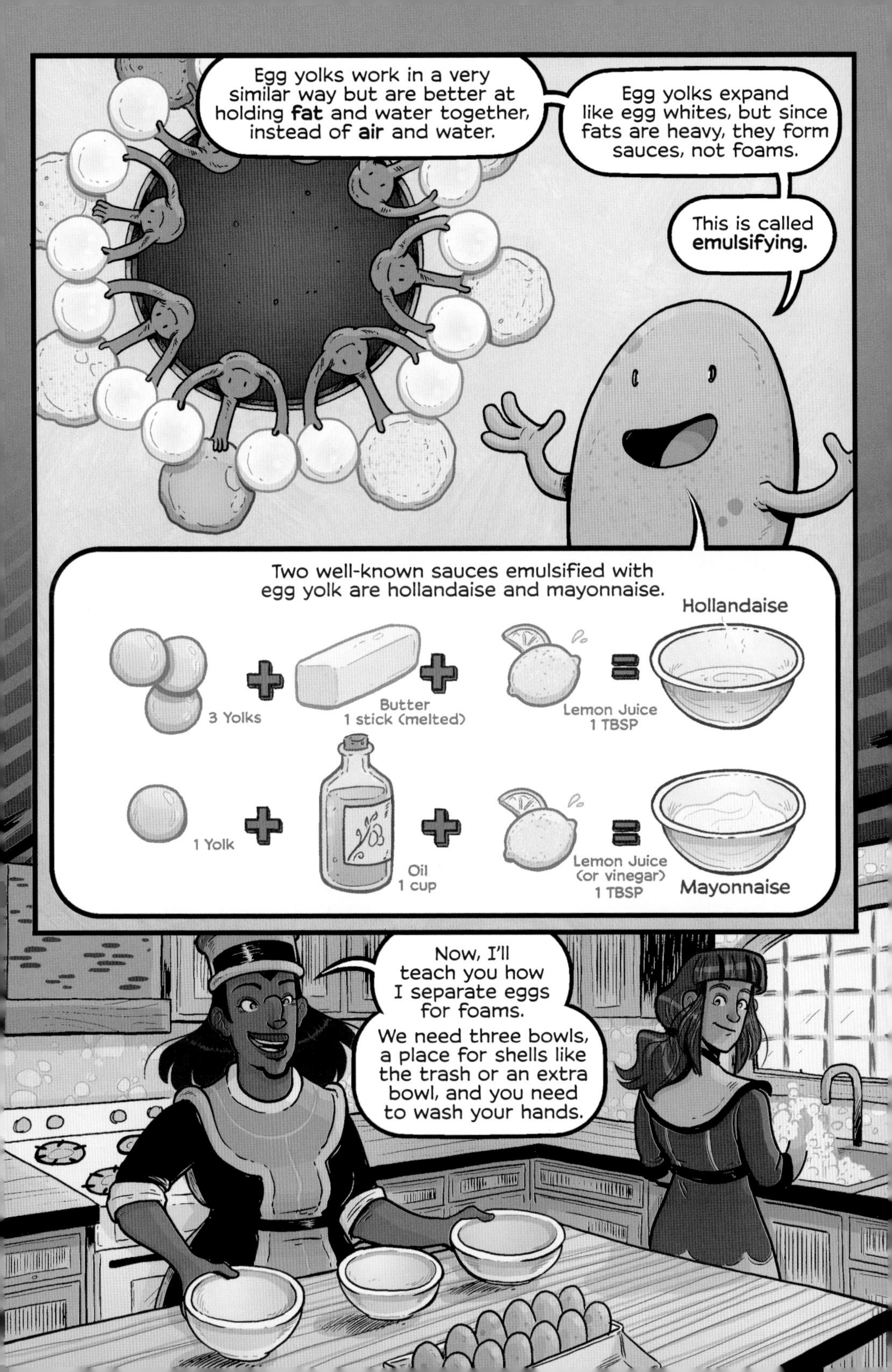

Egg yolks work in a very similar way but are better at holding **fat** and water together, instead of **air** and water.
Egg yolks expand like egg whites, but since fats are heavy, they form sauces, not foams.
This is called **emulsifying.**
Two well-known sauces emulsified with egg yolk are hollandaise and mayonnaise.
Hollandaise
3 Yolks
Butter
1 stick (melted)
Lemon Juice
1 TBSP
1 Yolk
Oil
1 cup
Lemon Juice
(or vinegar)
1 TBSP
Mayonnaise
Now, I'll teach you how I separate eggs for foams.
We need three bowls, a place for shells like the trash or an extra bowl, and you need to wash your hands.

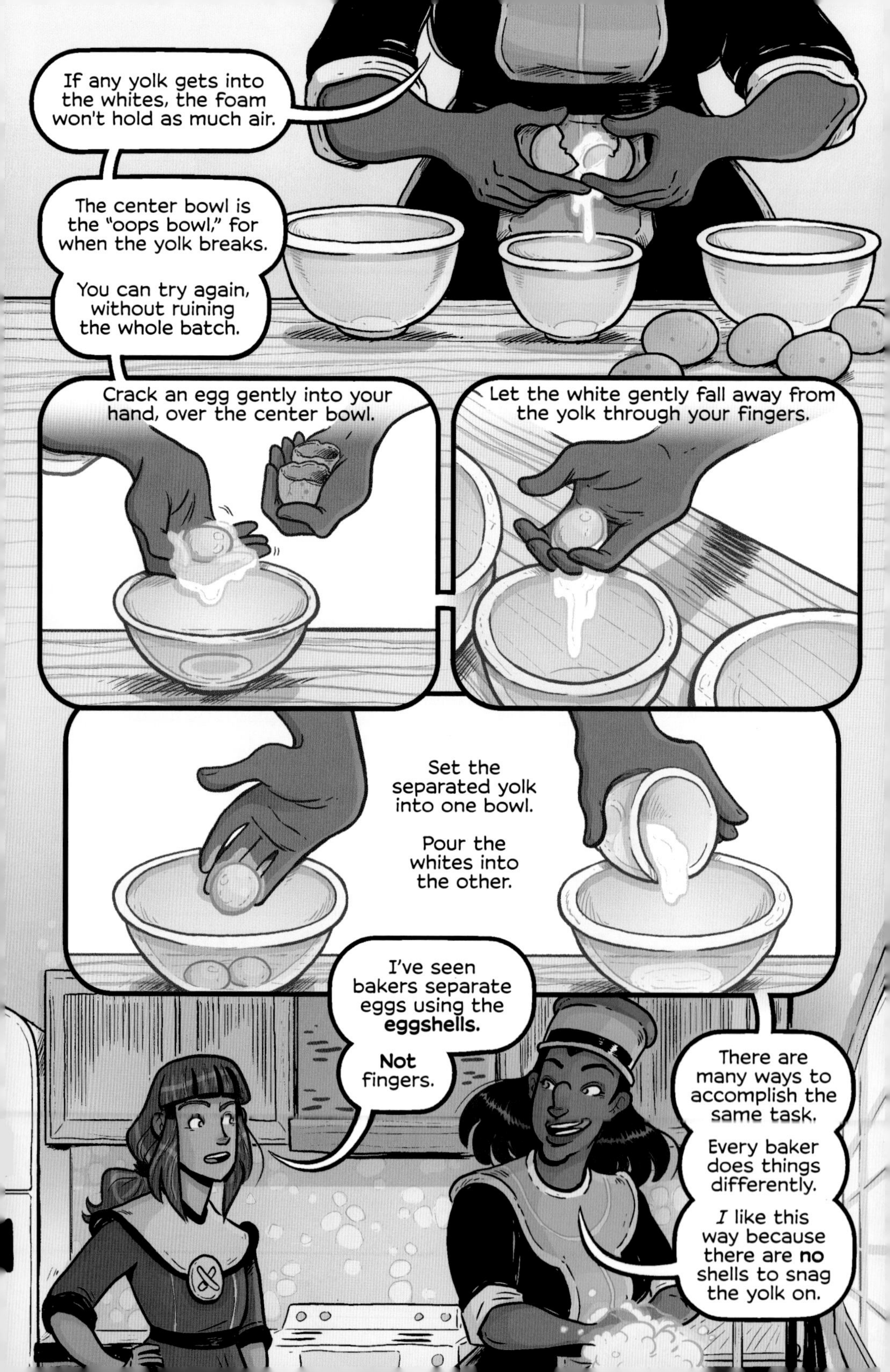
If any yolk gets into the whites, the foam won't hold as much air.
The center bowl is the "oops bowl," for when the yolk breaks.
You can try again, without ruining the whole batch.
Crack an egg gently into your hand, over the center bowl.
Let the white gently fall away from the yolk through your fingers.
Set the separated yolk into one bowl.
Pour the whites into the other.
I've seen bakers separate eggs using the **eggshells.**
Not fingers.
There are many ways to accomplish the same task.
Every baker does things differently.
I like this way because there are **no** shells to snag the yolk on.

SPONGE CAKE

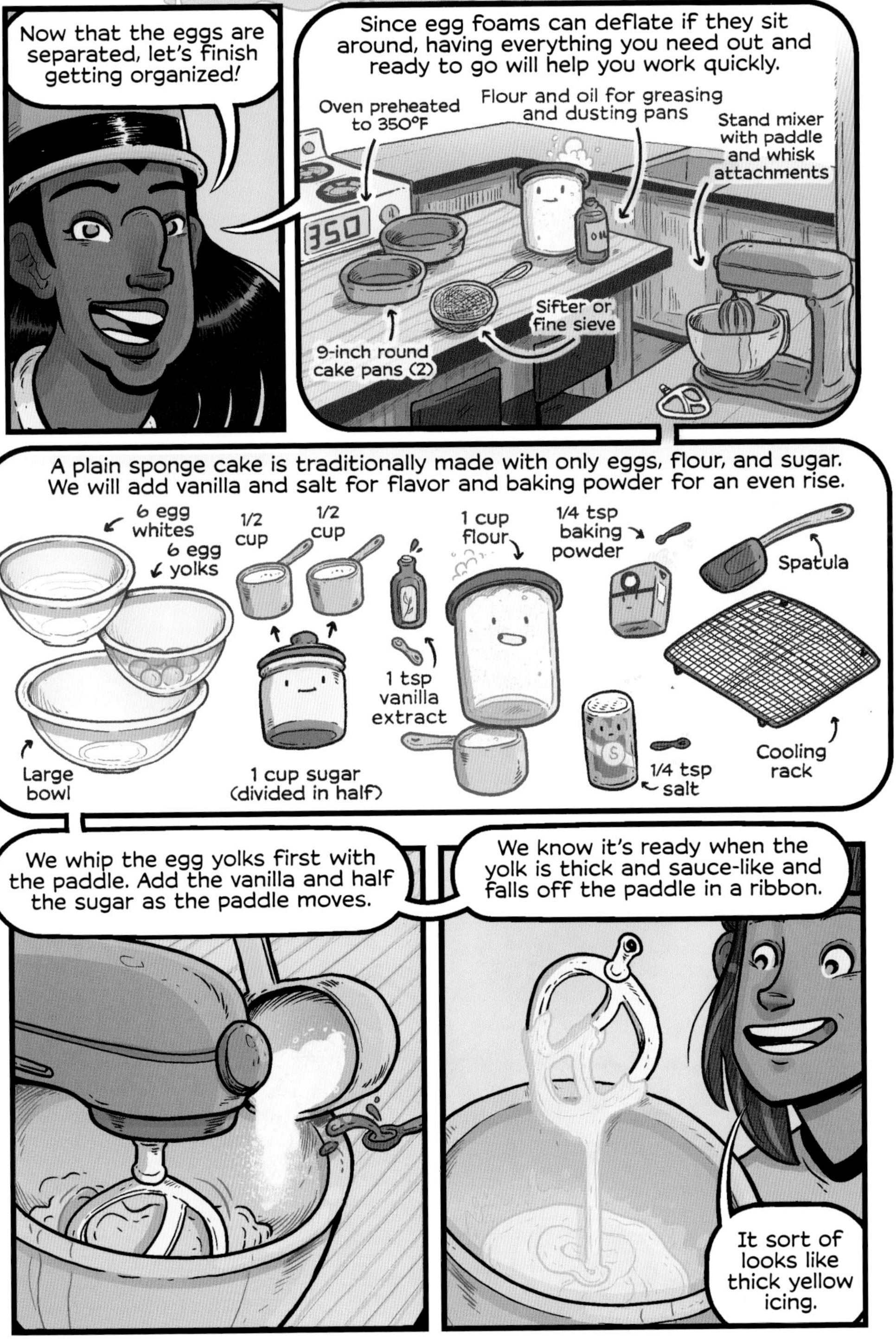

Now that the eggs are separated, let's finish getting organized!
Since egg foams can deflate if they sit around, having everything you need out and ready to go will help you work quickly.
Oven preheated to 350°F
Flour and oil for greasing and dusting pans
Stand mixer with paddle and whisk attachments
350
9-inch round cake pans (2)
Sifter or fine sieve
A plain sponge cake is traditionally made with only eggs, flour, and sugar. We will add vanilla and salt for flavor and baking powder for an even rise.
6 egg whites
6 egg yolks
Large bowl
1/2 cup
1/2 cup
1 cup sugar (divided in half)
1 tsp vanilla extract
1 cup flour
1/4 tsp baking powder
1/4 tsp salt
Spatula
Cooling rack
We whip the egg yolks first with the paddle. Add the vanilla and half the sugar as the paddle moves.
We know it's ready when the yolk is thick and sauce-like and falls off the paddle in a ribbon.
It sort of looks like thick yellow icing.

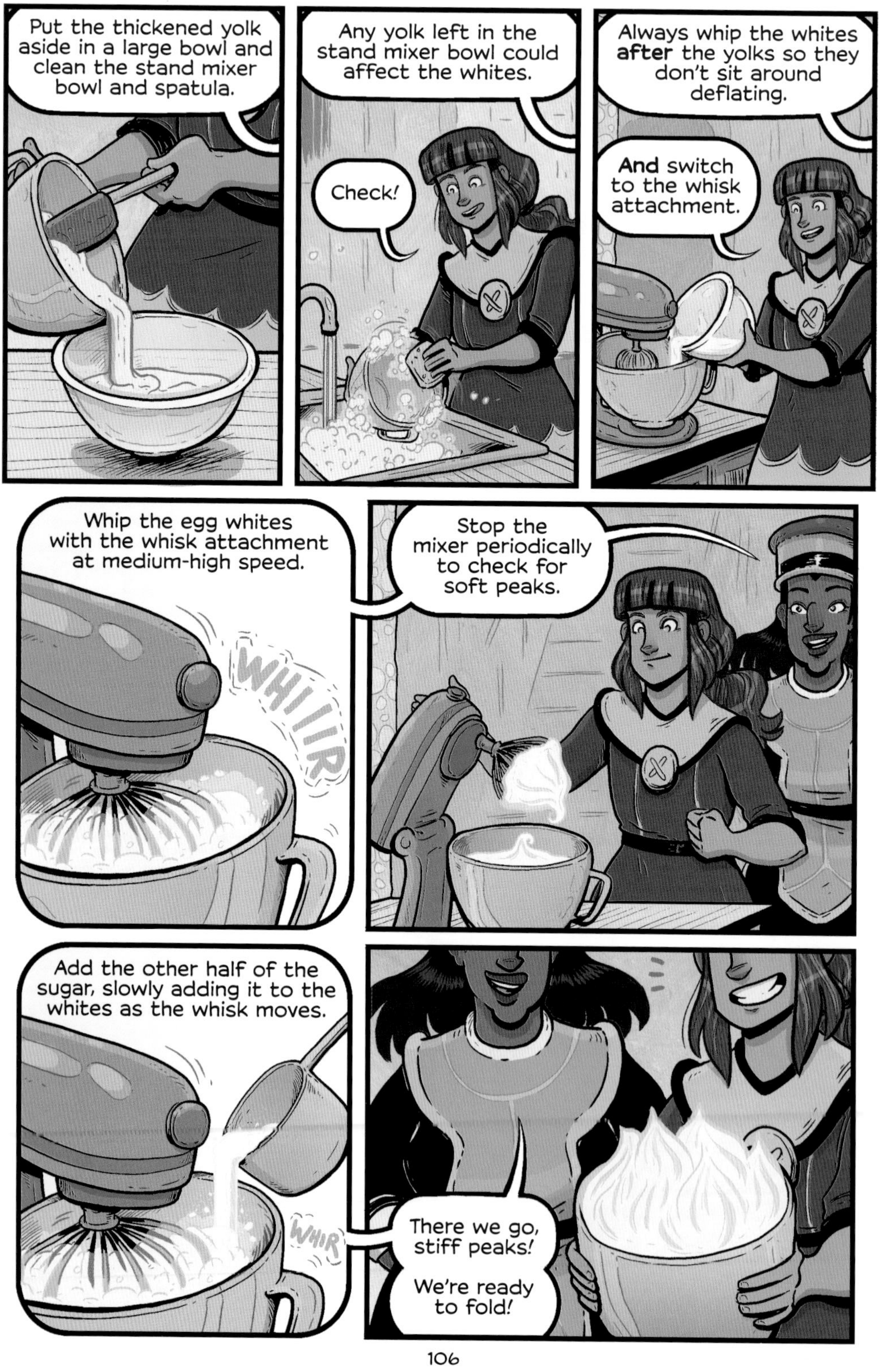
Put the thickened yolk aside in a large bowl and clean the stand mixer bowl and spatula.
Any yolk left in the stand mixer bowl could affect the whites.
Check!
Always whip the whites **after** the yolks so they don't sit around deflating.
And switch to the whisk attachment.
Whip the egg whites with the whisk attachment at medium-high speed.
WHIIIR
Stop the mixer periodically to check for soft peaks.
Add the other half of the sugar, slowly adding it to the whites as the whisk moves.
WHIR
There we go, stiff peaks!
We're ready to fold!

To keep as much air in as possible, there's a special fold to gently incorporate everything together using the spatula.

Add **half** the egg white foam to the thickened yolk. Adding it all at once can deflate it.

PLOP

Plunge:
Cut through the center with the spatula to the bottom of the bowl.

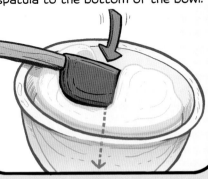

Fold over:
Then scoop from the bottom up and fold over the top like a blanket.

Turn:
Quarter turn the bowl as you scrape along the side, clearing it of foam.

Repeat the plunge, fold, and turn, until the egg white foam is mostly, *but not fully* incorporated.

plunge　　　　　fold over　　　　　turn

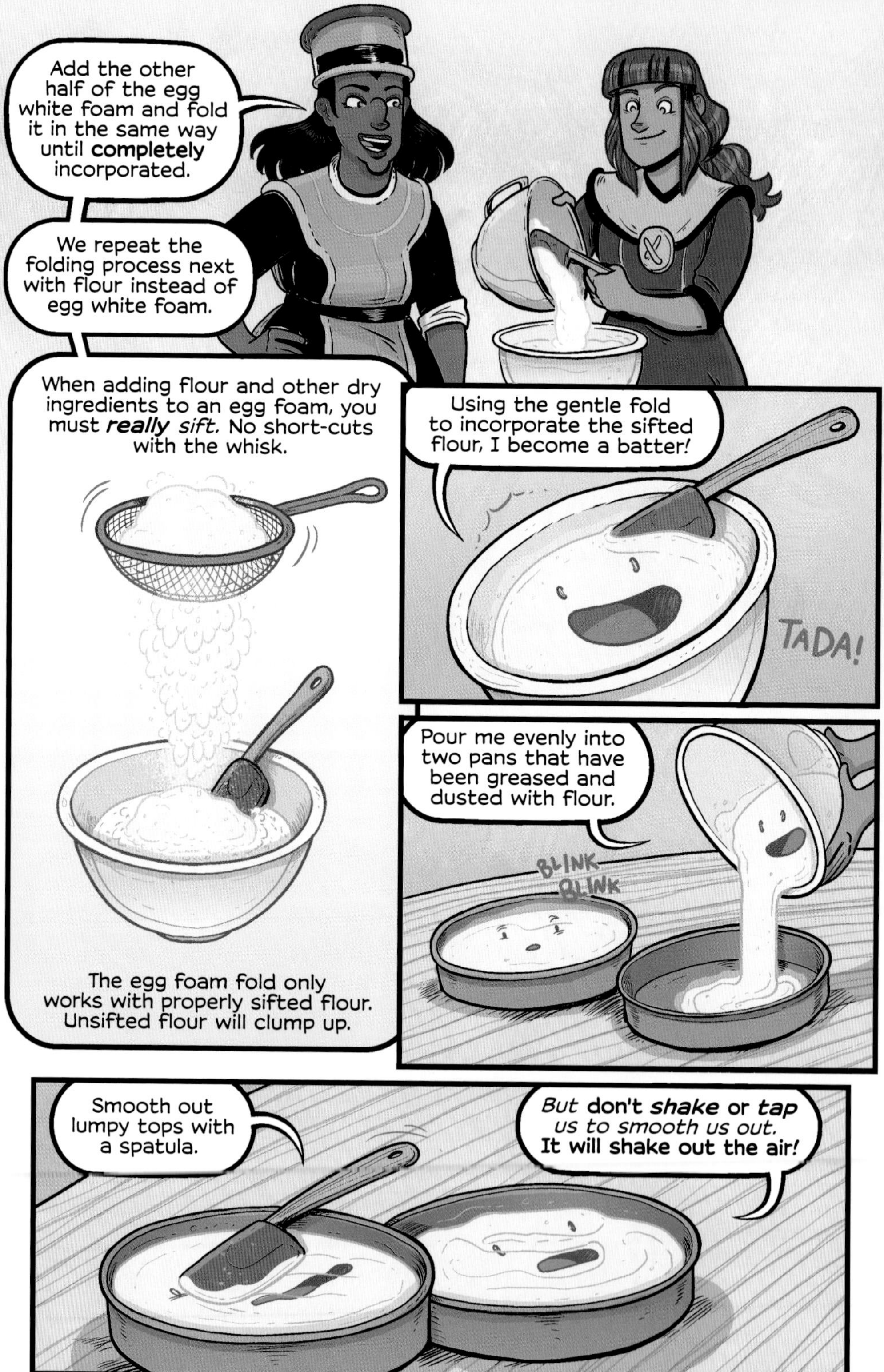
Add the other half of the egg white foam and fold it in the same way until **completely** incorporated.
We repeat the folding process next with flour instead of egg white foam.
When adding flour and other dry ingredients to an egg foam, you must ***really*** *sift.* No short-cuts with the whisk.
The egg foam fold only works with properly sifted flour. Unsifted flour will clump up.
Using the gentle fold to incorporate the sifted flour, I become a batter!
TADA!
Pour me evenly into two pans that have been greased and dusted with flour.
BLINK BLINK
Smooth out lumpy tops with a spatula.
But **don't *shake* or *tap*** *us to smooth us out.* **It will shake out the air!**

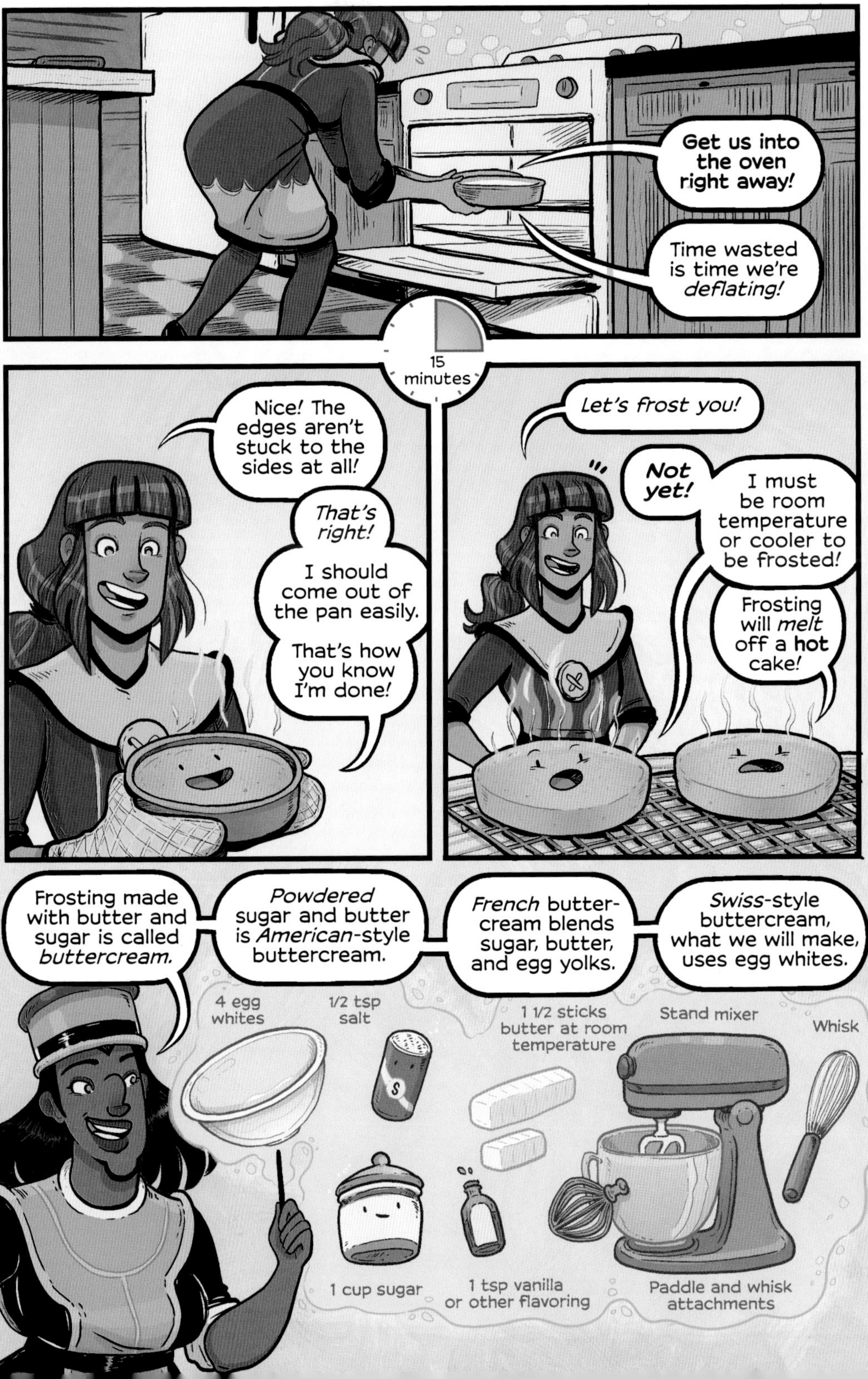

Get us into the oven right away!
Time wasted is time we're *deflating!*
15 minutes
Nice! The edges aren't stuck to the sides at all!
That's right!
I should come out of the pan easily.
That's how you know I'm done!
Let's frost you!
Not yet!
I must be room temperature or cooler to be frosted!
Frosting will *melt* off a **hot** cake!
Frosting made with butter and sugar is called *buttercream.*
Powdered sugar and butter is *American*-style buttercream.
French butter-cream blends sugar, butter, and egg yolks.
Swiss-style buttercream, what we will make, uses egg whites.
4 egg whites
1/2 tsp salt
1 1/2 sticks butter at room temperature
Stand mixer
Whisk
1 cup sugar
1 tsp vanilla or other flavoring
Paddle and whisk attachments

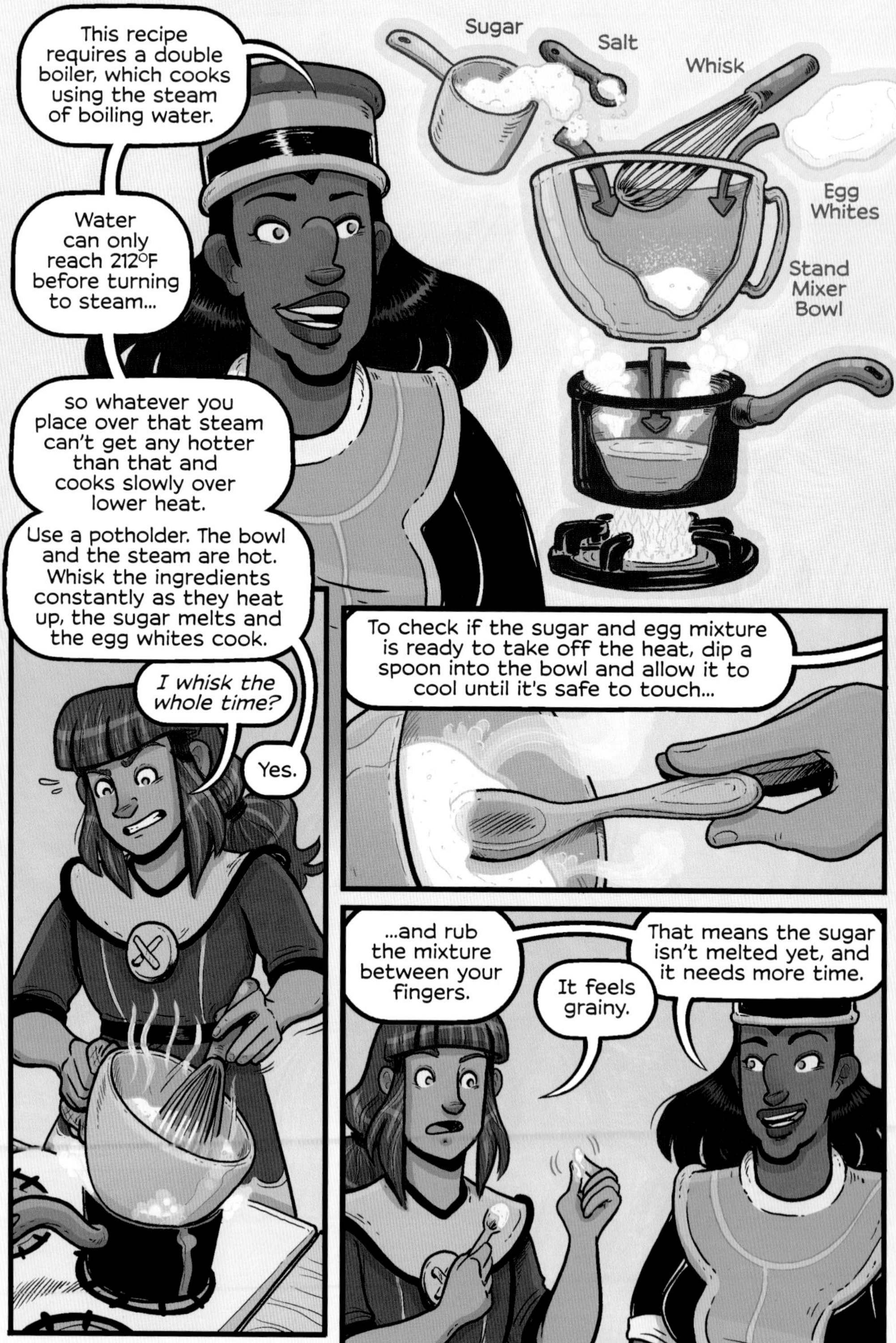
This recipe requires a double boiler, which cooks using the steam of boiling water.
Sugar
Salt
Whisk
Egg Whites
Stand Mixer Bowl
Water can only reach 212°F before turning to steam...
so whatever you place over that steam can't get any hotter than that and cooks slowly over lower heat.
Use a potholder. The bowl and the steam are hot. Whisk the ingredients constantly as they heat up, the sugar melts and the egg whites cook.
I whisk the whole time?
Yes.
To check if the sugar and egg mixture is ready to take off the heat, dip a spoon into the bowl and allow it to cool until it's safe to touch...
...and rub the mixture between your fingers.
It feels grainy.
That means the sugar isn't melted yet, and it needs more time.

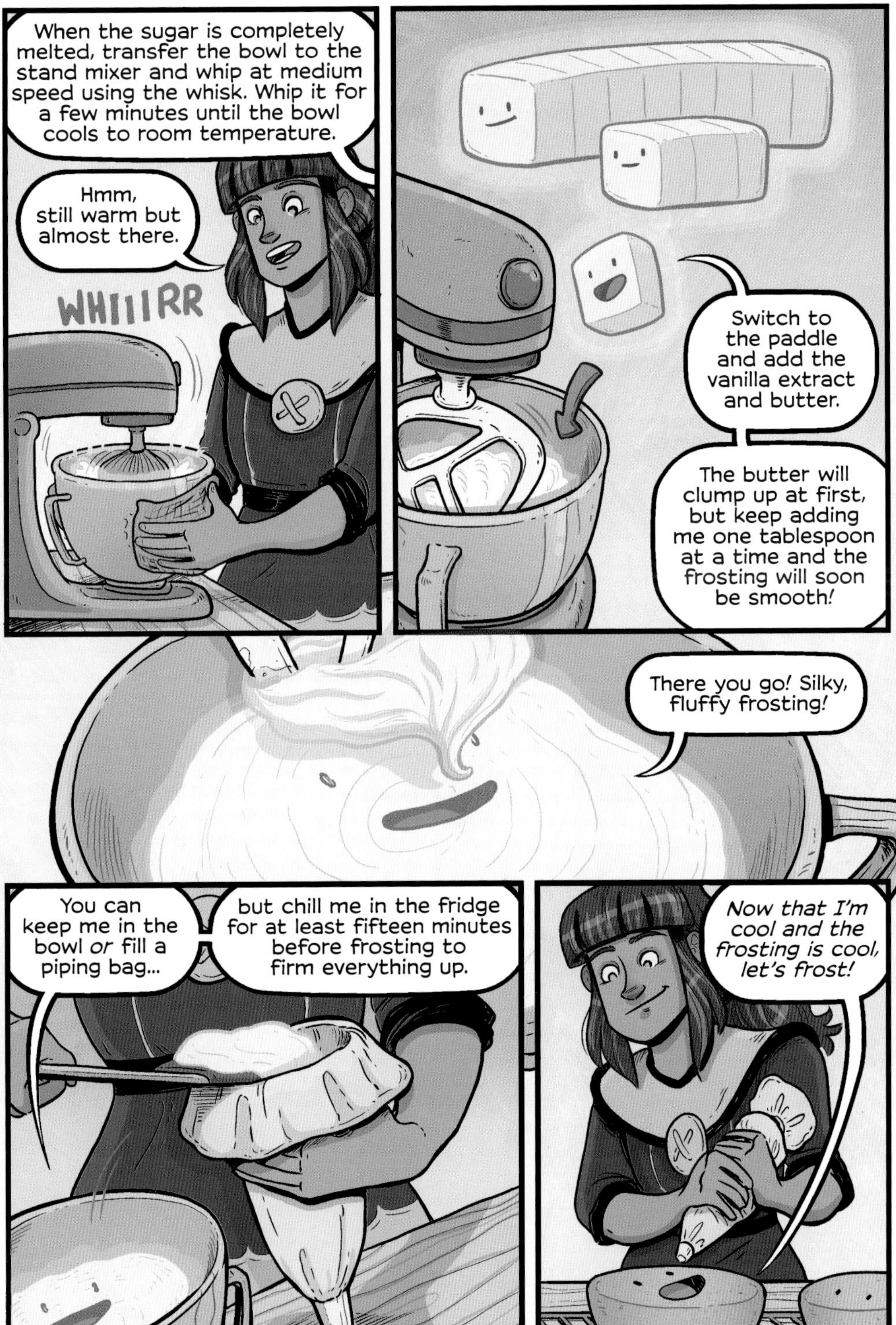
When the sugar is completely melted, transfer the bowl to the stand mixer and whip at medium speed using the whisk. Whip it for a few minutes until the bowl cools to room temperature.
Hmm, still warm but almost there.
WHIIIRR
Switch to the paddle and add the vanilla extract and butter.
The butter will clump up at first, but keep adding me one tablespoon at a time and the frosting will soon be smooth!
There you go! Silky, fluffy frosting!
You can keep me in the bowl *or* fill a piping bag...
but chill me in the fridge for at least fifteen minutes before frosting to firm everything up.
Now that I'm cool and the frosting is cool, let's frost!

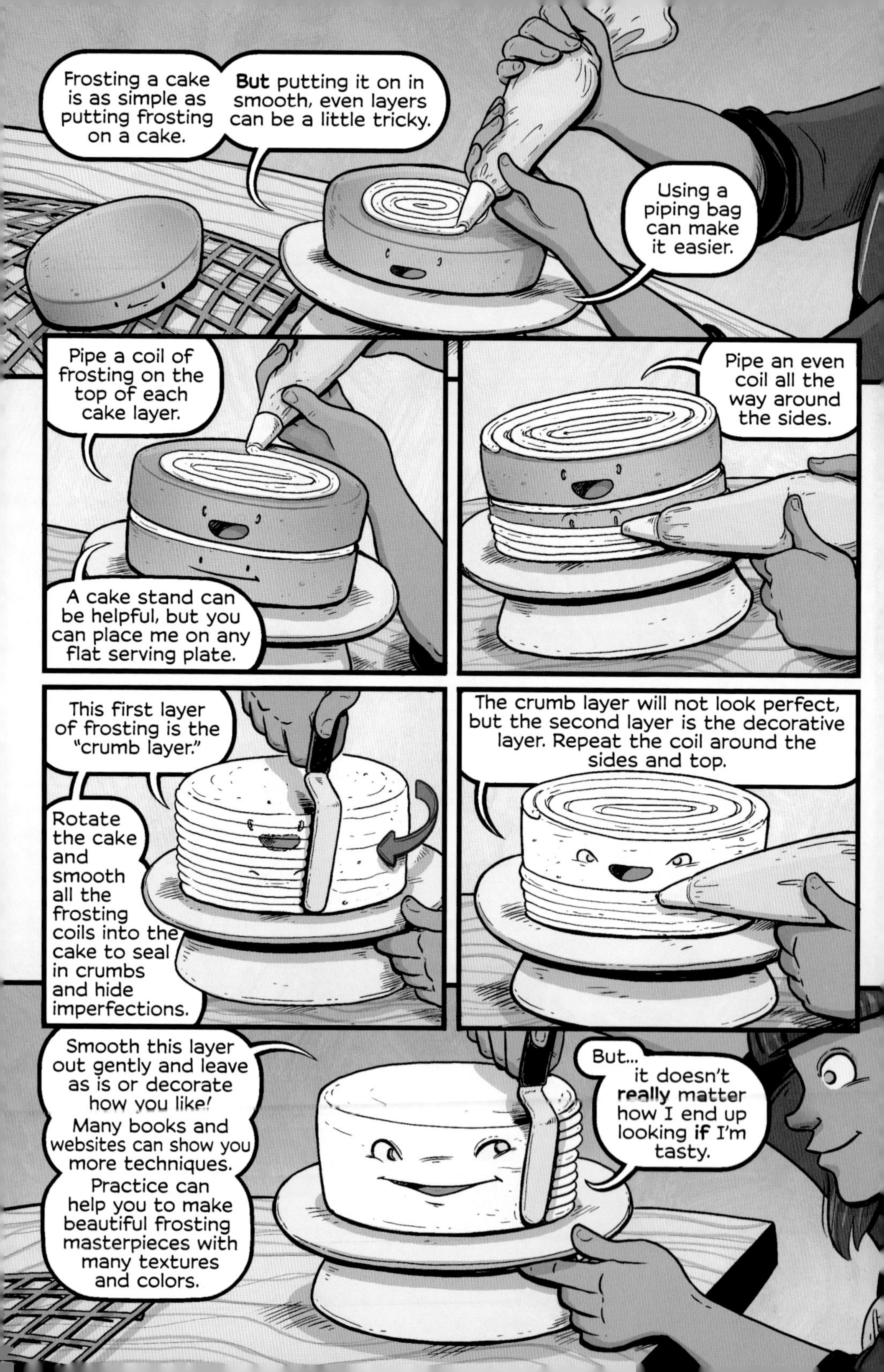
Frosting a cake is as simple as putting frosting on a cake.
But putting it on in smooth, even layers can be a little tricky.
Using a piping bag can make it easier.
Pipe a coil of frosting on the top of each cake layer.
A cake stand can be helpful, but you can place me on any flat serving plate.
Pipe an even coil all the way around the sides.
This first layer of frosting is the "crumb layer."
Rotate the cake and smooth all the frosting coils into the cake to seal in crumbs and hide imperfections.
The crumb layer will not look perfect, but the second layer is the decorative layer. Repeat the coil around the sides and top.
Smooth this layer out gently and leave as is or decorate how you like!
Many books and websites can show you more techniques.
Practice can help you to make beautiful frosting masterpieces with many textures and colors.
But... it doesn't **really** matter how I end up looking **if** I'm tasty.

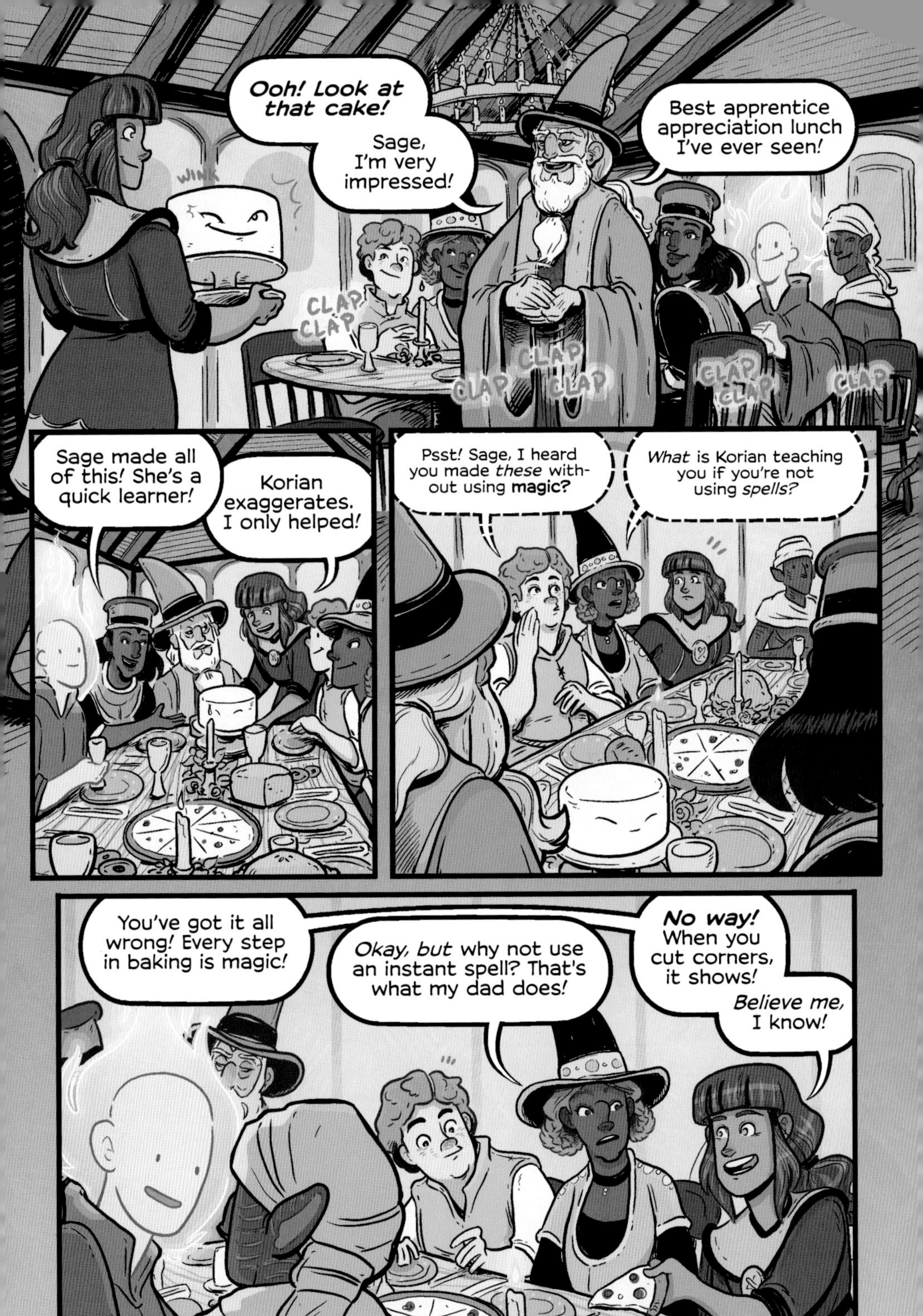

Ooh! Look at that cake!
Sage, I'm very impressed!
Best apprentice appreciation lunch I've ever seen!
WINK
CLAP CLAP
CLAP CLAP CLAP
CLAP CLAP
CLAP
Sage made all of this! She's a quick learner!
Korian exaggerates. I only helped!
Psst! Sage, I heard you made *these* with-out using **magic?**
What is Korian teaching you if you're not using *spells?*
You've got it all wrong! Every step in baking is magic!
Okay, but why not use an instant spell? That's what my dad does!
No way! When you cut corners, it shows!
Believe me, I know!

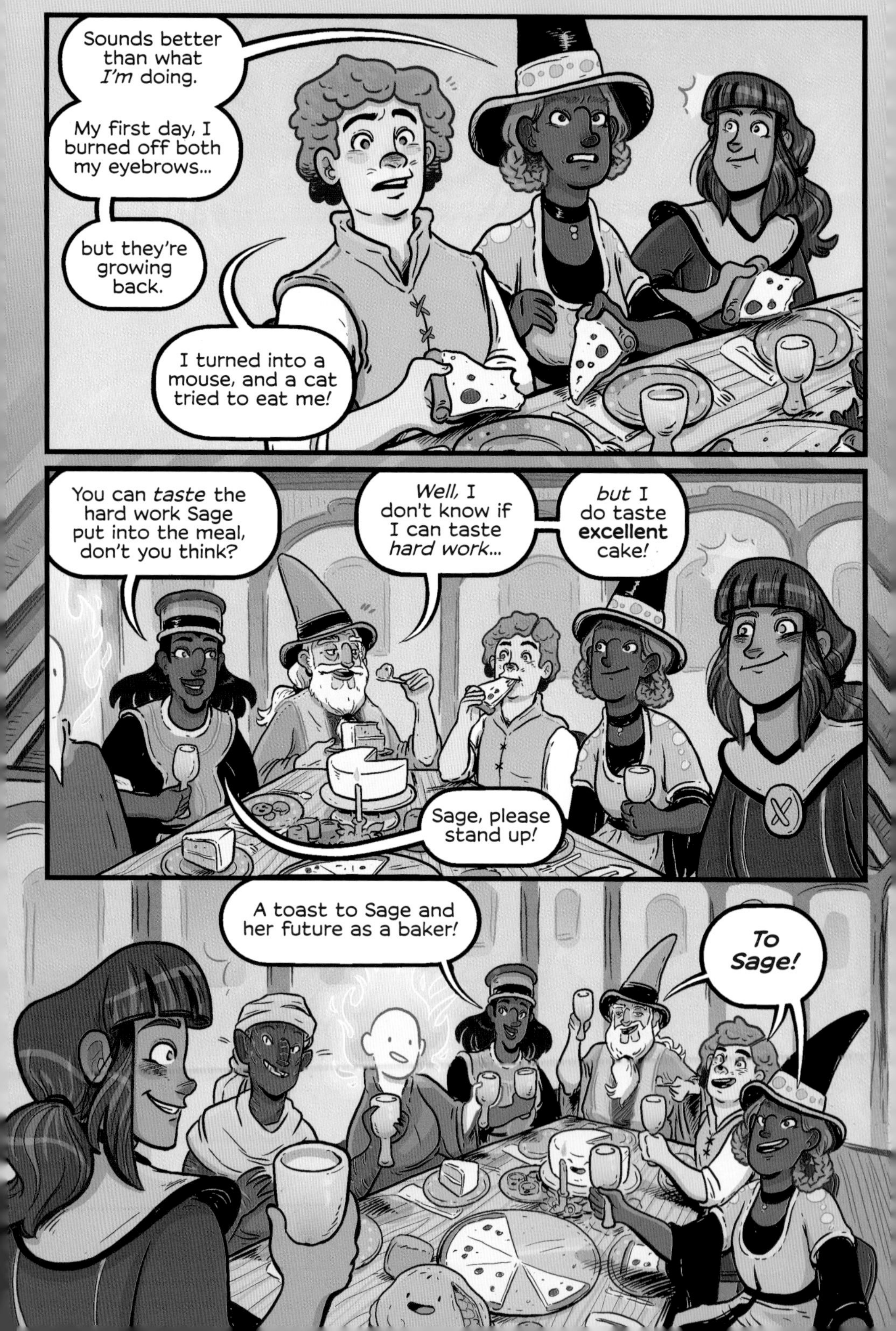
Sounds better than what *I'm* doing.
My first day, I burned off both my eyebrows...
but they're growing back.
I turned into a mouse, and a cat tried to eat me!
You can *taste* the hard work Sage put into the meal, don't you think?
Well, I don't know if I can taste *hard work*...
but I do taste **excellent** cake!
Sage, please stand up!
A toast to Sage and her future as a baker!
To Sage!

Here are the recipes Sage and Korian made in the book, in the order in which they appeared. You'll also find helpful baking tips, facts, and reminders.

The Baking Methods

Egg Foam Method
- Separate egg yolk & white as needed
- Whip separated egg
- Sift dry ingredients together
- Fold together as directed
- Bake

Biscuit Method
- Cut cold fat into dry ingredients
- Combine with liquid to create dough
- Rest
- Roll or shape
- Bake

Creaming Method
- Cream butter and white sugar
- Add eggs one at a time
- Add wet ingredients
- Add dry (or alternate wet/dry)
- Bake

Dough Method (with yeast)
- Bloom yeast if needed
- Combine dry ingredients with liquid and yeast
- Knead
- Rise (proof / punch / fold / rest)
- Shape (and score as needed)
- Bake

Muffin Method
- Sift dry ingredients together
- Mix wet ingredients together
- Combine wet and dry
- Bake

Bonus Method: Custard Method
- Uses tempering: Hot milk is added slowly to eggs, cooking them
- Is not a batter or dough
- Doesn't always require an oven

Classic Pound Cake
Makes one loaf or bundt cake.

Ingredients
- 1 cup butter
- 1 cup sugar
- 4 eggs
- 1 tsp vanilla extract
- 1/2 cup whole milk
- 2 cups flour
- 1 tsp baking powder
- 1/2 tsp salt

Special Tools
- Stand mixer with paddle attachment
- Wire cooling rack

Organize
1. Preheat oven to 350°F.
2. Grease and flour loaf pan or bundt pan.
3. Make sure butter is close to room temp, slightly soft.
4. Measure and sift together all dry ingredients: flour, baking powder, and salt.
5. Measure out and mix milk and vanilla.
6. Crack all eggs in a bowl together and whisk lightly.

Prepare
7. Put butter in stand mixing bowl with paddle attachment and beat on medium speed for 2 minutes.
8. Add sugar slowly and cream mixture together till fluffy.
9. Add eggs slowly, making sure they are fully incorporated.
10. Add vanilla extract.
11. Add about 1/3 of the dry ingredients and mix.
12. Add about 1/2 of the milk and mix until incorporated.
13. Repeat: 1/3 more dry, rest of milk, then rest of dry.
14. Make sure mixture is fully blended.

Bake
15. Pour into pan; smooth top with spoon but don't shake.
16. Bake 1 hour or until center is cooked.
17. Cool cake inside pan 15 minutes.
18. Carefully remove from pan and cool on wire rack.

Decorate with icing, fruit, honey, or powdered sugar.

What happens when cookies bake in the oven

Use your favorite cookie recipe and watch the magic happen.

92°F	+92°F	144°F	212°F	310°F	+360°F
Oven spring: Dough spreads, edges set.	Gases expand, steam rises and escapes.	Proteins and starch set to final shape.	Sugar liquefies from heat.	Maillard reaction: proteins brown.	Sugar caramelizes if oven is set hot enough.

Cooling solidifies sugar, and the dough deflates.

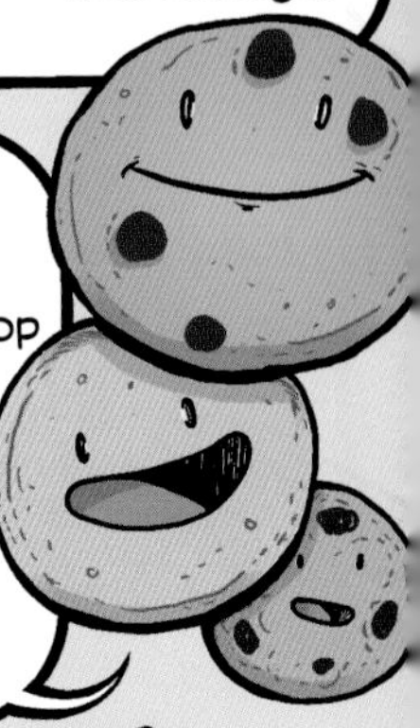

Effects of ingredients on cookies

Fat
- Butter: more tender
- Shortening: denser, chewier

Eggs
- Extra egg white: taller, fluffy
- Extra egg yolk: fudgier, denser

Sugar
- All white sugar: thin and crispy
- All brown sugar: tall and moist

Chemical Leavening
- Only baking soda: craggy top
- Only baking powder: smooth top

Flour
- Less flour: crispier cookie
- More flour: doughy cookie
- Bread flour: chewy cookie
- Cake flour: softer cookie

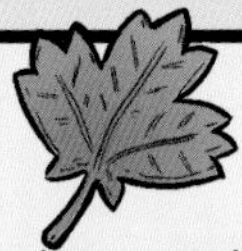

Replacing Sugar

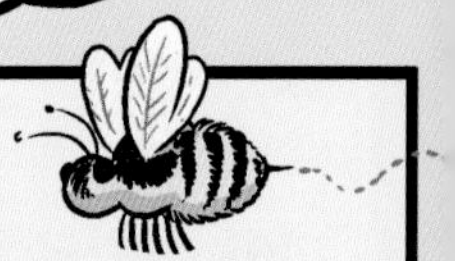

To use honey, agave, or maple syrup instead of granulated sugar, follow a few simple steps.

Lower temperature (syrup burns faster)
Reduce temperature by 25°F.

Reduce liquid (syrup has more water)
For every 1 cup syrup, use 1/4 cup less liquid.

Add baking soda (needs extra lift)
For every 1 cup syrup, add 1/3 teaspoon.

Reduce sugar (syrup is sweeter)
For every 1 cup sugar, use 2/3 cup syrup.

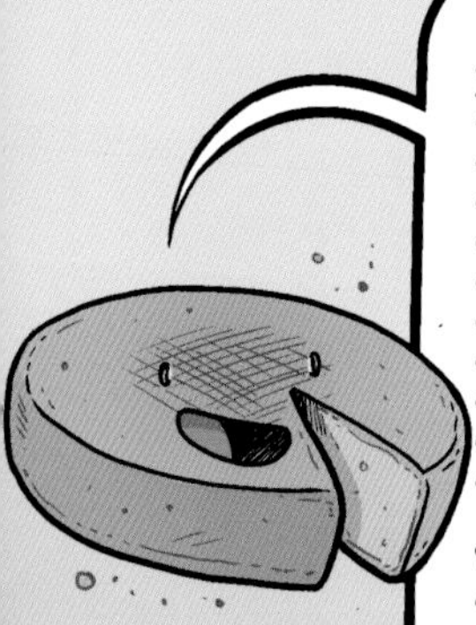

Savory Corn Bread

Makes 9 muffins or one 9-inch pan.

Ingredients
- 1 cup flour
- 2 cups cornmeal
- 1/4 cup sugar
- 1 TBSP baking powder
- 1/2 tsp baking soda
- 1 tsp salt
- 1/2 cup melted butter
- 3 whole eggs
- 1 1/2 cups buttermilk
- 1/2 cup whole milk

Vegan
- 1 cup all-purpose flour
- 2 cups cornmeal
- 1/4 cup sugar
- 1 TBSP baking powder
- 1/2 tsp baking soda
- 1 tsp salt
- 1/2 cup oil
- 1/2 can creamed corn
- 2 cups milk alternative (unsweetend)
- 2 TBSP white vinegar

Organize
1. Preheat oven to 375°F.
2. Grease pan of your choice.
3. Butter and eggs to room temperature.

Prepare
4. Combine and whisk all dry ingredients: flour, cornmeal, baking powder, baking soda, and salt.
5. In a large bowl, combine and whisk all wet ingredients: sugar, melted butter, eggs, buttermilk, and whole milk.
6. Mix dry ingredients into wet ingredients and mix until incorporated.
7. Do not overmix; lumpy is good.

Bake
8. Pour batter into pan or muffin tray.
9. Bake for 20 to 30 minutes (test for doneness).
10. Cool for 15 minutes in pan before removing.

Best served warm and fresh.

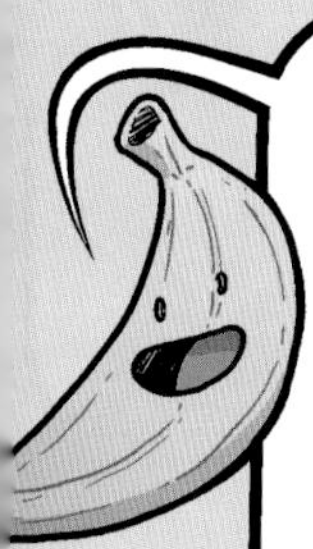

Banana Bread
Makes one loaf.

Ingredients
- 1 stick butter, at room temperature
- 2/3 cup packed brown sugar
- 2–4 very ripe bananas (1 1/2 cups)
- 1/3 cup sour cream
- 2 eggs
- 1 1/2 cups flour
- 1 tsp salt
- 1 tsp baking soda
- 1/2 cup chopped walnuts (optional)

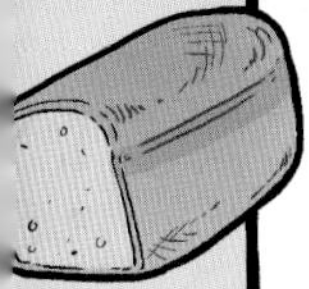

Special Tools
- Stand mixer with paddle attachment (if available)
- 9 x 5 inch loaf pan
- Wire cooling rack

Organize
1. Preheat oven to 350°F.
2. Grease the pan.
3. Combine eggs and sour cream.
4. Combine sugar, butter, and banana.
5. Combine and sift all dry ingredients (flour, baking soda, and salt).
6. Measure walnuts and set aside (optional).

Prepare
7. Cream butter, sugar, and banana using the paddle attachment for 2 minutes.
8. Add sour cream and eggs; mix thoroughly.
9. Add dry ingredients to wet ingredients, only mixing enough to incorporate while leaving lumps.
10. Gently stir in walnuts.

Bake
11. Pour in greased pan.
12. Bake about 60 minutes and test for doneness.
13. Cool in pan for 15 minutes.
14. Remove from pan and cool on rack.

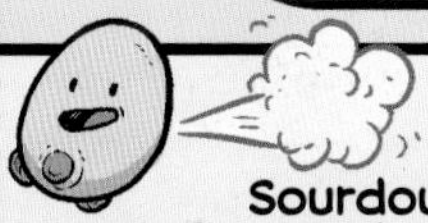

Four ways to add yeast to your bread

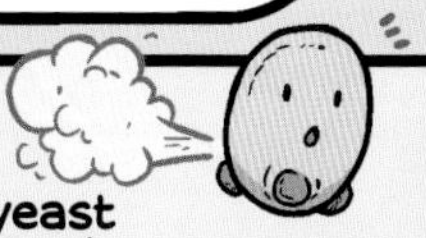

Sourdough starter
A loose flour and water mix, which natural yeast will collect and grow on. Takes days.

Active dry yeast
Granulated dried yeast. Needs warm water to wake up or bloom from its dormant state.

Fresh yeast cake
Similar to a sourdough starter in texture, must be refrigerated, not widely available.

Instant yeast
Powdered dried yeast that will wake up immediately with moisture of any kind.

Bread techniques
Pizza dough is easy to make because it does not need to be perfect, but many breads are defined by careful shaping and scoring and by their crust.

Shape
- Shape affects the texture of the dough. Large, round loaves will have more soft bread inside; long, thin loaves have more crust.
- Shape is determined by factors like the type of flour used, how it's eaten, how it's cooked, and regional traditions.

Scoring
- Scoring is making cuts in the dough before it is baked. Most free-formed or nonpan loaves are scored.
- Gluten on the outside of the dough has more tension; the cuts break the outer gluten, permitting more oven spring while controlling the rise and shape while baking.

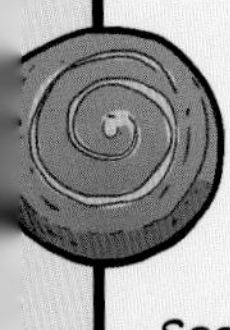

Crust
- Steaming bread with water while it's baking creates a thick crust. The water lowers the outer temperature of the bread, cooking it more slowly than the inside. This also hardens the starches that are cooking and drying on the surface.
- Sometimes glazes, like egg yolk or milk, are brushed on to create shine on crust.

Scoring, shaping, crusts, and glazes may also be used to identify the bread to both the baker and buyer visually, without having to ask or label them.

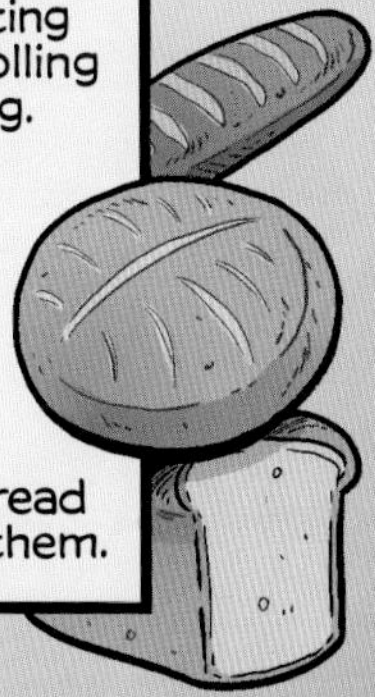

Pizza Crust (Part 1)
Makes one medium pizza crust or two personal sized.

Ingredients
- 1 cup warm water (90°F to 110°F)
- 1 tsp sugar
- 1 envelope dry **active** yeast (if using **instant** yeast, "blooming" is not neccesary)
- 2 TBSP olive oil
- 3 cups all-purpose flour
- 1 tsp salt

Special Tools
- Large mixing bowls (not metal)
- Cling wrap

Organize
1. Make sure all surfaces are dry and clean.
2. Mix and sift dry ingredients (flour and salt).
3. Mix warm water, sugar, oil, and yeast in a clean bowl and let it "bloom" for 10 minutes.
4. Use olive oil to grease a large bowl and set aside.

Prepare
5. Make a shallow "well" or crater with dry ingredients on the table or inside a bowl.
6. Pour the yeast water into the center.
7. Mix wet into dry using a fork, working around the edges of the well first.
8. Switch to using using your hands once most liquid is mixed in.
9. The dough should be smooth and slightly tacky, but not sticky and wet or dry and crumbly.
10. If very wet, add more flour (1–2 TBSP).
11. If very dry, add more water (1–2 TBSP).
12. Knead the dough for about 10 minutes.
13. Form the dough into a smooth ball and place in the large oiled bowl.
14. Cover bowl tightly with cling wrap and place in a warm area to proof (around 80°F is ideal).
15. Leave for 1 hour; should double in size.
16. Refrigerate for 4 hours or overnight.

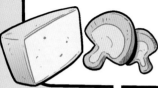

Pizza Crust (Part 2)

Ingredients
- All-purpose flour (as needed)
- Semolina flour (as needed)

Special Tools
- Cookie sheet
- Pizza stone if available
- Cast-iron cookware if available inside oven

Organize
1. Take dough out of fridge at least an hour before use to warm up.
2. Preheat your oven to 475°F.
3. Preheat pizza stone in oven if using.
4. Keep dough whole for one pizza or cut dough in half for two smaller pizzas.

Prepare
5. Flour your work surface and knead dough for 2 minutes.
6. Press with fingers or roll out to a round shape half the size of your final pizza.
7. If it's very stretchy and won't stay shaped, cover with cling wrap and let rest 10 minutes.
8. Hold part of the dough up by gently placing fingers underneath the edge and carefully stretching it up and out, section by section.
9. Dust a cookie sheet with semolina and place dough on top.
10. Add toppings of your choice (sauce, cheese, etc).

Bake
11. If using a pizza stone, carefully take out (it will be extremely hot) and slide the pizza onto it from the cookie sheet; return to oven right away.
12. If no pizza stone available, put the cookie sheet with the pizza on it directly into the oven.
13. If the pizza is thin, bake for 10–15 minutes.
14. Bake thicker crusts with more toppings 20-25 minutes.
15. When finished, let it cool a few minutes, but serve warm.

Cheddar Biscuits

Makes 5 to 7 biscuits.

Ingredients

- 2 cups all-purpose flour
- 2 tsp sugar
- 1 TBSP baking powder
- 1 tsp salt
- 1 tsp garlic powder
- 1/4 tsp cayenne
- 1/4 tsp paprika
- 1 stick butter, cold (plus extra to melt)
- 1 cup buttermilk
- 1/2 cup shredded cheddar cheese
- 1 TBSP fresh chopped parsley

Special Tools

- Baking sheet
- Wire cooling rack
- Rolling pin
- Round cookie cutter

Organize

1. Preheat oven to 475°F.
2. Measure buttermilk and cheese out, then keep cold.
3. Chop cold butter into uneaven pea-size (or smaller) pieces and then keep cold.

Prepare

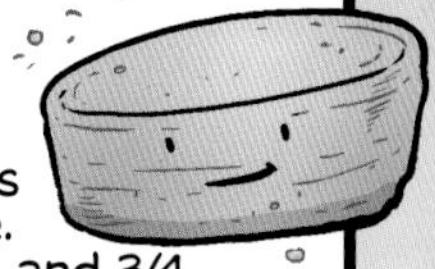

4. Combine and sift all dry ingredients in a large bowl, spices included.
5. "Cut" cold butter into dry with fingers or pastry blender till "shaggy" texture.
6. Add cheddar cheese, half the parsley, and 3/4 of the buttermilk to the shaggy mixture. (Add the rest of the buttermilk if it seems too dry.)
7. Use a spatula to combine, folding the wet batter onto itself; finish with hands if desired.
8. For best results, cover dough with cling wrap and rest in fridge for 30 minutes.
9. Flour surface and rolling pin well.
10. Roll out with rolling pin on clean surface.
11. Fold dough over in thirds.
12. Lightly roll again, 3/4- to 1-inch thickness.
13. Cut out square shapes with a knife or use a circle-shaped cutter, about 2 1/2" diameter.

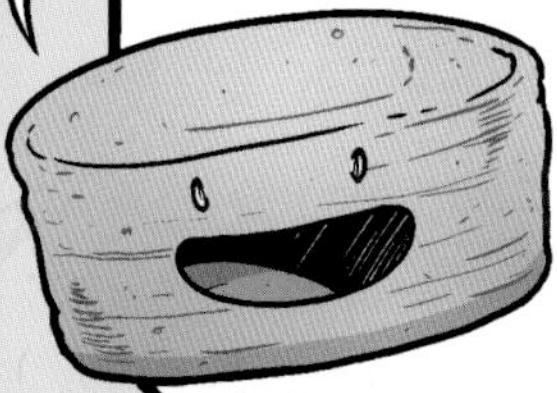

Bake

14. Transfer to baking sheet, keeping them close together.
15. Bake 10–15 minutes.
16. Let cool on baking sheet for 2 minutes.
17. Brush with melted butter and sprinkle with parsley (optional).
18. Serve warm or transfer to cooling rack.

Apple Pie Filling

Makes filling for one double crust pie.

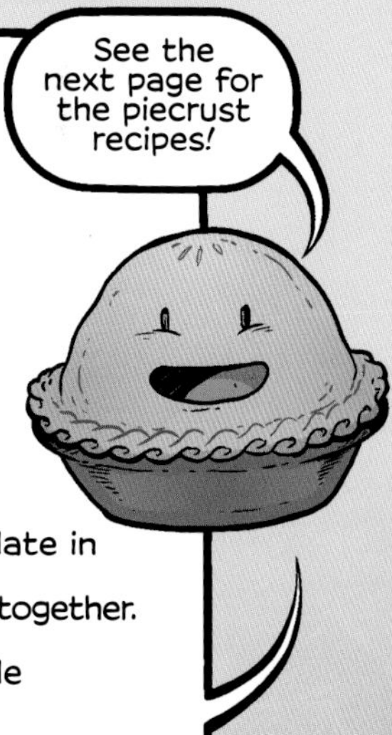
See the next page for the piecrust recipes!

Ingredients

- Double crust pie dough
- 1/4 cup all-purpose flour
- 1 cup white sugar
- 1/2 tsp cinnamon
- 1/2 tsp salt
- 1/4 tsp ground nutmeg
- 2 TBSP lemon juice
- 2 TBSP butter, chilled and cubed
- 6 large or 8 medium-sized apples

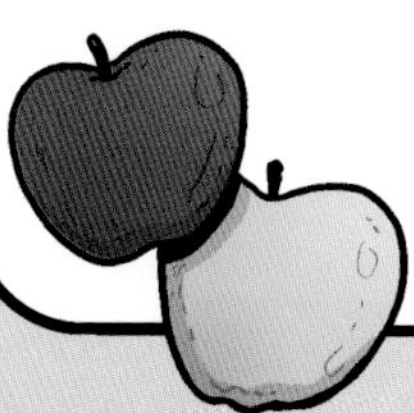

Organize

1. Preheat oven to 475°F.
2. Keep dough cold while making filling.
3. Peel, core, and slice apples.
4. Mix flour, sugar, spices, and salt.
5. Mix apples, lemon juice, and butter.

Prepare

6. Combine the flour mixture into the apple mixture in batches, so the apples are evenly coated.
7. Get pie dough ready for filling.
8. Place apples inside the dough and pie plate in a domed shape.
9. Cover with top dough and seal the crusts together.
10. Make a few steam vents on the top.
11. Brush crust with beaten egg and sprinkle with white sugar (optional).

Bake

12. Bake at 475°F for 15 minutes.
13. Lower temperature to 350°F; continue to bake for 30–45 more minutes till golden.
14. Only open oven if edges are cooking fast, to cover them with tinfoil to prevent burning.
15. Let cool for an hour before serving.

Double Piecrust
Makes one double crust pie.

Ingredients

Crust
- 2 1/2 cups all-purpose flour
- 1 tsp salt
- 2 sticks cold butter
- 1/2 cup cold water

Filling of your choice

Special Tools
- Rolling pin

Organize
1. Rough chop cold butter into uneaven pea-size (or smaller) pieces; keep cold.
2. Measure water and keep cold.
3. Combine and sift dry ingredients (flour and salt).
4. Oven temperature will depend on the filling; check with your recipe.
5. Have the filling of your choice prepared and ready.

Prepare
6. "Cut" butter into dry ingredients with fingers or pastry blender till "shaggy."
7. Add half the water to butter/flour mixture.
8. Use a spatula or hands to incorporate ingredients, folding it onto itself and making sure all water is absorbed.
9. If it's very dry, add more water. If it's too wet, add more flour.
10. Cover with cling wrap and rest in fridge for at least one hour.
11. Flour surface and rolling pin well.
12. Roll dough thin, fold over in thirds, and repeat till rolled larger than two pie plates (for top and bottom).
13. Cut two circles of dough out at least 2 inches larger in diameter than the pie plate being used.
14. Lay the bottom crust into the pie plate and gently press it in.
15. Fill with filling of your choice.
16. Cover with top crust and seal edges by using fingers to pinch together or by pressing with a fork.

Bake
17. Egg wash or crust decoration is optional.
18. Oven temperature and time will depend on the filling; bake according to your recipe and filling.

Single Piecrust
Makes one single-crust pie or tart.

Ingredients
- the same as double crust recipe, but cut amounts in half
- add 2 tsp of sugar for sweeter crust (optional)

Special Tools
- Pie weights or dry beans
- Parchment paper

Organize
1. Preheat oven to 350°F.
2. Same organizing as a double crust.

Prepare
3. Prepare crust the same as double crust, but only cut out one circle.
4. The crust must be laid into the pie plate and cut, shaped, or crimped exactly as you want the finished product to look.

Bake
5. Lay parchment paper into your shaped dough.
6. Fill evenly with pie weights or dry beans.
7. Bake 15–20 minutes; you want a little color, but not a full bake.
8. Let cool before filling and baking again according to the filling recipe.

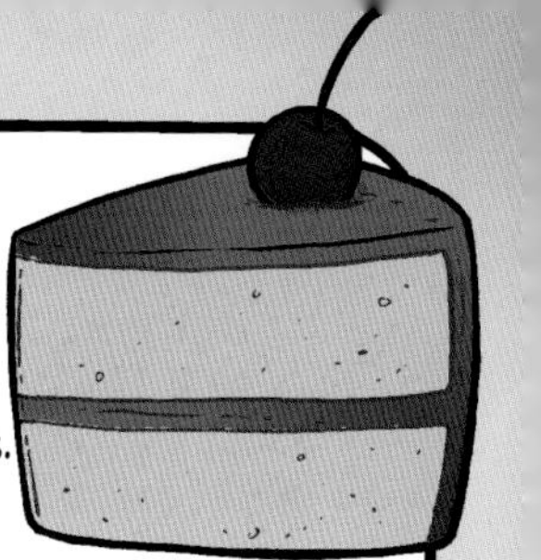

Simple Sponge Cake

Makes one two-tiered cake.

Ingredients
- 6 eggs, room temperature
- 1 cup white sugar, divided in half
- 1 tsp vanilla extract
- 1 cup flour
- 1/4 tsp baking powder
- 1/4 tsp salt

Special Tools
- Stand mixer with both paddle and whisk attachments
- 9-inch round cake pans (1 or 2)
- Wire cooling rack
- Sifter or fine mesh strainer

Organize

1. Combine and sift dry ingredients.
2. Preheat oven to 350°F.
3. Separate eggs into whites and yolks.
4. Grease and dust two 9-inch round cake pans.

Prepare

5. Put 6 yolks in stand mixer bowl and use paddle attachment at medium-high speed.
6. Slowly pour in half the white sugar (1/2 cup) and vanilla as you beat.
7. Continue to beat until the yolk lightens in color, and when the paddle is removed, a thick "ribbon" of yolk should fall off of it.
8. Transfer yolk mixture to a large clean bowl.
9. Thoroughly clean all tools used, so no yolk remains.
10. Add 6 egg whites to clean stand mixer bowl.
11. Use whisk attachment at medium-high speed and watch for a light foam or froth to start to form.
12. Slowly add the other half of the sugar while continuing to whisk.
13. Once stiff peaks appear, take half the egg white foam and fold into yolk mixture.
14. When mostly combined, fold in the rest of egg white foam.
15. Sift the dry ingredients into the egg mixture and fold in till fully incorporated and batter forms.

Bake

17. Divide the batter evenly between the cake pans.
18. Smooth batter if needed but don't tap or shake.
19. Bake for 15-20 minutes.
20. If baking unevenly, rotate inside oven halfway through.
21. When fully cooked, the edges should come away from the pan.
22. Let rest in pan for 5 minutes, then invert onto wire rack to cool completely.

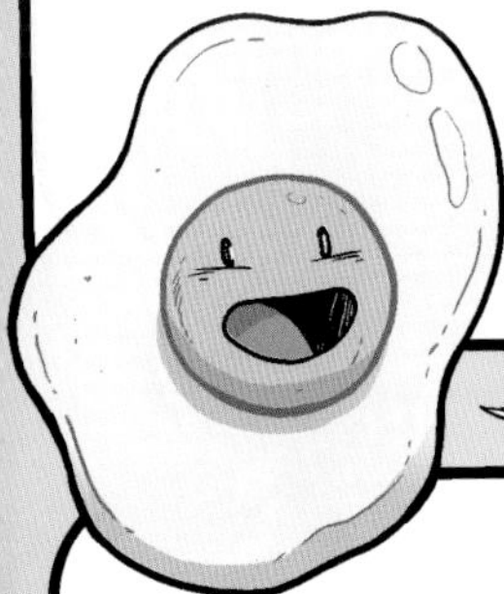

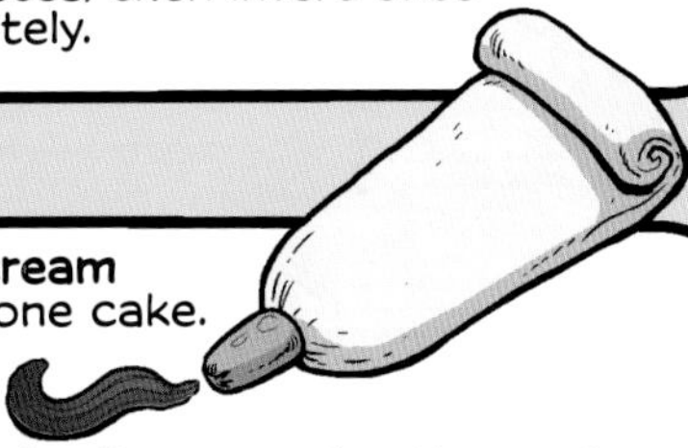

Swiss Meringue Buttercream

Makes enough frosting for one cake.

Ingredients
- 4 egg whites
- 1 cup white sugar
- 1/2 tsp salt
- 1 1/2 sticks butter at room temperature
- 1 tsp vanilla or other flavoring

Special tools
- Stand mixer with both paddle and whisk attachments
- Thermometer if available
- Pot for double boiler
- Regular whisk

Organize

1. Separate eggs and discard yolks or use in other recipes.
2. Cut butter into tablespoons.
3. Fill pot halfway with water and bring to a boil on stove.

Prepare

4. Put egg whites, sugar, and salt in stand mixer bowl, and put on top of boiling water to create a double boiler.
5. Whisk constantly as the sugar heats up and melts, cooking the egg whites.
6. Make sure it doesn't go over 180°F, or feel with your fingers for graininess of unmelted sugar.
7. When 170°F–180°F and sugar is completely melted, transfer to stand mixer.
8. Whip on medium speed with whisk attachment, till bowl is cool to the touch and very stiff peaks can form.
9. Switch whisk attachment for paddle.
10. Add butter (a tablespoon at a time) and vanilla extract while paddle moves.
11. Leave in bowl or fill piping bag.
12. Chill in fridge for 15 minutes before use.

Lemon Meringue Pie

Combine methods with this bonus recipe using a blind-baked crust, custard filling, and egg foam topping.

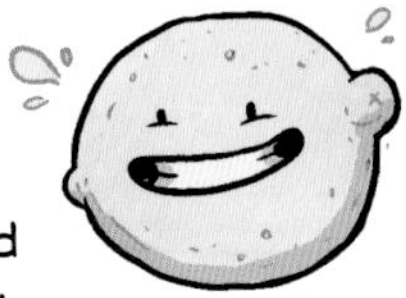

Ingredients

Single piecrust, blind-baked and cooled

Lemon Filling
- 1 1/4 cup sugar
- 1/3 cup cornstarch
- 1/4 tsp salt
- 1 1/2 cups milk
- 2 TBSP butter at room temperature
- 4 egg yolks
- 1/2 cup lemon juice
- 1 TBSP lemon zest

Meringue Topping
- 4 egg whites
- 6 TBSP sugar
- 1/4 tsp cream of tartar
- 1/2 tsp vanilla

Special Tools
- Hand or stand mixer with whisk

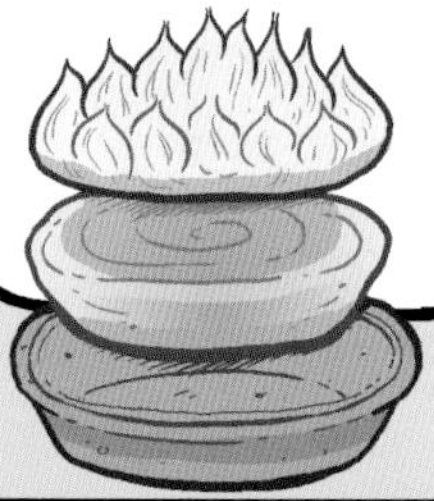

Organize
1. Oven preheated to 375°F.
2. Egg yolks and whites separated and in large bowls.

Prepare

Lemon Filling

3. Combine sugar, cornstarch, salt, and milk in heavy pot over medium heat.
4. Whisk constantly until it starts to steam.
5. Pour half of hot milk mixture slowly into the egg yolks while whisking.
6. Slowly pour the egg and milk mixture into the remaining hot milk over heat while whisking.
7. Continue to whisk and cook until the mixture becomes a thick pudding consistency.
8. Remove from the heat and add lemon juice, lemon zest, and butter, whisking until combined.
9. Pour the filling into the cooled blind-baked piecrust.

Meringue Topping

10. Beat egg whites till foamy.
11. Add cream of tartar and vanilla and continue to beat.
12. Add sugar slowly while continuing to beat.
13. Beat till shiny, smooth, stiff peaks form.

Bake
14. Top lemon filling with meringue.
15. Bake 5-10 minutes till the meringue turns golden brown on the edges.

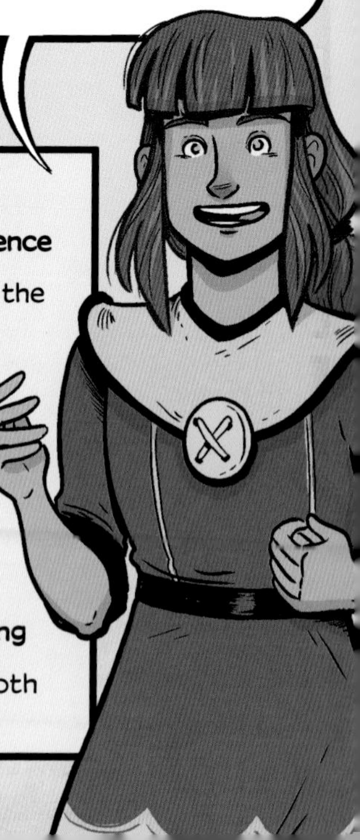

Continued Reading

How Baking Works: Exploring the Fundamentals of Baking Science
Paula Figoni (John Wiley & Sons, 2010)
A chemistry-based analysis of baking and recipes, including the science of baking without sugar or gluten.

The Baking Bible
Rose Levy Beranbaum (Houghton Mifflin Harcourt, 2014)
A beautiful and slightly more advanced cookbook, with clear, straightforward ingredient lists and instructions.

The Dessert Bible: The Best of American Home Cooking
Christopher Kimball (Little, Brown and Company, 2015)
Hundreds of recipes with clearly described techniques and an analysis of what tools and tips work best in practical use.

I'm Just Here for More Food: Food x Mixing + Heat = Baking
Alton Brown (Stewart, Tabori & Chang, 2004)
A clear analysis of baking from a scientific viewpoint, in both its approach to ingredients and the techniques used.

Conversions and Measurements

Abbreviations	
°F	degrees Fahrenheit
°C	degrees Celsius
fl oz	fluid ounce
oz	ounce
tsp	teaspoon
TBSP	tablespoon
g	gram
lb	pound
pt	pint
qt	quart
gal	gallon
ml	milliliter

Fahrenheit to Celsius
275°F · 140°C
300°F · 150°C
325°F · 165°C
350°F · 180°C
375°F · 190°C
400°F · 200°C
425°F · 220°C
450°F · 230°C
475°F · 240°C

Weight Conversions
1 oz · 28 g
1 lb · 454 g

Dry Measurements	
1/16 tsp	"A pinch"
1/8 tsp	"A dash"
3 tsp	1 TBSP
1/8 cup	2 TBSP
1/4 cup	4 TBSP
1/3 cup	5 TBSP + 1 tsp
1/2 cup	8 TBSP
3/4 cup	12 TBSP
1 cup	16 TBSP
1 lb	16 oz

Liquid Measurements		
8 fl oz	1 cup	
1 pt	2 cup	16 fl oz
1 qt	2 pt	4 cup
1 gal	4 qt	16 cup

US and Metric Conversions		
1/5 tsp		1 ml
1 tsp		5 ml
1 TBSP		15 ml
1 fl oz		30 ml
1/5 cup		50 ml
1 cup		240 ml
2 cup	1 pt	470 ml
4 cup	1 qt	.95 liter
4 qt	1 gal	3.8 liters

Butter				
1 TBSP	14 g			
1 stick	4 oz	113 g	8 TBSP	1/2 cup
4 stick	16 oz	452 g	32 TBSP	2 cups

Lemons & Limes (Approximate)		
1 lemon	1–3 TBSP juice	1 TBSP zest
4 lemon	1/2 cup juice	1/4 cup zest

Chocolate		
1 oz	1/4 cup grated	40 g
6 oz chips	1 cup	160 g
1 cup powder	115 g	

First Second

All instructions included in this book are provided as a resource for parents and children. While all due care has been taken, we recommend that an adult supervise children at all times when following the instructions in this book. The projects in this book are not recommended for children three years and under due to potential choking hazard. Neither the authors nor the publisher accept any responsibility for any loss, injury, or damages sustained by anyone resulting from the instructions contained in this book.

Published by First Second
First Second is an imprint of Roaring Brook Press,
a division of Holtzbrinck Publishing Holdings Limited Partnership
175 Fifth Avenue, New York, NY 10010
All rights reserved

Library of Congress Control Number: 2018938072

Paperback ISBN: 978-1-250-15006-6
Hardcover ISBN: 978-1-250-15005-9

Our books may be purchased in bulk for promotional, educational, or business use. Please contact your local bookseller or the Macmillan Corporate and Premium Sales Department at (800) 221-7945 ext. 5442 or by e-mail at MacmillanSpecialMarkets@macmillan.com.

First edition, 2019
Edited by Robyn Chapman and Bethany Bryan
Expert consultant: Kelly Vass
Book design by Rob Steen

Printed in China by 1010 Printing International Limited, Kwun Tong, Hong Kong

Penciled, inked, and colored in Photoshop with Kyle Webster digital brushes Drawing Box: Non Photo Blue Pro and Inkbox: Pocket Brush 1 along with a variety of other Photoshop brushes.

Paperback: 10 9 8 7 6 5
Hardcover: 10 9 8 7 6 5 4 3 2 1